*The Painted King*

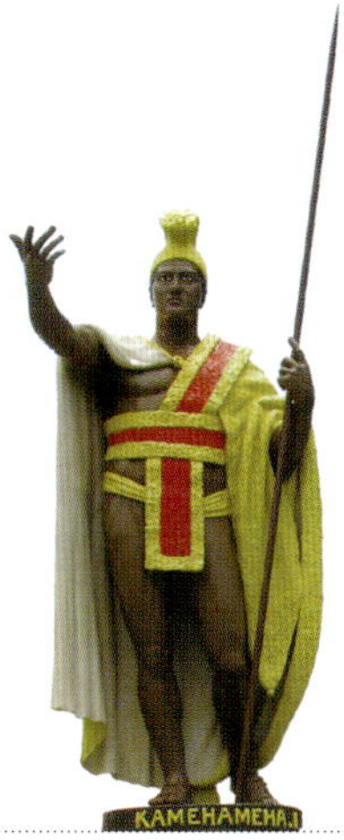


# The Painted King

## ART, ACTIVISM, AND AUTHENTICITY IN HAWAI'I

GLENN WHARTON

HAWAI

UNIVERSITY OF HAWAI'I PRESS
HONOLULU

Printed in China
17 16 15 14 13 12 6 5 4 3 2 1

**Library of Congress Cataloging-in-Publication Data**
Wharton, Glenn.
The painted king : art, activism, and authenticity in Hawaiʻi / Glenn Wharton.
p. cm.
Includes bibliographical references and index.
ISBN 978-0-8248-3495-1 (cloth : alk. paper)
ISBN 978-0-8248-3612-2 (pbk. : alk. paper)
1. Kamehameha I, the Great, King of the Hawaiian Islands, d. 1819—Statues. 2. Kapaau (Hawaii)—Buildings, structures, etc.—Conservation and restoration. 3. Public sculpture—Conservation and restoration—Hawaii—Kapaau—Citizen participation. I. Title.
NB230.H3W53 2011
730.9969—dc23
2011020891

*Published with the support of the Maurice J. Sullivan & Family Fund in the University of Hawaiʻi Foundation.*

University of Hawaiʻi Press books are printed on acid-free paper and meet the guidelines for permanence and durability of the Council on Library Resources.

Designed by Julie Matsuo-Chun
Printed by Everbest Printing Co., Ltd.

*For Alexander and Paul*

# *Contents*

## *Acknowledgments*

I THANK THE RESIDENTS OF North Kohala, who took this project to their hearts and developed its participatory aspects within their community. Among the many people who affected me deeply are Boyd Bond, Hilton Nalani Cabrera, Stephanie Cabinis, Fred Cachola, Emma Glory, Randee Golden, Sharon Hayden, Raylene Ha'alelea Lancaster, Daniel Otake, Kealoha Sugiyama, Nani Svendsen, and Audrey Veloria. The special lessons I learned about Hawaiian culture from Marie Solomon and John Keola Lake, now deceased, will be with me forever. We could not have conducted the project without the guidance and support from members of our project team on O'ahu, including Marilyn Cristofori, Lei Ahsing, Mary Tuti Baker, and Michael Jones.

I interviewed and worked with many people elsewhere in Hawai'i who are not mentioned in the book. They include Peter Apo, Edward Halealoha Ayau, Kehau Cachola-Abad, Ross Cordy, Billy Fields, Sahoa Todd Fukushima, Linda Hee, Kiyoshi Ikeda, Marion Kelly, Downy Manoukian, Jeffrey Melrose, Puakea Nogelmeier, Jon Osorio, Kalena Silva, Miriam Stark, Ricardo Trimillos, and Geoff White.

I owe deep gratitude to my partner, Harvey Molotch, for his insightful advice and tireless support on the home front as I performed lengthy site visits and wrote and rewrote the text for this book. Other scholars gave me guidance along the way, including Mitchell Duneier and Howard Becker, who helped me analyze the social worlds at play, David Lowenthal, who challenged me to justify heritage conservation in the face of postmodern criticism, and Ian Hodder, who pushed me toward intellectual bravery when I was in doubt. Janey Bennett, Michael Denneny, and Amy McCulloch helped me with editing the text and processing the images. And finally, my warm thanks to Carol Hasegawa, who got me into all this in the first place and remains a lifelong friend.

I gratefully acknowledge financial support from the Samuel H. Kress Conservation Publication Fellowship program, administered through the Foundation for the American Institute for Conservation of Historic and Artistic Works (FAIC). Funding for the participatory conservation project and seed money for the documentary film was provided by the following: the Americans for the Arts' Animating Democracy Lab funded by the Ford Foundation, the Atherton Family Foundation, the Getty Trust, the Hawai'i Community Foundation, the National Center for Preservation Technology & Training of the National Park Service, the National Endowment for the Arts, Pacific Islanders in Communications, and Save Outdoor Sculpture! of Heritage Preservation and the Smithsonian American Art Museum.

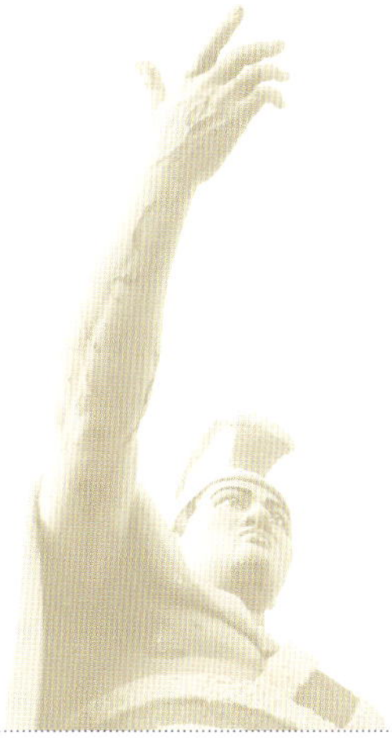

# 1 *A Painted King*

I FIRST SAW THE SCULPTURE in the spring of 1996. Fearful I would drive right by it, I proceeded carefully through the small town of Kapaʻau, scanning the land around each of the historic buildings. I knew it stood in front of an 1893 courthouse from the sugar plantation days. When the dramatic image appeared on a grassy mound in the distance, curiously gesturing out to the sleepy highway, I realized I could not have missed it.

I parked my small rental car across the street and stared at the figure. Here was the first in a series of monuments to King Kamehameha[1]—the chief celebrated for uniting the Hawaiian archipelago in the late eighteenth century and who later became Hawaiʻi's first king. Located near his birthplace in this semirural town on the northwest tip of the island of Hawaiʻi, the heroic figure stood on its lava-rock pedestal like a Roman emperor. It looked as out of place as I felt.

As I got out of the car and crossed the street, gusty winds bent the surrounding palms towards the colossal figure. Despite the strong tropical sun, a light shower blew through with the wind. I set my tools under the deep overhang of the courthouse *lanai* (porch) in order to investigate other objects in the little park, including three large stones with carved depressions from the ancient Hawaiian game of *kōnane.* Sounds of a ukulele came from

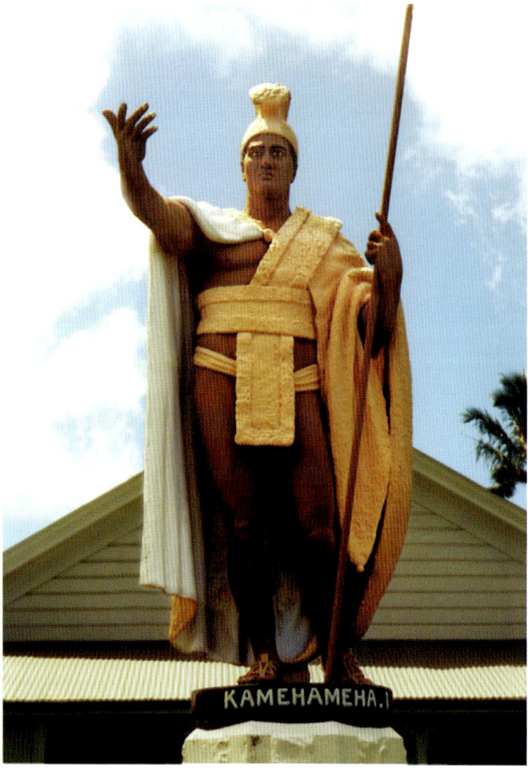


The Kamehameha sculpture as it appeared in June 1996. The over-lifesize figure is eight feet five inches in height, mounted on a seven-foot-nine-inch bluestone base.

the courthouse. Peering inside the wide-open windows, I saw a small group of older women and men playing music and dancing hula. Their stares made me uncomfortable, so I quickly turned around to get to work.

As a sculpture conservator from California, I occasionally worked in Hawai'i, but never before on a project like this. My work usually takes me to urban museums and parks, where I repair sculptures and other historic objects. I work alongside curators and public art managers, developing methods for removing corrosion and adjusting the surface appearance. Bronze sculptures usually have green, black, and brown corrosion. We discuss whether to remove the corrosion or leave it as it is. When we decide to leave the green layer, we argue for honoring change that occurs over time. When we decide to remove it, we are trying to restore the original, typically brown surface tones. This debate between honoring the effects of time versus the original appearance of an artwork often stirs strong feelings. It extends to the cleaning of paintings, restoring musical instruments to playable condition, and stripping corrosion from archaeological objects to reveal surface decoration.

But this sculpture was startling in appearance. Far from the influence of

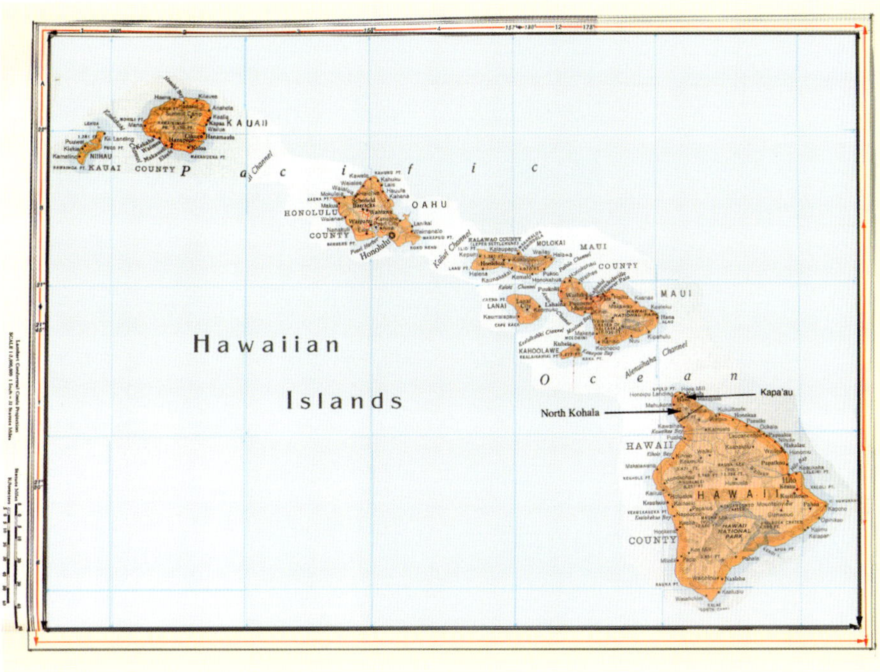


Map of the Hawaiian Islands, indicating the North Kohala district on the island of Hawai'i and the town of Kapa'au where the sculpture is installed.

professional art circles, local residents had painted the figure in bright colors. Kamehameha's skin was brown, his hair was black, and his cloak was yellow. He had white toenails and fingernails and penetrating black eyes with small white brush strokes for highlights. I had never seen a sculpture like this. It looked more like a piece of folk art than a nineteenth-century heroic monument.

I was surprised. Honolulu administrators told me there was paint on the figure, but why would anyone completely paint a bronze sculpture like this? My traditional training as a conservator took over. I wanted to remove the paint and return it to its nineteenth-century appearance. After all, my directive from Honolulu was to do just that: research the original appearance and recommend methods for removing the paint. My report would list steps for "restoring" the artist's initial coatings. No one knew what it originally looked like, but some art historians suggested that the skin was chemically patinated brown and the feathered garments were gold-leafed, like the second in the Kamehameha sculpture series, a cast copy erected in Honolulu. I was familiar with the Honolulu cast, after having regilt it with a team of other conservators in 1994.

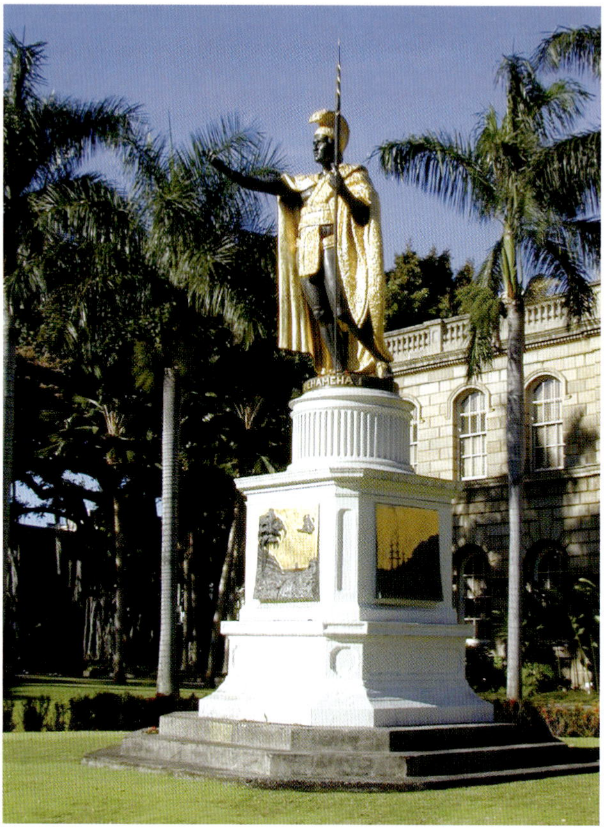

The second cast of the sculpture in front of the Ali'iolani Hale government building in Honolulu.

This was standard forensic research for a sculpture conservator. We often get involved in technical studies to authenticate suspected forgeries or determine when a sculpture was made. My purpose here was to take samples for analysis to see if I could reconstruct the sculpture's technical history and then develop methods for removing the paint. During my few hours at the site, I had to think through logistics of the future project. How could I strip up to a quarter of an inch of paint buildup from an eight-foot-five-inch sculpture on top of a seven-foot-nine-inch pedestal? In this public setting, my mind went to the safety hazards associated with gallons of chemicals and the steam-blasting required to remove the thick paint film. I also worried about the powerful trade winds, locally known as ʻĀpaʻapaʻa. Would they blow the solvent vapors and overspray onto the street? But if we covered the scaffolding with tarps to protect our work from the winds, would the entire scaffolding blow over, hitting the sculpture?

I took photographs to document the sculpture's condition. The 120 years of exposure to North Kohala's[2] winds had taken their toll. The paint on the sculpture was faded and "chalked" from the intense ultraviolet rays of the subtropical sun. I used a ladder I had borrowed from the state maintenance department to get a closer look. Aside from the expected bird guano, gecko poop, spider nests, and soiling, in some crevices I saw residues of floral lei and other organic offerings from the public. From these residues grew small spots of black fungus. I saw many chips of lifting paint. In some sections, the paint had actually peeled off the surface, revealing underlying corrosion. Small spots of powdery green corrosion on the exposed metal alarmed me. This could only mean one thing: bronze disease, a rapid form of copper alloy corrosion. I had seen bronze disease before on sculptures in Hawai'i, most notably on the severely corroded Mahatma Gandhi figure in the Kapi'olani Park in Honolulu. This could be serious.

Bronze disease forms pits on a sculpture's surface. It is an acid-producing reaction, driven by salts in active corrosion cells. If a sculpture isn't intensively washed, treated with corrosion inhibitors, and protected with wax, paint, or lacquer, bronze disease eats its way into the structure of the metal. The result is a deeply pitted and disfigured surface, not unlike the festering skin of a leper. Hence, the reference to disease. In fact, bronze disease is a specific form of corrosion that occurs on copper, brass, and bronze in the presence of chloride salts, water, and oxygen. I had heard that the sculpture sank in a shipwreck on its way to Hawai'i, which certainly exposed it to ocean salts that could cause this form of corrosion. One of my first thoughts was whether the thick layer of paint had actually protected the metal surface from these chlorides over the years. The only way to know the extent of corrosion would be to strip off the paint.

In addition to the green spotted corrosion, red-brown stains ran down the

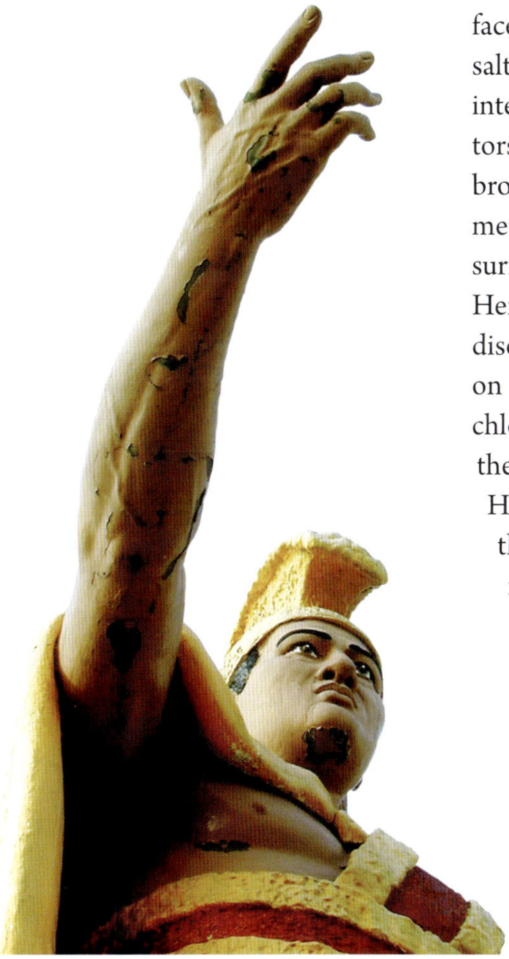

Details of peeling paint and corrosion.

base from some sort of interior iron corrosion, probably from the armature, or support system. Also alarming was a deep crack in the metal base. This might be from early damage or more recent earthquake activity, and it could indicate that the sculpture was in danger of toppling. Stripping the paint off and assessing all this damage seemed like a prudent first step, regardless of final surface coatings.

I was on a tight schedule and could only spend half a day in Kapaʻau. Carol Hasegawa, the conservation manager for public art in Honolulu, contracted me on a grant to assess the condition of four sculptures.[3] Carol explained that she chose this sculpture because of its apparent poor condition and question of legal ownership by the state. At the time I didn't know what she meant, but I gladly added the Kamehameha sculpture on the island of Hawaiʻi as a quick side trip from my work in Honolulu. In spite of my hurried schedule, I wanted to speak with someone in town about the paint. I wandered across the street to a small store. Before I had a chance to say anything, the shopkeeper approached me. Looking me in the eye, she asked,

"What were you doing across the street on the ladder?"

"I'm a sculpture conservator, and I've been contracted to assess the condition of the sculpture."

"Who contracted you?"

"The city of Honolulu."

"What for?"

"Well, the state may want to restore it."

"Whatever you do, don't remove the paint!"

"Why?"

"Because here in town we like him painted. Every year on Kamehameha Day we have a parade, and people in the parade stop to offer him gifts. The paint helps us relate to him as a human being. At sunrise on Kamehameha Day, we offer him chants and drape lei over his shoulders."

"Do most people in the community feel this way?"

"Everyone."

I was unprepared for this. I offered my aloha and walked out of the store, confused. This brief conversation had a powerful effect on me. People rarely have strong feelings about preserving public artworks, yet here was a situation where a community not only cared, but also had a parade in front of their altered sculpture and provided it with gifts.

Part of me felt that painting it with bright colors was a sacrilege, like adding a mustache to the Mona Lisa. Yet I also recognized that a local custom had somehow set in. Should this custom be honored, even if the artist hadn't wanted the sculpture painted? Who was I as an outsider to recommend that layers of paint and history be stripped away? At the time I knew little about the community's relationship with the sculpture or to its Native Hawaiian past. I also had no idea what Thomas R. Gould, the nineteenth-century American sculptor, had in mind when he first designed the image in Florence in 1878–1879 and had it cast in Paris in 1880.

I had the technical skills and capabilities to research the original materials used by Barbedienne, the Paris foundry that cast it, yet I was not equipped to address these concerns of local residents. These thoughts went into my report several weeks later. I recommended standard technical and archival research prior to a decision, but I also recommended involving the community in deciding whether to repaint it after addressing the corrosion and structural problems.

After submitting my report I moved on to other conservation projects. I ran a practice based in Santa Barbara with five people on staff, and we were involved in many museum and public art projects. Putting the Hawaiʻi survey to bed meant I could turn my attention to a damaged sculpture at the San Francisco Museum of Modern Art. At the time I was also preparing maintenance training for outdoor sculpture at the Taiwan Museum of Art and the San Diego Museum of Art. My mind was diverted to these other projects and their deadlines. We were always overbooked and stressed, but fortunately our brilliant office manager, Shirley Purcilly, kept clients at bay and books balanced while the rest of us repaired the sculptures in the workshop and maintained a steady flow of photographs and reports to document our work. Shirley protected us: "We are so glad you called to find out when your sculpture will be returned, but they are working on it right now in the back and can't come to the phone."

During the year that followed, my mind often wandered to the Kamehameha sculpture. Who was Kamehameha, and why is the sculpture in the remote town of Kapaʻau? I began reading about his life and legacy. Depending on what you read, he was born sometime between 1738 and 1761, and died in 1819.[4] Known by some as Kamehameha the Great, he was an ambitious local chief from the Kohala region who is celebrated for first uniting the Hawaiian islands under one rule in 1810, after a long series of bloody battles and political negotiation. He established a monarchy and united the legal and tax systems to strengthen his reign and those of his descendants. He was also present when Captain James Cook first arrived on the Hawaiian Islands, and later promoted trade as contact increased between Hawaiʻi, the United States, and Europe.

I learned Kamehameha's legends: born on a beach, rescued from an attack by soldiers intending to prevent his succession to the throne, and hidden by his caregiver in a remote mountain village until his fifth year.

I read that the Hawaiian legislature commissioned the sculpture in 1878 to honor the centennial of Captain James Cook's "discovery" of the Hawaiian Islands. From this dubious beginning, a complicated series of fortuitous accidents and political decisions led to making two casts of the same sculpture. The reigning King Kalākaua and the legislature that commissioned the work decided to install the second cast, which was in better condition, in front of the Aliʻiolani Hale government building in Honolulu, and the first cast in Kohala, near Kamehameha's birthplace. This was in part to appease local residents. Like their modern-day descendants, they combined a fierce local pride with a distrust of Honolulu. Many were angry at the legislature for commissioning the sculpture for Honolulu in the first place, rather than Kohala.

Nothing I read provided me with the answer to my central question—why was the Honolulu cast gold-leafed and the North Kohala cast painted? Was it always this way, or did something happen that caused people to paint the original cast? I asked people I knew in Honolulu, but the reply was always the same—it has been painted for as long as anyone could remember.

In a stroke of good timing (at least for me), a strong wind knocked over some tents at a social function at the Parker Ranch Museum, a historic cattle ranch in nearby Waimea, in December 1995. The director contacted me to repair two eighteenth-century English lead garden sculptures that were bent over by the tent. This brought me back to the island in the summer of 1996 and provided me with time to visit the Kamehameha sculpture again. While I worked with two assistants to reshape the damaged English sculptures and replace their corroded armature, I heard that a volunteer in North Kohala had just repainted the Kamehameha sculpture. Curious, I found his number and called him. His name was Kealoha Sugiyama, and he was about to become my first local contact. After I had described the project and my hopes for community involvement, there was a long silence on the phone. Finally, he asked me to meet him at the sculpture. "I will know from Kamehameha if you are the right person to do this work."

The next weekend I drove the twenty miles over the extinct Kohala volcano, down the mountain from the open plains of Waimea into the lush district of North Kohala. I drove to the courthouse and parked in back, next to the police department. Wearing shorts, sandals, and the only *aloha* shirt I brought on the trip, I walked around to the front of the building and saw the newly painted figure of Kamehameha. To my surprise, the yellow painted sash now had a bright red stripe running down the center. Next to the sculpture stood Kealoha, who warmly greeted me with a lei and the ubiquitous Hawaiian hug and "aloha." His Hawaiian first name and Japanese last name, combined with piles of braided green lei and brightly colored flowing garments, made him appear exotic to me.

I nervously began telling him about my analysis and how unusual it is for a community to change the original appearance of a work of art. I spoke about the field of art conservation and how we try to honor the artist's original aesthetic intentions. I could see that he wasn't fully listening. He stopped me and quietly told me to look at the figure. After a long silence, he asked if I saw anything different. "The red stripe?" "Yes." He then launched into his own tale about being angry with the state maintenance team for abandoning their regular maintenance and painting back in 1988. He had noticed the faded and peeling paint and complained to Ali Fujii, the district building maintenance supervisor for the state. They came to an agreement that if Kealoha would volunteer to paint it, the agency would pay for the paint, provide scaffolding, and prepare the surface by water blasting. While carefully watching my reactions, he described his own research process:

> I stood in front of the Kamehameha statue and dialogued with it that I was going to paint it, and lo and behold I was across the street at the Bond Library. I borrowed a few books about Kamehameha and the next day I stood in front of Kamehameha again. I looked at one book about cloaks and feathers, and I saw a picture of the Līloa Sash and to my astonishment, it was red with gold trimming. I showed Kamehameha this regal sash and I said is this what you wanted me to know? And I wasn't sent back to the library so I knew that if I was going to paint the statue, Kamehameha wanted me to paint the Līloa Sash in the right color. I took the picture to a group of kahuna [priests, spiritual leaders] at the Puʻukoholā Heiau and I shared my story, and they agreed that it would be *pono* [proper procedure, righteous] to paint it red.

I was stunned. This conversation, more than any other, made me realize how much I had to learn if I was going to understand the people in North Kohala and their relationships with the sculpture. He had just told me that

Kamehameha guided him to paint the sash red and that spiritual leaders agreed that he should follow this direction. We chatted for a while longer, then I thanked him and returned to Waimea, promising to be in touch. I had no idea what he thought about me or whether I was the right person to conserve the sculpture. There was another world of knowledge I would have to open myself to in order to understand the sculpture and its community.

After returning to California once more, I gradually started outlining a project in my mind to involve the community in deciding how Kamehameha should look. My interest in activist public art and relational aesthetics[5] led me to think about an activist form of conservation. It seemed that if people cared about the sculpture as much as Kealoha Sugiyama and the shopkeeper indicated, and if the question of how to conserve it was open for debate, this could be an ideal situation for wide public discussion on larger questions about representing the Native Hawaiian past—a discussion not only about caring for the sculpture, but about who Kamehameha was and what he means to the multicultural community of Native Hawaiian and plantation descendants, along with the mainland transplants that surround him today.

The project could build on discussions that were already taking place in the heritage industry about opening up professional authority and empowering communities in representing the past. It could also provide an opportunity for cultural analysis. For instance, what effect do ethnicity and religion have on how people think about the depiction of Kamehameha? A community-based, participatory form of conservation could force questions of authenticity at a moment in which efforts to identify truth in conservation have been destabilized.[6]

The thought of such a project was both exhilarating and frightening. I had no idea what an activist conservation would look like. As the name might imply, art conservation is a field with a focus on objects from the past. We are trained as scientists to understand how materials interact with their environment, how objects are made, and how they deteriorate. We develop strategies for slowing down or halting this deterioration. Artifact conservation always treads a narrow path between material and culture. We do material research to understand the object physically, and we perform cultural and aesthetic research to learn how it should look, according to the artist who made it or the people who originally used it. We work with curators, anthropologists, archaeologists, and other professionals to decide how to clean, repair, and replace missing elements. Despite this combination of scientific and cultural research, we haven't developed ways to embrace communities around these objects—especially people who bring new meanings to them and want to change how they look. The idea of sharing research and decision making outside of professional circles was something new. And just how to do this was not clear.

I began asking myself if something was wrong with the way I normally did my work. I campaigned for years to increase public awareness of unattended outdoor sculptures and monuments, and here was a sculpture somehow adopted by its community. Not only did they care for it, but they painted it in ways the artist certainly never imagined. Following the ethics of my profession, it seemed that my duty was to research the original appearance, then strip the paint off and replace it with nineteenth-century finishes. My instinct told me that this approach missed something important, but I knew I did not have the skills to conduct a form of conservation that embraced community.

As I described the idea of a community-based conservation to my colleagues, some enthusiastically encouraged me to go on. Others warned me that if I went too far in opening conservation to the public I would sacrifice my role as an "unbiased" outside expert. One colleague rolled his eyes and warned me not to "go native," as some conservators of Native American artifacts do by giving nonprofessionals a strong voice in deciding how to care for museum collections.

I mentioned the project to several arts administrators I knew in Honolulu. Most were enthusiastic and encouraged me to pursue my plans. One, however, caught me off guard. Sitting in her office one day, she told me that we absolutely must respect the artist's original conception. If we learn that it was originally gold-leafed, then we should strip the paint off and gold-leaf it. "When I first got involved with it over twenty-five years ago, I kept asking 'Why are you painting it?' The answer I got back was 'Because we like it that way.' And this was from an older Hawaiian woman. I find it a little offensive. Every time I look at that statue and I look at those white eyeballs, it just turns me off."

The project was already getting a mixed response even before it was underway. In addition to these cultural issues, there were financial and logistical concerns. I knew the project would require funding far beyond what state agencies ordinarily provide for conservation. I also knew that we needed local participation to bring it off and that I had essentially no knowledge of the community. Would I even be accepted as a conservator from the mainland asking a lot of difficult cultural questions? Having no contacts in North Kohala, I looked for a nonprofit arts organization in Honolulu that could umbrella the project and help find local people and groups to become partners in our efforts.

After several people suggested the Hawai'i Alliance for Arts Education, I contacted Marilyn Cristofori, their executive director. With a personal background in performance arts and a professional mission to build community through the arts, she understood immediately what I wanted to do. In our early phone conversations, she began mapping out a project that would involve students, teachers, artists, and elders. She and Lei Ahsing, their program director, spoke about community arts workshops and classroom art projects as a way to spark local interest. They widened the project beyond my limited imagination. We were off and running . . . or so we thought.

Months went by, and my e-mails to the State Foundation for Culture and the Arts about project development went unanswered. I began to worry that I was developing a project in my own imagination without actually having the support of state agencies. In December 1997, I finally decided to call the director of the Art in Public Places program. He effectively shattered all of our plans. In a long and decisive monologue, he explained that since the sculpture was commissioned before the founding of the State Foundation for Culture and the Arts, it is not under their jurisdiction. In fact, since it was commissioned by the constitutional monarchy before Hawai'i was part of the United States, it isn't officially under any agency in the current government. He then described their workload, including their need to perform a complete inventory before they could assign priority and add new works to the long list of public artworks they care for. In effect, he warned me off. He concluded the conversation by saying, "You have no idea what you would be getting yourself into." I didn't have the nerve to remind him that this was Hawai'i's first sculpture or that the state does take care of the second cast in Honolulu. In fact, his agency organized our 1994 project to regild it.

After this devastating call, I contacted Marilyn Cristofori and told her that the project was off. I could see no way of proceeding without state support. Another year went by. Then I received an e-mail from Susan Nichols, director of the Save Outdoor Sculpture! (SOS!) project in Washington, D.C., that funded my initial survey. This Smithsonian American Art Museum/Heritage Preservation joint project coordinated a volunteer effort to inventory all the outdoor sculpture across the nation. She told me that their next project was to launch a grant program to fund community-driven conservation projects in every state. Hawai'i was one of the few states that had not submitted an application, and, knowing I had worked in Hawai'i, she wondered if I knew of a sculpture in poor condition that the community could rally behind. I quickly e-mailed back, "Susan, do I have a project for you!"

After I explained the local involvement with the Kamehameha sculpture and the state resistance to a community-based project, Susan, in her unflappable style, asked for the phone number of the Art in Public Places director. The next time I heard from her, Susan had negotiated the framing for a project that could be administered by another state agency, the King Kamehameha Celebration Commission. I contacted the Hawai'i Arts Alliance with this news, and together we started drafting funding proposals.

The stage was almost set. The next vital step was finding local residents to partner with. Marilyn Cristofori and Lei Ahsing took charge. Through their contacts, they found local organizations that work in culture and the arts. They also identified Native Hawaiian community groups. Through a series of interviews with local residents, they decided we should work with leaders from four groups: the Kamehameha Day Celebration Committee, the Kohala Hawaiian Civic Club, the Kohala Senior Citizens Club, and the Halau 'O Ha'alelea hula group.

Buoyed by initial funding success from our grant proposals, we sent additional requests to more agencies and foundations. Little by little, we received funding for arts programming and community projects that extended well beyond the costs of the technical conservation work on the scaffolding. In addition to an SOS! grant, other support came from the Ford Foundation, the Getty Trust, the National Park Service, the National Endowment for the Arts, the Hawai'i Community Foundation, Pacific Islanders in Communications, and the Atherton Family Foundation.

The project began to take shape with input from the community organizations, the Hawai'i Alliance for Arts Education, myself, and our funders. The King Kamehameha Celebration Commission in Honolulu retained state authority to accept or reject the local decision on the sculpture's conservation. They were aware of "anti-Honolulu" sentiments, however, and chose to maintain a distance from project activities. Their staff would not visit North Kohala during the project. We decided to create a documentary film about the project and contracted filmmaker Mary Tuti Baker and her Ki'i Productions crew. Since part of her family came from the region, "Tuti" would have a certain local entrée and respect.

As the project funding and organization proceeded, I thought about my own role, working in a remote Hawaiian community. This was new territory for me. It felt like the right thing to do, but it was contrary to the way conservation usually works. I was more than a little concerned about opening up a conservation question to wide-scale public debate. As a haole (Caucasian) from the mainland I suspected I might not be received with open arms.

In August 1999, I began my research by spending three weeks in Honolulu, searching the Hawai'i State Archives, the Bishop Museum, and the University of Hawai'i library for historic documents and literature relating to the sculpture's history. I also sent my samples from 1996 to David Scott, at the J. Paul Getty Museum, and James Martin, first at the Williamstown Art Conservation Center and later at Orion Analytical in Williamstown, Massachusetts, to learn what the sculpture was made of, how it was made, the layering of the paint over time, and the corrosion underneath the paint. Their methods of analysis included stereomicroscopy, polarized light microscopy, fluorescence microscopy, x-ray fluorescence, x-ray diffraction, environmental scanning electron microscopy, and scanning electron microscopy with energy-dispersive x-ray fluorescence spectrometry. Small pieces of paint I had removed with scalpels were set in plastic and polished on the side to provide an image in the microscope of the layered paint buildup.

In addition to this standard conservation research, I wanted to learn more about local culture before the project began. While I was in Honolulu, I spoke with friends and a few university researchers about outsiders like myself working in Hawaiian communities. Some people began to take me in. I was taken to a cultural sensitivity workshop in which participants performed exercises that played on misconceptions of others. Native Hawaiians reminded me of Captain Cook's unfortunate experience—first celebrated, then killed in a confusing set of events still debated and very much alive in the minds of many. I was directed to one of the most important debates in contemporary anthropology, in which Marshall Sahlins and Gananath Obeyesekere argue the role of mythology in his death, the ability of outsiders to give voice to indigenous cultures, and who is or is not an "outsider."[7]

This was a warning of the cultural misunderstandings that arise when researchers try to lay a preconceived project onto a Hawaiian community. My status as an outsider needed to be carefully navigated in order to gain trust, and I was told that I could only gain trust by slowing down, spending time, and listening. Keahi Allen of the King Kamehameha Celebration Commission commented on her experience, "Because I don't come from there, it's none of my business. I am not there, even though our family comes from there. Even I am considered an outsider."

I was further advised that locals would be skeptical of my motivations.

Fred Cachola, a historian who was raised in North Kohala but moved to Honolulu, warned me "as a community, people in Kohala have been acted upon by the plantations, missionaries, and others who have come and gone." He explained that people in North Kohala prefer projects and opinions that come from inside the community, not outside. The advice I received wasn't all bleak. I was also told of the *aloha* spirit, which is much more than a warm greeting and offering of lei to outsiders. If trust and reciprocity are established, Hawaiians gradually shed their reservations and welcome people with an openness rarely seen in other cultures.

Given these warnings from all sides, I decided that my role during the initial period of community activities and decision making would be to provide information from my research and discuss the technical concerns of gold leaf and paint, but not to express my personal preference for paint or gold. Once the community decided this central issue, I would select either the paint or gold materials that would withstand the harsh subtropical environment, then work with residents to make more detailed decisions such as the exact color of Kamehameha's skin. Once the project was set up, I could immerse myself in historical research about the sculpture and hopefully learn whether it was originally gold-leafed or painted.

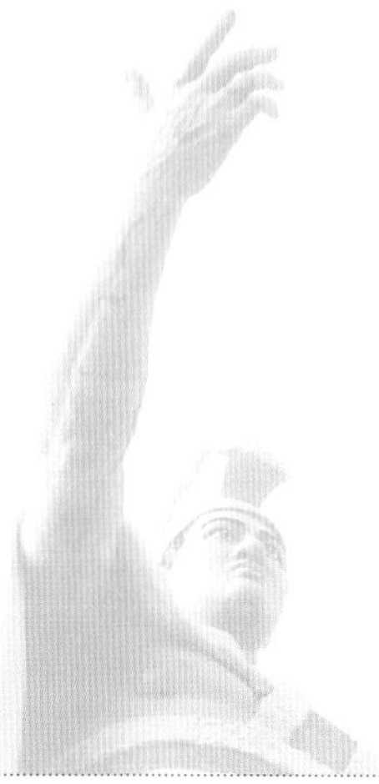

# 2 *Creating a "Pacific Hero"*

MOST OF THE ORIGINAL DOCUMENTS about the sculpture's commission reside in several well-guarded boxes in the Hawai'i State Archives in Honolulu.[1] I often research old correspondence to prepare my recommendations for conservation, but this was a rare treasure trove. The handwritten letters between the artist and the commissioning body are mixed in with photographs, newspaper articles, and other papers that have accumulated since the late nineteenth century. They are stored in an underground vault on the grounds of 'Iolani Palace. This extravagant gilt structure was built between the time the sculpture was commissioned in 1878 and its final installation five years later, on May 8, 1883. Knowing this fact enhanced the feeling of history as I visited the facility and spoke with state archivist Jeff White about the political and social turmoil during the late days of the Hawaiian kingdom.

At first I wasn't sure what I was looking for, other than any documentation that remained from the commission. The staff archivists didn't know what they would find, but they became interested in my quest to learn about the material and social history of the sculpture. Once they started searching, they produced box after box of material for me to sort through. I quickly discovered that the original letters were intact—and nearly all legible. The two key players whose letters I read were the artist, Thomas Ridgeway Gould, and the primary mover within the Hawaiian legislature, Walter Murray Gibson.

As I read through the boxes and sorted through microfiche archives, an almost unbelievable set of events came alive. I pieced together the steps of the process as well as hidden and not-so-hidden agendas that produced this unusual sculpture. The bias of newspaper articles also helped reveal how the heated politics of the day fed into its design. I learned of Gould's neoclassical obsessions as a sculptor, Gibson's personal ambitions to align himself with the struggling Hawaiian monarchy, and the interest of the reigning king, David Kalākaua, in associating himself with Kamehameha, the originator of the dynasty. The documents revealed a struggle across the Atlantic and Pacific to get the figure "right," in terms established by their joint vision. This vision reflected the political, economic, and cultural forces of the day, and in turn shaped the way people related to the sculpture through its history, leading to the unusual present-day practices of veneration and maintenance.

In one of his letters, the artist described the image as a "Pacific Hero"—a combination of words that signals a deliberate blending of Hawaiian and Western values. During its design and fabrication, Gould, Kalākaua, and the Hawaiian legislature's commissioning body fused cross-cultural elements to achieve their goals. To understand these goals, I read about the power dynamics at play in Hawai'i at the time of the sculpture's commission. It was a time when the emerging power of sugar barons, the threats of U.S. annexation, and the waning influence of Hawaiian royalty all coalesced.

King David Kalākaua (1836–1891) came to the throne in 1874 and reigned with a constitutional monarchy that replaced the absolute monarchy established by Kamehameha. Under Kalākaua, an elected legislature and a House of Nobles shared authority with the king. To strengthen his position vis-à-vis the U.S. government, as well as with the British and other colonial powers threatening the independence of the islands, Kalākaua negotiated trade deals with sugar barons such as Claus Spreckels of San Francisco. Among his overtures to the United States were the Reciprocity Treaty of 1875, which encouraged trade and large-scale investment by American entrepreneurs, and an 1887 amendment that allowed the United States to develop a naval base at Pearl Harbor.

The demographic and social conditions in the islands changed dramatically as U.S. business interests strengthened in Hawai'i. During the one hundred years following Captain Cook's arrival in 1778, descendants of early Polynesian settlers dwindled from a robust 800,000 to 47,508 due to infectious diseases brought by missionaries, sailors, and merchants.[2] The 1848 Māhele enactment of landed property rights turned much of the land over from Native Hawaiians to missionary descendants and U.S. businessmen, which radically altered traditional Hawaiian relationships to the land.[3] This facilitated the development of the sugar plantations. With the rapidly shrinking pool of Native labor and the increasing need for agricultural workers, haole (Caucasian) businessmen imported large numbers of Asian immigrants, thereby dramatically altering the cultural, political, and economic landscape of Hawai'i.

Racial antagonism intensified during Kalākaua's reign, with the king involved in a fragile balancing of opponents. Three groups were in rivalry: Native Hawaiians, part-Native Hawaiians, and haoles. Kalākaua increased his support among Native Hawaiians by promoting a revival of Hawaiian music, hula (Hawaiian dance), and other cultural forms that zealous missionaries had forced into secrecy. He also called for Hawaiians to *ho'oulu lāhui* (increase and preserve the race).

The Kamehameha sculpture was yet another way to promote the Native monarchy. I was shocked to learn that its commission was to honor the centennial of Captain Cook's "discovery" of the Hawaiian Islands. Yet it was in keeping with other sorts of cultural fusion, such as Kalākaua's European displays of pomp and power. The "Merrie Monarch," as he is sometimes remembered, not only sponsored dance and music festivals in the Native traditions but also engaged in courtly extravagance in grand European mode. He nearly bankrupted the kingdom with his elaborate reconstruction of the 'Iolani Palace in American/Italian style with electric lighting and gilt ornament. Shaping his regime to imply power and authority analogous to European monarchies was an effort to generate such power and authority. As it turned out, these measures had little effect. Toward the end of his life in 1887, members of the secretive and pro-American Hawaiian League and others forced him to sign a new constitution. This "Bayonet Constitution" effectively stripped him of power and restricted the voting rights of Native Hawaiians, further solidifying haole control.

Understanding these political, economic, and cultural tensions enriched what I learned about the design and fabrication of the sculpture. Because of the complex series of steps leading to the sculpture's final installation, I include a chronology in Appendix 2. Walter Murray Gibson (1822–1888) played a crucial role in all phases of the sculpture's early life. As a member of the Hawaiian legislature, he was one of only four haoles elected in 1878. Increasingly significant in Kalākaua's tight circle of power, he moved up to prime minister and minister of foreign affairs by the time the sculpture was installed in 1883.[4] In addition to his relentless efforts at commercial self-aggrandizement, Gibson was strong in his support of King Kalākaua and was a prominent advocate of Native Hawaiian traditions. Born in the southern United States, he learned to speak Hawaiian and even established a Hawaiian-language newspaper (*Ka nuhou o Hawaii*). In 1880 he purchased the English-language *Pacific Commercial Advertiser,* giving him a strong voice in the haole media as well.

I found an astounding speech given by Gibson in 1878 in which he lobbied to allocate funds for the sculpture:

> [W]hat is the most notable event, and character, apart from discovery, in this century, for Hawaiians to commemorate: What else but the consolidation of the archipelago by the hero Kamehameha? The warrior chief of Kohala towers far above any other one of his race in all Oceanica. . . . Therefore let Hawaiians, especially you Hawaiian Nobles and Representatives, lift up your hero before the eyes of the people, not only in story, but in everlasting bronze.[5]

He contrasted European monarchy with his vision of an unruly and violent Hawaiian past:

> You, representatives of the people, gathered here in orderly assemblage—in this noble hall, panoplied with the insignia, the crown, the sceptre, and banner of free and enlightened government. . . . We can imagine in 1778, on the site where we are assembled, a crowd of half-naked savages, mingling their loud, discordant cries with the dissonant beat of the ancient rude drum. The smoke for a sacrifice ascends, and we can picture an uplifted club falling upon a human victim to beat out his brains, where now the mallet of our worthy President only strikes to preserve peace and good will. This, O Hawaiians! this stride from savage disorder to our present order, is something worthy of your commemoration.

Gibson continued his oration by placing Kamehameha at the fulcrum of change. He implied that after a violent establishment of power, Kamehameha embraced European values of the Enlightenment:

> He began our century with savage war and massacre, and yet he was chiefly the destroyer of cruelty and superstition, and waded through human blood

> for the sake of enduring peace within his native isles. . . . He met destiny with the mind of a philosopher and a patriot, and Kamehameha, the barbarian conqueror, welcomed the new era with the spirit of an enlightened statesman; he made the white men his friends.

Gibson went on to associate the "young" nation of Hawai'i with ancient classical models, and he further argued for the need to mark this similarity with an appropriate monument:

> All nations keep their epochs and their eras. Rome dated from her foundation, and Greece from her Olympic games . . . nations mark the commemoration with some monument or memorial. . . . The British Parliament and the American Congress, and other representative bodies of enlightened States, have each voted hundreds of thousands of dollars for monuments to their great chiefs and teachers. . . . The Hawaiian Legislature must now prove its enlightenment in a similar recognition of the heroes of its history.

Following this remarkable presentation, the legislature duly allocated ten thousand dollars to commission the sculpture and formed a Commemorative Monument Committee to implement the process. Not surprisingly, Gibson was chairman. Four other members of the legislature assisted him, three of whom were Native Hawaiian.[6] Gibson traveled to New York, Boston, and other U.S. cities in search of an appropriate sculptor. There is no mention in the archives of considering Hawaiians to either design or produce the sculpture.

In September 1878, Gibson met Thomas Ridgeway Gould in Boston and selected him to be the artist. Born into a prominent New England family, Gould had connections that helped him receive important commissions, including busts of Ralph Waldo Emerson (now at Harvard Library) and John Hancock. In 1868, he moved his primary studio to Florence, where he continued to develop his work in the contemporary neoclassical style. The Kamehameha sculpture dominated the last three years of Gould's life. It was his largest and most important commission.

I found references to the commission in the U.S. media. Boston papers found Gould appropriate for the task:

> The legislative assembly . . . composed largely of descendants of Kamehameha's warriors, many grandsons of tattooed chiefs who carried

> on savage warfare . . . voted unanimously . . . for a work of art to commemorate their country's hero. . . . It has been thought fitting that Boston, which first sent Christian teachers and ships of commerce to the Islands, should have the honor of furnishing this commemorative monument.

Gibson appointed two Bostonians to oversee the legal and logistical arrangements.[7]

When Gibson returned to Honolulu, he wrote a report for King Kalākaua reiterating the nature of the contract "with Thomas R. Gould, sculptor of Boston, to design and construct a bronze statue of Kamehameha the Conqueror, of heroic size, or about seven feet in height to be finished within one year, or fifteen months at the farthest from date of contract." The artist followed the conventions of the day in the design and fabrication process: he began with an initial sketch and a small clay maquette (model). He then took molds off the clay maquette, and cast it in plaster. Gould sent photographs of the plaster cast to the committee in Honolulu for approval. He next enlarged the plaster model to a full-size clay model, then a full-size plaster cast. He sent additional photographs for approval by his client. In 1880 he shipped the plaster to the Barbedienne foundry in Paris for final casting and finishing.

One consequence of the lengthy process across the Pacific and Atlantic was a bond that formed between Gibson and Gould. As Gould wrote to Gibson, "You and I know that you were the prime mover and final victor in the fight for the statue. It is our statue, and shall be forever." The scrawled letters in the archive revealed that Gould and Gibson both had personal and political ambitions at stake. They worked intensely to "get it right" in their own terms.

John Charlot argues convincingly that Gould used the Roman sculpture of Augustus Caesar from Prima Porta—a sculpture well known in the United States and Italy at the time—as inspiration for the design.[8] Gould described improvements in the maquette by reporting to Gibson that "I have increased the likeness, lightened the body and raised the left hand higher up on the spear. He begins to look heroic." Indeed, Kamehameha's right arm in Gould's sculpture is lifted higher than the arm in the Augustus sculpture. The Kamehameha sculpture carries the spear in his left hand, like Augustus' scepter, even though Kamehameha is thought to have been right-handed. This classical inspiration found in Augustus Caesar was in keeping with Gould's other neoclassical work from the final years before his death.

Despite the Roman model, Gould and Gibson strove to create a likeness of Kamehameha's face, body, and clothing. This began with Gibson actively

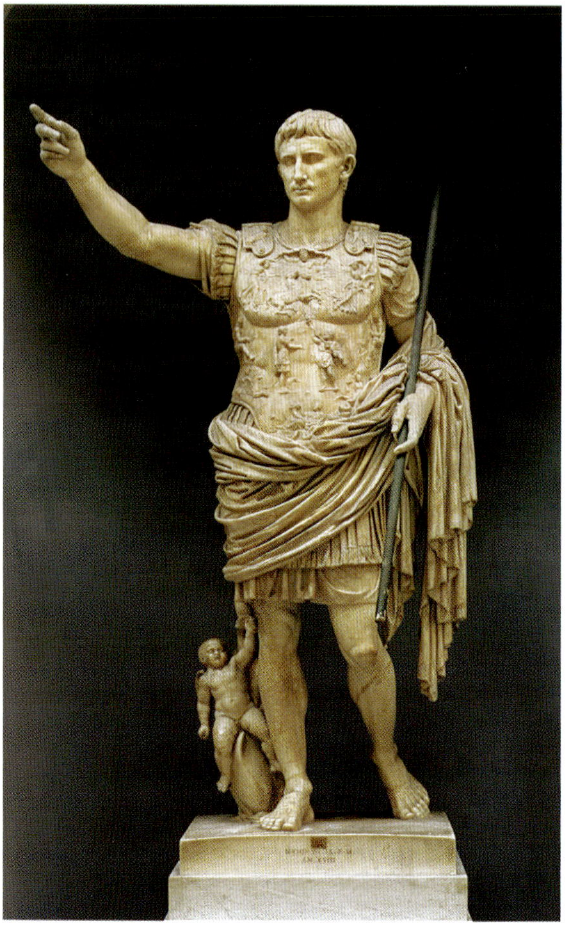

Augustus Caesar of Prima Porta. Six feet eight inches, Marble, c. 20 BC. Musei Vaticani, Vatican City, Italy. The Bridgeman Art Library.

engaging Gould in conversation over the initial sketch. A problem for all concerned was that no one knew exactly what Kamehameha looked like. On his trip to Boston, Gibson brought Gould a Kamehameha image that could only have been a rough approximation of his facial features. It was a French engraving that was a copy of a Chinese copy of a Russian artist's copy of his original portrait, executed in 1816. The Russian artist was Louis Choris, who was on board the Russian warship *Rurick* that came to the Hawaiian Islands in 1816 and 1817. Despite tensions between the Russians and Hawaiians due to previous acts of Russian aggression, Choris was able to get access and paint this portrait of Kamehameha on November 24, 1816. Before leaving Hawai'i, Choris gave Kamehameha two copies he had made back on his ship from his original portrait. Later, an American businessman borrowed one of these copies from Kamehameha and hired a Chinese artist to reproduce it for

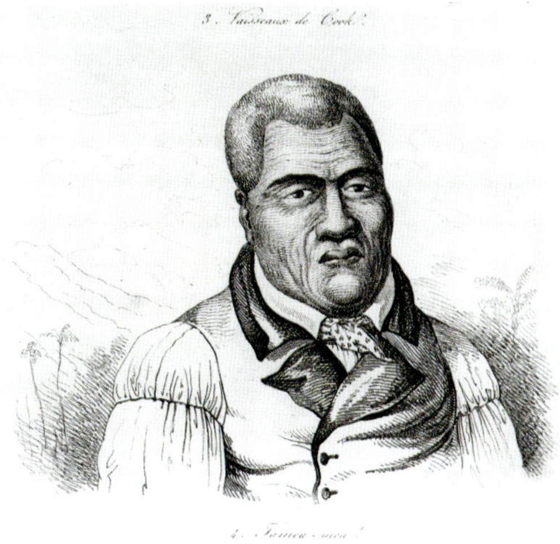

French engraving copied from a copy of a copy of a watercolor portrait of Kamehameha by Louis Choris, 1816. From *Voyage Pittoresque* by Dumont D'urville. Stanford University Library.

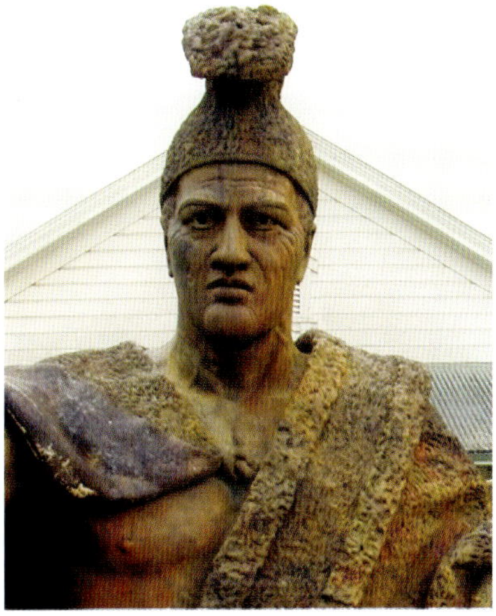

Detail of the Kamehameha sculpture after we stripped the paint off the surface in March 2001.

commercial purposes. The French traveler Dumont D'urville acquired one of these Chinese copies and copied it again in Paris as an engraving for his book, *Voyage Pittoresque.* Later, I found an original copy of this book in the archives at Stanford University and asked their photography department to scan it. This French engraving was the image that Gibson provided to Gould.

After seeing Gould's initial sketches, Gibson asked him to adjust Kamehameha's face to make him appear younger than D'urville's engraving. The goal was to make him about forty-five years old even though Kamehameha was about sixty-three in Choris' life portrait. Apparently the artist went too far in his modifications, causing Gibson to write after one of his studio visits that "the study which you undertook . . . is—in my opinion—a good design . . . but the chief correction must be in the face, which although designed to represent an earlier period should conform somewhat more in likeness to the engraved portrait which you have had for copy."

Besides the D'urville engraving, other sources entered into discussions of how the king should look. There was consensus that Kamehameha's heroic stature involved a certain degree of bulk. As Gibson wrote in the English-language newspaper he owned, "At the time Lieut. King (of Captain Cook's expedition) observed him, he was a young barbarian of unusual physical strength—All the traditions [*sic*] of him say that he had great breadth of shoulder and large abdomen, with long back, round massive head and a protruding chin of power."[9]

Another interesting set of images, created after Gould showed his early maquette to the Hawaiian Club of Boston, entered into the design process. Some of the members who had been to the islands complained to Gibson that the *malo* (loincloth) was inauthentic. This led to King Kalākaua's getting involved. He commissioned photographs of a "Native Hawaiian" dressed in Kamehameha's original feathered garments that had been handed down over the generations.

Through all of this communication over the design, Gould became increasingly distressed about not receiving his contract or initial payments for the commission:

> I am perplexed and disappointed by receiving from Mr. Brewer a letter in which he says he has received no authority from the Government Committee in Honolulu as regards the payment of first installment on Kamehameha Statue, nor any notice of approval or signature of the contract which I had signed and forwarded. Also that the photos of the Hawaiian with the original feather cloak on and of another nude Hawaiian. These delays delay the statue, particularly as warm weather is coming, and it is difficult to keep the clay moist in the summer heat. I have the iron skeleton of the figure already prepared and set up and all agencies ready for the work, but no news comes to me, no contract, no money.

Much delayed, Gould's final contract arrived with the five photographs commissioned by King Kalākaua. It describes their agreement:

> . . . a heroic, bronze statue of not less than seven feet and four inches in height, of King Kamehameha First, of the Hawaiian Islands, according to photographs sent to Thomas R. Gould, of native Hawaiian, robed in feather cloak, as worn by Hawaiian chiefs of the highest sovereign rank, and also having a helmet, baldric and other parts of costume of warrior chief of the old time in Hawaii, it being understood, that this costume shall be adhered to in the statue, but that the pose of spear in one hand, with the other hand extended, shall be in conformity with the study, or statuette, of Thomas R. Gould, as approved by the Chairman of the Committee when in Boston, and the head, arms and legs shall be represented nude as in said statuette.

Further reading surprised me once again. The photographs Kalākaua sent to Gould were not even of a full-blooded Native Hawaiian. There were in fact two men used as models: John Timoteo Baker, a member of the King's Guard, and Robert Hoapili Baker, his half-brother and first lieutenant in Kalākaua's troops. They were both personal friends of Kalākaua.

All this work to get the depiction of Kamehameha "right" suggests an effort to idealize him as an emperor-statesman with a strong body,[10] only partly based on Native Hawaiian models. John Timoteo was one quarter Native Hawaiian, one quarter Samoan, and half Caucasian. Robert Hoapili was half Native Hawaiian and half Caucasian. In Ms. Taylor's articles on the subject, she suggests that "King Kalākaua did not see anything peculiar about using a one-quarter Hawaiian as his model. He simply wanted the statue to be appealing to 'foreigners' and so selected the handsomest man in court."[11] These photographs represent another sort of fusion, cultural and biological, embedded in the sculpture as its makers sought to ensure their particular vision.

After examining debates in the literature over which half-brother modeled for which photographs, it seems likely that the model dressed in the cloak and other feathered garments is John Timoteo Baker and the "nude" model (actually garbed in what looks like long, dark underwear) is Robert Hoapili Baker. To add to the confusion, the photographs of John Timoteo Baker were in fact photomontages that grafted muscular legs of a local fisherman onto his torso.

Gibson and Kalākaua also paid close attention to Native Hawaiian artifacts and clothing on the sculpture that carry the insignia of high-ranking chiefs and the complex cultural system of *kūʻauhau* (genealogy), *kapu* (special privilege), and rank. Given the heightened criticism of the government by American businessmen, the press, and Native Hawaiian critics, gross errors in design would certainly evoke strong reactions.

King Kalākaua provided John Timoteo Baker with Kamehameha's *kāʻei* (sash), tied around the figure's waist and draped over his left shoulder, along with his *mahiole* (helmet) and *ʻahu ʻula* (cloak) to model in the photographs sent to Gould. The "Liliʻuokalani Sash" consists of thousands of tiny red and yellow feathers intricately secured to a woven support of *olonā* (*Touchardia latifolia*) bark.[12] It has a central band of red feathers flanked on each side and across the ends with yellow feathers. The central stripe of red feathers is what Kealoha Sugiyama represented in his 1996 paint job. They are most likely from the rare Hawaiian honey-creeper *ʻiʻiwi* (*Vestiaria coccinea*), and the yellow feathers are from the *ʻōʻō* (*Moho nobilis*). Human and fish teeth are arranged among the feathers along the end of the *kāʻei.* The *ʻahu ʻula* is

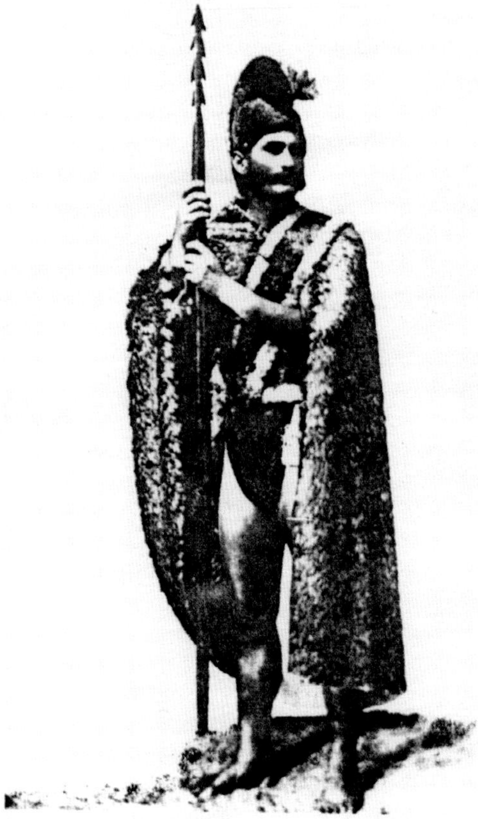

One of two photographs of John Timoteo Baker wearing Kamehameha's feathered garments sent to Thomas Ridgeway Gould. Photo attributed to J. J. Williams. Bishop Museum.

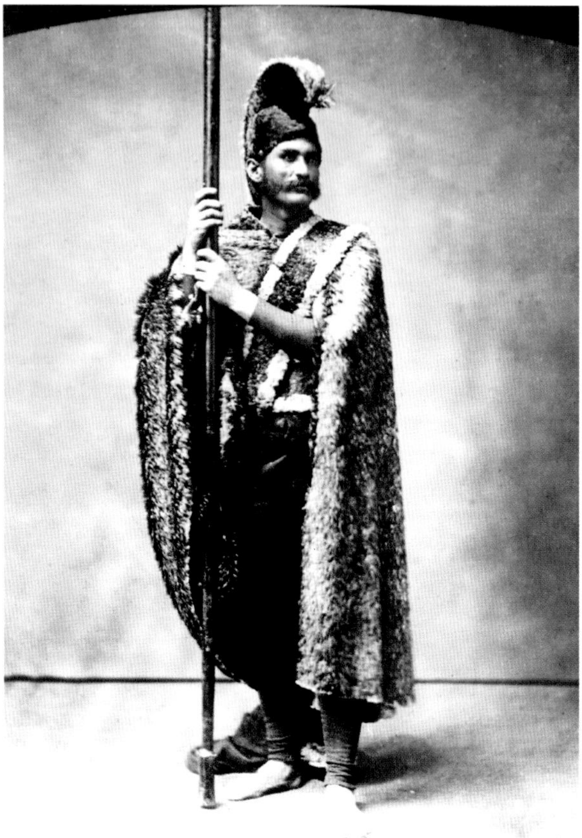

Original photograph of John Timoteo Baker wearing black stockings. M. Dickson, Bishop Museum.

composed of approximately 450,000 feathers from the now-extinct *mamo* tied to a net of fine mesh. On the sculpture, Gould curiously adorned the *'ahu 'ula* with a European tassel on its extension below the king's left arm. The helmet on the sculpture is believed to be the one that Kamehameha gave to his rival Kaumuali'i, chief of Kaua'i.[13]

The *pololū* (long spear) in Kamehameha's left hand is an inexact replacement of the original from a restoration campaign in 1883. Gould's original spear was barbed at the end, not straight. The *ali'i* (chiefs) in Hawai'i used long spears for both war and sport, whereas the barbed spear in Gould's design signifies peace. According to Taylor, Princess Likelike owned the *pololū* in the photographs that Kalākaua sent to the artist.

Despite the makers' efforts to get it right by their various and sometimes

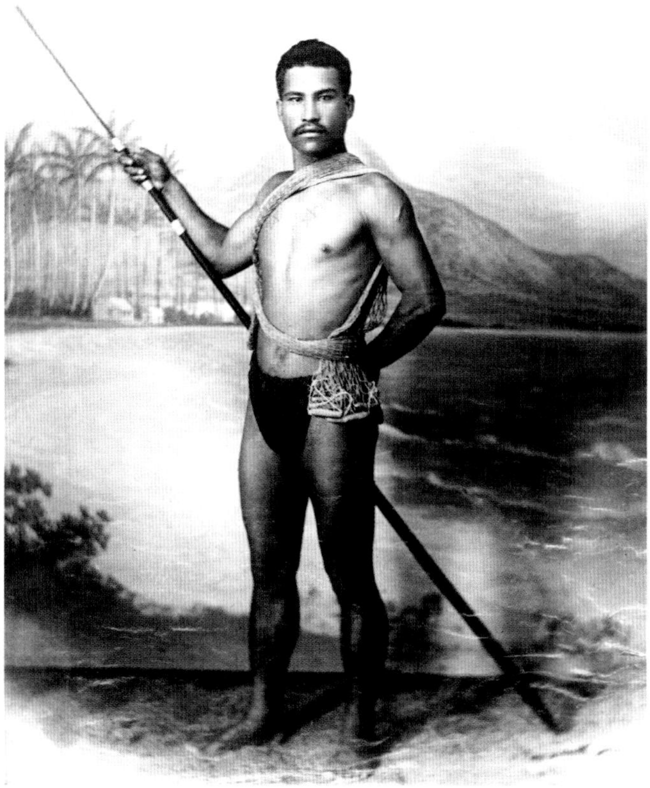

Photograph of a Hawaiian fisherman. His legs were spliced onto the original image of Baker to create the photomontage seen in figue opposite page, left. Bishop Museum.

conflicting principles, virtually from the beginning members of the press and the local population found fault with the result. Some of these same complaints persist in North Kohala today, often mentioned in connection with foreign mistakes in representing Hawaiian culture.

The most frequently mentioned mistake, then and now, are the sandals. Sandals were worn by Hawaiians, but only when traveling long distances on rough terrain. They made them from tough plant fibers of *ti* leaves or *kapa,* either twisted or braided. The artist made no effort to model Hawaiian-style sandals. In fact, the Commemorative Monument Committee asked the artist to modify a first version of the sandals, apparently already Roman in design, to give them a more classic look.

After the sandals, the next most noticed faults are the European-style tassel on the *'ahu 'ula* and the arrangement of the *kā'ei*. The *kā'ei* drags on the ground behind Kamehameha like a royal European train. This is not only considered degrading for one of the most important symbols of royal authority, but the delicate feathers would never survive abrasion from trailing behind their wearer. Changes were made during the design of the *kā'ei* to satisfy various parties, but as later observers pointed out, its arrangement is impossible without being two separate sashes.[14] Robert Hoapili Baker, one of the models for the photographs, described the arrangement of two sashes. A netted sash was "worn passed twice around the waist with the ends hanging down in front" while a feather sash "was brought over the shoulder and caught in the band in the small of the waist."

Surprisingly, I found no early complaints about the sculpture's right-hand gesture, since today people have a lot to say about it. According to John Keola Lake, a participant in our conservation project, Kamehameha would never use an open-hand gesture in this manner:

> In Hawaiian circles they only used an open hand in several instances. When there is a ritual that calls upon Kū,[15] when priests are convening . . . and asking for the powers above. That is the only time the hand gesture is done with the hand facing up, *huli kilima I lalo hana kapo'e o hana kanoke,* when the hand is turned downwards, he is prepared to work. When the hand is turned upwards, he rests, he has nothing to do. So it would be very un-Hawaiian for him to greet people beckoning with the hand up. To beckon is with the hand down. This gesture is offensive. Hawaiians would never greet people the way the sculpture is gesturing. That is an expression between the *ali'i* and his god.

The sculpture also has a problem in its materiality, both in the sense of long-term durability and of being true to Native Hawaiian practices. Gibson wanted to communicate material permanence in the European

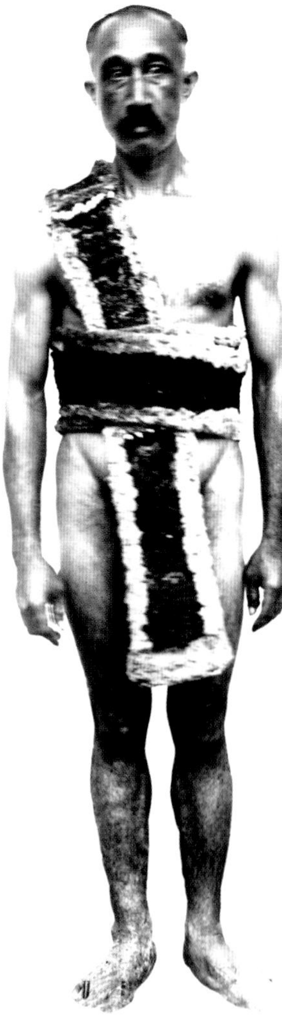

Undated photograph of a Hawaiian man wearing the feather sash of King Liloa, Hawaii. Bishop Museum. Photograph SP 126,642.

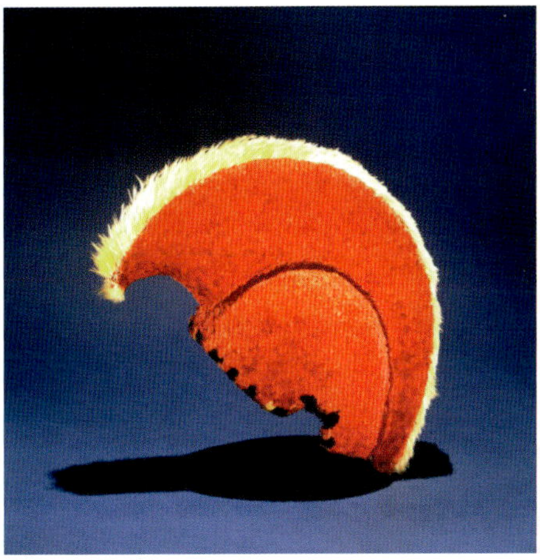

The "Kaumuali'i Helmet" used as a model for the Kamehameha sculpture. Bishop Museum. Accession No. 959.

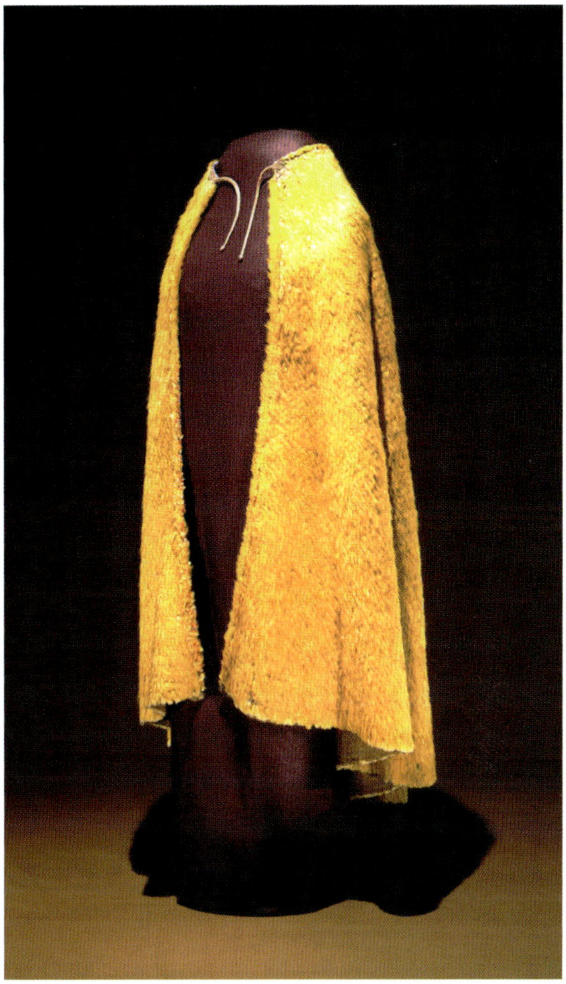

The "Kamehameha Cloak" used as a model for the sculpture (without the added European-style tassel). Bishop Museum. Accession No. 6828.

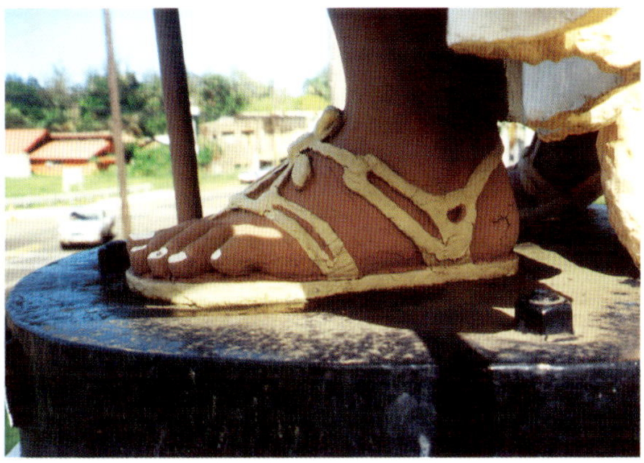

Detail of the classical-style sandals on the Kamehameha sculpture.

tradition of heroic representation. Figurative sculpture existed in Hawai'i, but wood was used almost exclusively, sometimes with the addition of feathers and other natural materials (see page 78). Temple sculptures were not installed on plinths. They were brought out under strict *kapu* (taboo) or during times of war. Sometimes they were burned after their usable life expired.[16]

Wood was not considered for the Pacific Hero. Surprisingly, the alloy analysis we performed from a small sample I took determined that it was cast in brass rather than bronze,[17] despite the constant reference to "bronze" during all stages of commissioning, design, and manufacture. Like bronze, brass is a copper alloy but one whose secondary constituent is zinc. It was used with some frequency in nineteenth-century France. Its physical behavior is similar to bronze, and after exposure to the elements, only analysis can distinguish the two alloys. Either alloy was a good choice for a durable sculpture in climates of Europe and North America. As I already knew from other projects in Hawai'i, the mid-Pacific subtropical environment is not favorable to either.

The use of European technology served as an advertisement for European ways. For those abroad, it communicated Hawai'i's participation in European conventions. The Barbedienne foundry was known for its high-quality casting and was used by Rodin, Barye, and other important sculptors of the time. The sculpture is well executed. It is hollow-cast over an internal iron armature support and welded onto a circular copper alloy base. Gould exhibited the cast in Paris before transporting it to Germany for shipment to Honolulu. According to a Honolulu news report quite likely authored by Gibson, it was seen by "sculptors and other scientific men, and it had really been an interesting advertisement for this country."

But none of this technology nor the larger aspirations had anything to do with Hawaiian traditions. Hawaiians did not create monuments to commemorate heroes. Whereas the foundry welded the letters "KAMEHAMEHA I" on the front of the circular base, precontact Hawaiians used pictographs to communicate. The foundry incised the sculptor's name and date of the final design in Italy on the base: "T.R. GOULD Inv, et Fecit / FLORENCE 1879." They also identified themselves with an incised inscription below the left foot: "F. BARBEDIENNE, Fondeur / PARIS." Hawaiian tradition does not record names of people who create sculptures. Any such effort is an affront to the spirit, or *mana,* inhabiting the object.

The mixed messages I discovered in the design of the Kamehameha sculpture are a result of intentional manipulation of Hawaiian and Western materials and symbols to achieve desired effects. The stance of a Roman

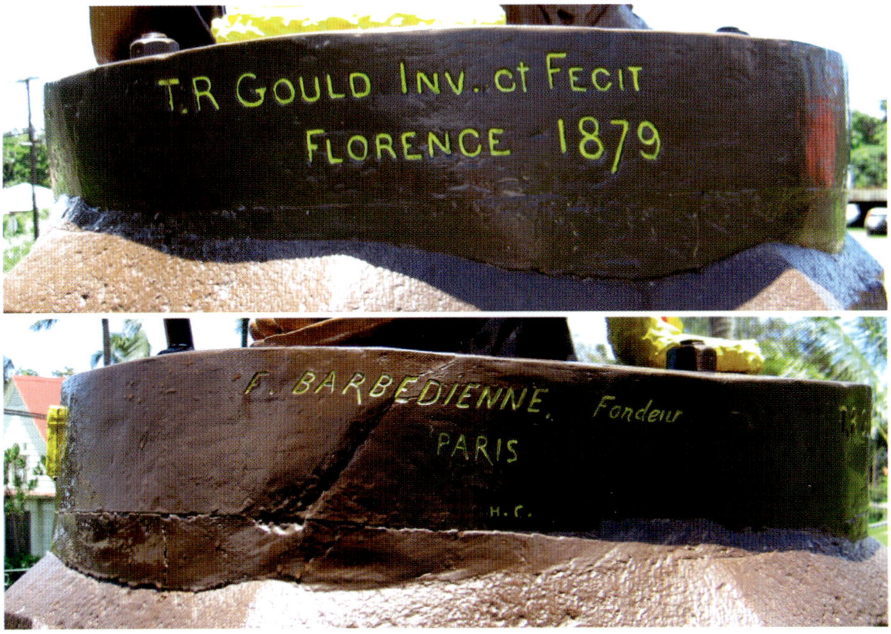


Inscriptions on the circular base.

emperor communicates European technology and ideology, yet he is cloaked in the most highly venerated feathered vestments of Hawaiian royalty. The design and fabrication was a European project grafted onto Native Hawaiian cultural traditions. But as I learned in the archives, this transcultural construction was not a simple melding of two traditions. It was a deliberate effort to celebrate a Hawaiian conversion to European values, while retaining sanitized versions of both cultural traditions. Implicit in the undertaking was a desire to create a classical-style sculpture that recalls indigenous cultural roots yet distances itself from the "savage" and "barbaric" past by association with North American and European political ideology. Gibson, Kalākaua, and Gould reconstructed Kamehameha as the Pacific Hero who set the stage for transition from "barbarism" to a Christian republic.

At one point during my research in the archives, it dawned on me that I was only reading documents from the sculpture's makers and the mainstream Honolulu press. After this realization, I contacted Puakea Nogelmeier, chair of the Hawaiian Language Department at the University of Hawai'i at Mānoa, to ask about Hawaiian newspapers from that time. He explained that most of the Hawaiian press hadn't survived, and most of what exists remains untranslated. By the end of our meeting, he convinced me to contract one of his students,

Sahoa Todd Fukushima, to search the archives for me and translate relevant articles. This suggestion paid off—from his research and translations I learned of other points of view not communicated in the boxes of English documents I was going through. In one instance, Fukushima found complaints from Kohala about the location chosen for the sculpture.[18] Local residents argued that it should not be installed in Honolulu, but at a site more appropriate to Kamehameha's life in Kohala. I learned that when King Kalākaua visited Kohala in December 1880, members of a local audience protested, requesting that a sculpture also be made for Kohala. Little did they know that their wish would come true.

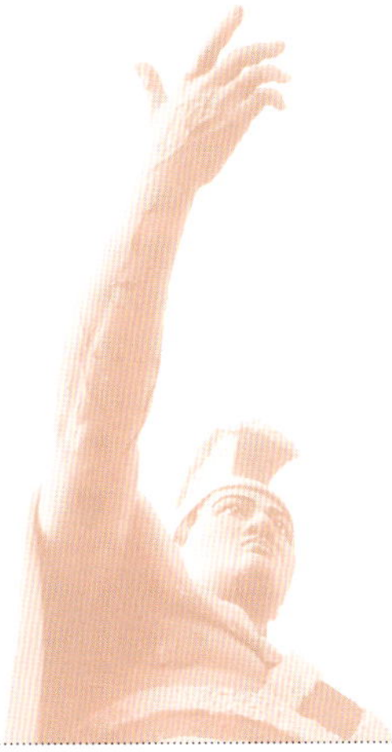

# 3 *Shipwreck*

ON AUGUST 21, 1880, the sculpture left Bremen, Germany, en route to Honolulu aboard the ship *George F. Haendel.* Although details in the accounts I found vary, the ship encountered a storm in the south Atlantic off the coast of Argentina. A fire broke out, then the ship struck a reef and sank to the bottom of the sea near the Falkland Islands. All the cargo went down, including the nine-and-a-half ton crate on the deck containing the sculpture.

The news traveled quickly to Honolulu. Fortunately the Hawaiian legislature had insured the sculpture for 50,000 marks (approximately $12,000), and with the insurance settlement the legislature commissioned a second cast for $7,000. The foundry made this second cast by taking new molds from Gould's plaster model. With an additional sum of $4,000 from insurance money, Gould and Gibson decided to add something they had always wanted: four partial-gilt bronze bas-relief panels depicting scenes from Kamehameha's life for the sides of the pedestal.

Gibson wanted to use these panels as propaganda, like Trajan's Column and other classical monuments that portray heroic battles. Gould returned to Florence and started work on the four bas-reliefs. He completed the maquette for the first relief, but died of a heart attack on November 26, 1881, at his house

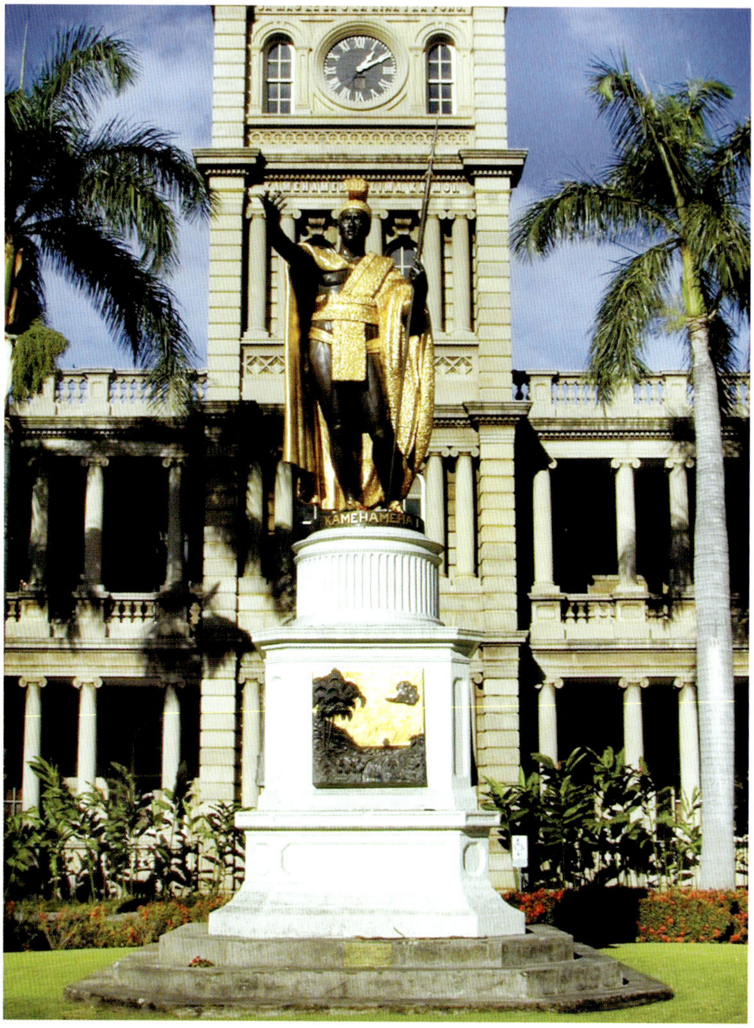


The second cast of the sculpture, standing in front of the Ali'iolani Hale government building in Honolulu.

and studio in the Poggio Imperiale of Florence, before completing the other maquettes.[1] Marshall S. Gould, the artist's son and also a sculptor, assumed the task of completing all four reliefs. As described in a letter I found in the archive from the artist's wife: "My Husband left his tool embedded in the clay of the second relief, and my boy modeled [and finished] them." The bas-reliefs mounted on the base of the Honolulu sculpture depict historic scenes from Kamehameha's life to help create an image of him as a Pacific Hero in

a b

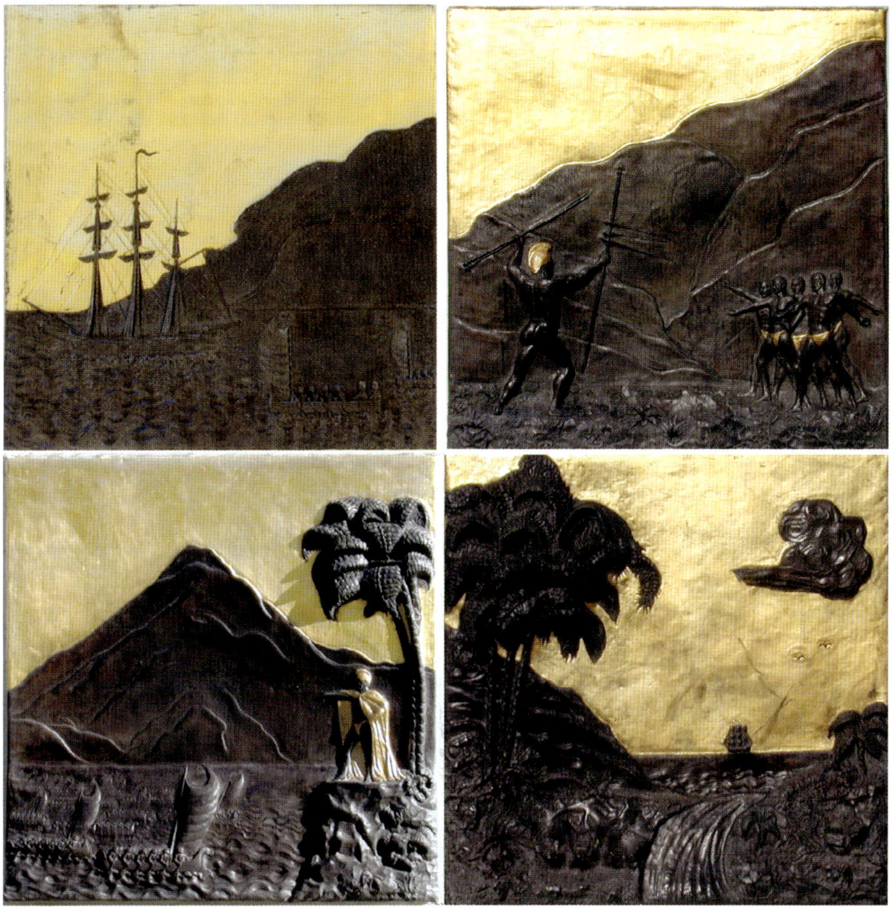

c d

Bas-relief panels on the plinth of the Honolulu cast, designed by Thomas Ridgeway Gould. 1881.

*a.* The young chief Kamehameha's first encounter with Captain James Cook, on board the *Resolution* off Lahaina in 1778.

*b.* The warrior Kamehameha warding off five spears hurled at one time.

*c.* Kamehameha's review of the *peleleu* war fleet off the coast of Kohala.

*d.* People rest along a road, illustrating Kamehameha's "Law of the Splintered Paddle," or Māmalahoe, in which he guaranteed free and safe access to roadways.

the Roman tradition. There is some debate whether Kamehameha was even at some of the historic events.

To the surprise of Honolulu officials, news came from the harbor on March 27, 1882, that the sculpture had arrived earlier than expected, aboard the *Earl of Dalhousie.* Upon inspection, Gibson and others found that it wasn't the second cast, but the original, retrieved from the bottom of the sea. Conflicting versions about what actually happened quickly spread throughout

Honolulu. Stories about the storm, the fire, the shipwreck, and the rescue all became part of the sculpture's history, complicating the already mixed message of its origins as a neoclassical Hawaiian king in celebration of Cook's Pacific "discovery."

I found various accounts of the rescue in contemporary newspapers, but it seems that a fisherman brought it up from the sea by tying ropes around its waist and lifting it on board his boat. A wrecker purchased it from the fisherman and sold it to an "old junk dealer," who placed it in front of his store in Port Stanley on East Falkland Island. On an eight-day stopover at the port, Captain Jarvis of the British ship *Earl of Dalhousie* recognized it as the lost Kamehameha sculpture and paid an equivalent of $300 or $500 (reports differ) on speculation of selling it for a higher price upon his arrival in Honolulu.

The sculpture lost its right forearm and spear during the recovery and experienced a deep gouge in the back of the cloak. The port pilot from Port Stanley revealed years later that "[w]hile loading it onto the ship [*Earl of Dalhousie*], one of the hands was broken off." Gibson manipulated the story to help achieve his political intentions in his newspaper, the *Pacific Commercial Advertiser:*

> The condition of the original statue is very good, considering its extraordinary experience. The right outstretched hand is melted off [*sic*] near the wrist, a small hole is broken into the feather cloak, and the spear held in the left hand is gone, but the feathers, and the feather helmet have not suffered in any way. The anatomy of the physique of the noble figure is finely displayed; and we wonder that the raging fury of the flames of a burning ship should have so slightly scathed the bronze warrior. The statue was placed on the deck of the *Geo. F. Haendel,* and this will account somewhat for the slight injuries it received. It will be no difficult matter to replace the lost palm, to mend the cloak and to put a new spear in the hero's hand. Then when set upon his pedestal he will stand up before admiring Hawaiians, as their Conquering Chieftain, coming forth from the flames, and rising up out of the sea, a harbinger of fresh hope and life unto his people and State.
>
> It is a very generally expressed opinion among the people, that the mutilated bronze warrior should be set up without repairs, except the replacing of the spear.

After assessing the damaged figure and negotiating with Captain Jarvis, the Hawaiian government purchased it for $875 or $1,200, depending on the source. It was temporarily taken to the Aliʻiolani Hale government building in Honolulu, and Gibson arranged for a shed to house it until restoration could take place. To replace the broken forearm, the legislature commissioned a new one from the artist's son, who had it cast at the Barbedienne foundry. This forearm arrived with the second sculpture and the four panels on January 3, 1883, on the British ship *Aberman.*

The Monument Committee decided to install the second cast, which was in better condition, at the original location in Honolulu. Where to install the original cast was up for debate. Representatives from Kohala asserted their claim to have it installed at Kamehameha's birthplace. The *Hawaiian Gazette,* critical of Gibson and his political aspirations, suggested that "Lānaʻi [the location of Gibson's ranch] would certainly be an appropriate resting place; but it is said Kohala desires to put in a claim. If it goes up to the latter place it is intended to put a placard underneath, explaining the loss of the hand. Our friend H suggests, 'burnt it, speculating on sugar!'"

I could not trace any details of the restoration process, but from my own examination of the sculpture, the major steps in the process are clear. Someone welded the new forearm onto the damaged sculpture shortly after it arrived in Honolulu and placed the new (unbarbed) spear through the sleeve created by his left hand.

Later newspaper articles mention fabrication of the replacement spear in Honolulu, not Paris. During technical analysis, I discovered material evidence of the restoration process, such as lead/tin solder welding material in the gouge on the cloak.

Despite the rich trove of documents and media accounts I found in Honolulu, I still hadn't found the answer to my central question about the statue's original finish. Since the sculpture spent fifteen months underwater and experienced damage of other sorts in transit, there was no easy way to know what the sculpture looked like after it was cast in Paris. Was it partial-gilt and chemically patinated like the second cast in Honolulu? Was it painted, as it was in 1996 when I first saw it? If so, what colors? Was it entirely chemically patinated like most bronze sculptures of the era? This common process involves heating acidic solutions on the metal surface with a torch to yield brown, black, or green colors. Or was it something else again? Gold was an appropriate choice to further align Kamehameha with European royalty and classical traditions, but it was expensive.

From Gould's and Gibsons' letters I learned that gilding was not part of the original budget, yet as Gibson wrote, "The artist suggests that the feather cloak, helmet, baldric and belt, be in gold bronze, which I cordially approve." They lobbied for additional money, but the correspondence provides no evidence that they procured funds for gilding. Perhaps the insurance settlement provided funds to gild the second cast, but Gould and Gibson hadn't won their argument for extra finances to gild the first.

Early descriptions of the first sculpture further cloud the issue. An article written shortly after it was cast but before it arrived in Honolulu implies that it was indeed gilt. "The feather mantle and helmet are a gold bronze, whilst the body is a dark bronze, thus forming a beautiful contrast." Yet a description upon unveiling clearly asserts that it was not:

> This, the original statue of Kamehameha I, of which the one that stands in front of Ali'iolani Hale is the replica, is all one color; that is to say, the feather cloak has not been gilded.

I found no mention in the archives of the surface color after the shipwreck or before restoration. The only known account of the retrieval from the ocean is a dubious story from Captain Radcliffe, then port pilot at Port Stanley. Thirty-two years later, in 1912, he came to Honolulu and provided the following story of events that centralizes his role in the dramatic story and implies an original gilt surface:

> Several months [after the shipwreck] a fisherman returned to port with the news that he had sighted the remains of the lost ship's hull . . . a few hundred yards off shore. . . . A diving crew was formed . . . with myself as leader. . . . After stumbling over boxes and wreckage, I came across what seemed to be a large bronze statue. I hastily knocked away the case in which it was packed, and sure enough, the statue of some warrior blazed forth in all his splendor.

My later conversations with residents in North Kohala shed no further light on the ambiguity I found in the archives. The rich stories about painting the sculpture, told by *kūpuna* (elders) and handed down across generations, contain no evidence of an original gilt appearance. No one I spoke with in North Kohala ever considered that it was originally gold-leafed. Everyone thought it had always been painted.

By the time the two casts arrived in Honolulu, the centennial of Captain Cook's "discovery" had come and gone. In arranging for the king's coronation

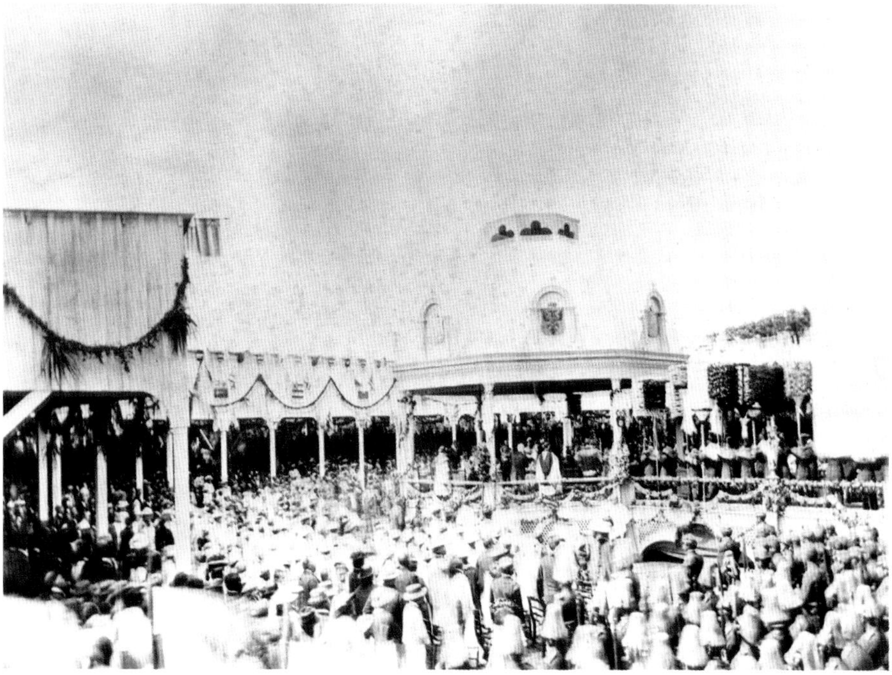

Coronation of King David Kalākaua. Ali'iolani Palace, Honolulu. February 12, 1883. Hawai'i State Archives.

celebration that was in fact slated for the ninth anniversary of Kalākaua's election to the throne, Gibson convinced Kalākaua to unveil the Honolulu cast as part of his coronation ceremony. This was a change from the legislature's original intention for the monument to mark Cook's encounter with the islands. Thus even before its unveiling, the sculpture multiplied into two casts and its central meaning shifted from celebrating Cook to celebrating Kalākaua. The coronation took place at the 'Iolani Palace on February 12, 1883.

Just as its makers combined Hawaiian and European traditions in designing the sculpture, the ceremonies for investiture and unveiling mixed the two worlds. The celebrations combined European royal pageantry and sacred Hawaiian ritual, with references to Christianity. The "Coronation of their Majesties the King and Queen of the Hawaiian Islands and the Unveiling of the Statue of Kamehameha I," a pamphlet based on text from an article in Gibson's *Pacific Commercial Adviser,* provides a typically approving account of the events:[2]

> The king wore the white uniform of the Guards, with a white helmet, and plume of white, red and blue. He wore the Grand Cordon, Star and

Collar of the Order of Kamehameha I.; the Star of the Imperial Order of the Chrysanthemum of Japan; the Star of the Order of St. Michael and St. George of England; the Star of the Order of the Conception of Portugal; and the Star of the Order of the Crown of Hawaii.

[There was a] procession bearing the King's jewels and decorations, the sceptre, the sword of state, the crowns, robes, the *palaoa* [whale tusk lei], the *pūloʻuloʻu* [tapa covered ball on a staff carried by a chief as insignia of taboo], the torch of Iwikauikaua, the Kāhili [feather standard, symbolic of royalty] of *Pili*. . . . The ceremony involved receiving the Kingly Sword, the Kamehameha cloak, the King's ring, the King's sceptre, and finally, the crown.

Then a Christian prayer:

Almighty Father, who crownest thy faithful servants with mercy and loving kindness, look down upon these, thy Servants, Kalakaua and Kapiolani, who now in lowly devotion bow their heads to Thy Divine Majesty; and as Thou dost this day set crowns of pure gold upon their heads, so enrich their royal hearts with Thy Heavenly Grace, and crown them with all princely virtues which may adorn the high stations wherein Thou has placed them, and Thine the honor and glory for ever and ever. Amen.

The non-Gibson-owned *Saturday Press* offers a less glowing, even scathing account titled *King Kalakaua's Koronation Kraze Komes to a Krisis!*:

The decorations of the pavilion are cheap, meager and ineffective . . . few native women received invitations. . . . One native woman rises and delivers a monotonous medley concerning fuss and feathers in general, and this fuss and those feathers in particular.

If the Hawaiian Government were intent on bringing royalty into discredit they could not better perform their task than by setting up their elaborate burlesque of medieval nonsense. In some particulars, the Hawaiian Kingdom is itself a burlesque. Its nationality is a thing of the past and its royal line is no longer on the throne. The chief revenues of the kingdom are derived from the property taxes of foreigners, and its Government is administered by shrewd Americans. . . .

[P]opular opinion and feeling which preceded and followed the event form one of the most dismal pictures ever recorded in the annals of the nation. How the aspirations of a vain monarch, led on by the plausible and persistent utterances of a glib-tongued but unscrupulous courtier

> [presumably Gibson], forced upon an unwilling people, an empty though costly ceremony . . . disquietude at home, and ridicule abroad, have been the results . . . his popularity among his own people has declined as a consequence of his coronation.

A similar diversity of cultural references and opinions comes from the sculpture's unveiling two days after the coronation. The ceremony included lines of troops, the king's guards in military finery, a horse brigade, the brass band, assembled school children, and various elements of Hawaiian royal regalia. *Thrum's Annual,* an almanac of events and statistics in Hawai'i, condemns the "nightly hula festivities that was a retrograde step of heathenism and a disgrace to the age. The feasts, regatta and races that were given proved a sad travesty on the spirit of enthusiastic loyalty which it aimed to bring forth."[3] The *Saturday Press* describes the sculpture as "an ideal barbaric hero" and "a daily center of attraction for a gathering of Hawaiian gazers."

As expected, Gibson's *Pacific Commercial Advertiser* provides more upbeat coverage, including a review of Gibson's own unveiling speech that strengthened associations between Kalākaua and Kamehameha:

> The first Monarch laid the foundation in the obscurity of a rude time, with his spear and strong arm. The seventh Monarch, who had just been crowned, perfects the national structure with all the enlightened and scientific appliances of our age. May the race of the great hero be preserved. May the Hawaiians be roused to the devotion to the nationality founded by the Conqueror.

An article translated from *Kū'oko'a,* a Hawaiian-language newspaper, celebrates the ceremony and marks Gibson's speech in a similar way:

> As the Hawaiian flags which covered the statue were removed, the prime minister, W. M. Gibson, opened the day's events relating to the statue, relating in English, the story of Kamehameha I and his famous deeds of bravery. Gibson said a few words in Hawaiian in front of the crowd about the statue thusly:
>
> 'Oh people of Hawai'i, behold today this bronze statue of Kamehameha I. This statue is somewhat like when Moses of the Israelites placed the bronze statue of the snake in the forest to give them life. Well, what of this statue? It gives life to the Hawaiians, etc.'

I wanted to know what Native Hawaiian people thought about the sculpture, but I found few references. Another article in *Kūʻokoʻa* that appeared ten days after the unveiling takes a dim view of community reaction:

> The ancient practices of the Hawaiians are not gone. Last Wednesday, when the statue of Kamehameha was unveiled, some people threw coins as offerings to the statue of Kamehameha. How funny! The ignorant deeds of long ago are still with us.

In contrast, the *Pacific Commercial Advertiser* provides a sympathetic reading of local response: "The Hawaiians appear to take great interest in the Statue of Kamehameha. Crowds of people were around it on Saturday night last and all day yesterday. Some of the old men and women gave vent to their feelings on looking at the Statue in chants and meles [songs or chants] in low tones."

About five weeks later, the paper gives more detailed commentary. Although given through the prism of Gibson's own newspaper, the following excerpt is one of the few examples I found that provides an indication of the political and spiritual meaning invested in the sculpture by Native Hawaiians at the time of its installation:

> There has not passed a day since its erection when there has not been crowds standing by and around it and engaged in a steady contemplation . . . we have heard frequent remarks made by those contemplating the statue, and were especially struck with one expression uttered in the Hawaiian language. "Will the chief let his people die?" This was the utterance, no doubt, of an anxious, patriotic soul, who, having been oppressed in heart with the frequent statement that his race was passing away.
>
> The statue is an ever-speaking history . . . we speak of this, not to set forth how, possibly, a simple people may be led by a superstitious influence to attach undue reverence to a work of art, but to show how a weak, suffering, and declining people may be aroused to a renewed hopefulness and to a better determination to strive for the improvement of themselves and their fellows, by a work of art which embodies great and noble qualities and a pre-eminent success.

A book of *mele*, published three years later, reflected the glories of the sculpture. As translated into English, one of the *mele* fervently commemorated it, fusing Gibson into its creation as the person who "carved" it:

Oh Kamehameha I
The great chief of us here
You died, but you live anew
On February 14
At Aliʻiōlani Hale.
The man-o-war bird soared on the Day of the Unveiling
Your cloak of mamo feathers
The feather helmet
Your spear like a spinning, challenging war club
You inspire me with fear
Oh great famous warrior of our Hawaiʻi.
The great chief Kamehameha lives
Carved by Gibson
Alleluia, Hip Hip Hooray![4]

After intense debate, the original cast was sent to Kohala. It arrived on May 1, 1883, following its Honolulu restoration. From the Māhukona port that was built up to export cane, the sculpture was transported on a railway built to service the plantations. Workers pulled the crate by steam power and wire rope onto a cane wagon that carried it to the planned location above the government-built road. The original site for its installation was the small village of Āinakea, a location having no relevance to Kamehameha's life—it was neither his birthplace, the location of his residence, nor the site of any significant military or ceremonial event. Āinakea was equidistant between two major sugar cane sites, the Star Mill and the Kohala Plantation. The Kohala Monument Committee chose the location in conjunction with the island's governess, Princess Kekaulike.

The May 8 unveiling in Kohala was smaller in scale than its Honolulu counterpart. Based on contemporary accounts, the ceremony had a stronger balance toward Native Hawaiian interests. King Kalākaua traveled from Honolulu on the Russian warship *Nayezdnik,* together with his Honor Guard and his Household Guard under Robert Hoapili Baker, the minister of the interior and one of the models used in the photographs for Gould, and the Royal Hawaiian Band. Since the concrete plinth wasn't fully set, the sculpture was suspended above it from a crane for the ceremony. As one witness reported:

> The King advanced and performed the act by pulling a string, the Hawaiian flag fell, and the crowd of people had the peculiar spectacle

> before [them of] the ancient conqueror suspended by his head to a fair model of a gallows, he being virtually hung in effigy.[5]

Reverend E. Bond, a descendant of first missionaries, offered a prayer in Hawaiian, and the Royal Hawaiian Band played the national anthem, *Hawai'i Pono'ī,* composed by Kalākaua during the first year of his reign.

Despite my desire to know how local people then, as now, responded to the sculpture, I found only a few references to Native Hawaiians' reactions—and from Honolulu media only. The *Honolulu Gazette,* politically opposed to Gibson on various fronts, gives an unfavorable description of the day's events and of Native Hawaiian participation:

> [A] succession of speeches and harangues from various native gentlemen of an apparently patriotic nature, then some more singing of the national air, then more speeches and graticculations [*sic*], all of which occupied nearly an hour, after this a feint [*sic*] attempt was made to raise a cheer but though often sought for, the majority were too apathetic to respond, so the will was taken for the deed, and then with much "pomp and circumstance," the order was given to unveil the work of art.
>
> As the work was now finished, the sight-seers dispersed rapidly, and soon but little was left to attract comment except the artistic work displayed. A few lingered to congratulate each other upon the successful termination of the event while others despatched trying to solve within their minds the problem of approximate values, and vast shrinkage of royalty.

The *Pacific Commercial Advertiser* provides a different account of community reaction in Kohala:

> Simultaneously with the exposure of the bronze figure, the band played *Hawai'i Pono'ī,* the assembled crowed cheered vociferously. Leis and wreaths of flowers and evergreens were placed at the feet of the statue and around the pedestal by the admiring Hawaiians.
>
> The concert [the evening before the unveiling] was followed by an impromptu dance which was kept up with spirit until midnight. This formed a grand climax to one of the most enjoyable evenings ever passed in the Kohala district.

Aside from Gibson's own paper, much of the English-language press expressed little sympathy for Kalākaua, Gibson, and the Hawaiian legislature's efforts to construct their Pacific Hero. It was a project associated with a particular faction of haole and Native Hawaiian society and its political and commercial elite in an attempt to use royal lineage and indigenous attributes to foster continued industrial expansion in the islands. It also corresponds to an ideology of stirring Native Hawaiian nationalism while reserving Hawai'i for certain pioneering haole residents, rather than sharing their commercial and political power with mainland groups, as might happen with U.S. annexation. With scarce representation in the media and a dearth of original sources in Kohala, I found it difficult to assess the real perceptions and associations of Native Hawaiians with this Pacific Hero project.

In the years immediately following the 1883 installation, Kalākaua's constitutional monarchy was destroyed following the forced signing of the "Bayonet Constitution" in 1887 that reduced his powers.[6] His sister, Queen Lili'uokalani, came to power after his death in 1891 but was dethroned and imprisoned with backing from the U.S. Navy. American businessmen and descendants of the missionary families staged a coup, seizing control of the government. A provisional government was initially established, which was transformed into the American-dominated Republic of Hawai'i in 1894. By 1898 the islands were officially annexed to the United States as the Territory of Hawai'i, which remained until 1959, when Hawai'i became a state of the union.

Over the years in North Kohala, the sculpture's symbolism gradually shifted with these political changes in Honolulu, along with more local currents in politics and culture. To better understand these relationships, I read about the dramatic changes in the economy and demographics of North Kohala since the mid-nineteenth century. The sugar industry almost entirely replaced the region's traditional agrarian subsistence and its system of local trade, with a cash-based economy linked to international markets.[7] In one form or another, by the time the sculpture arrived, sugar was everywhere. The sculpture stood at the edge of a cane field that was part of a vast plantation landscape. When the missionary school[8] located behind the sculpture closed its doors in 1912, local residents decided to move the sculpture from the cane field to its present location in the town of Kapa'au, which served the sugar industry as a place of local commerce.[9]

A plantation-based hierarchy emerged in North Kohala during the late

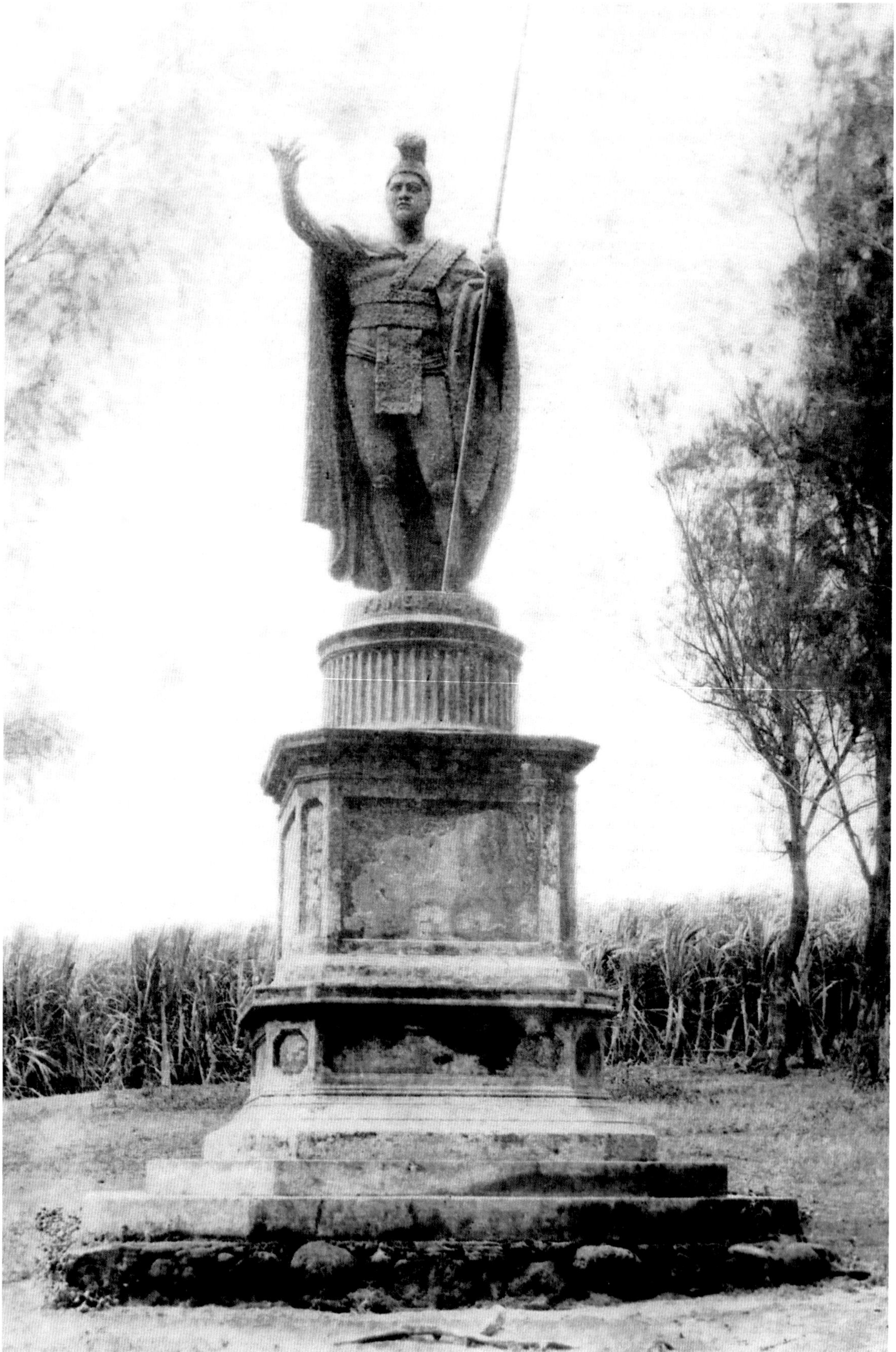

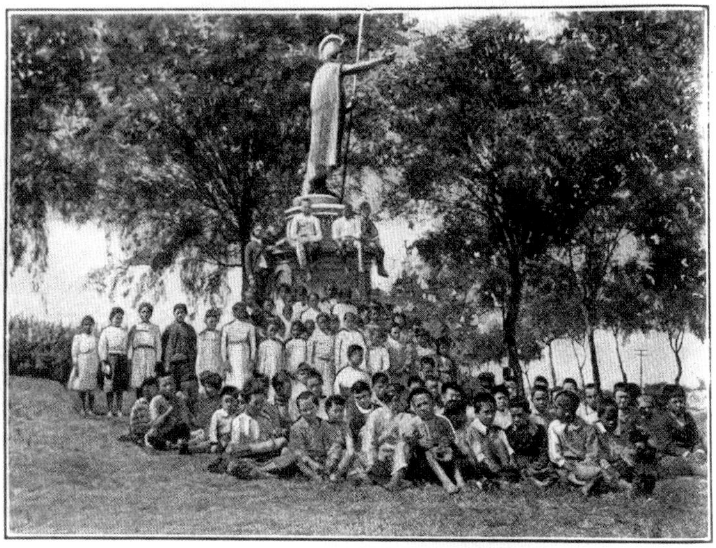

STATUE OF KAMEHAMEHA IN KOHALA.

Kamehameha sculpture with students from the adjacent missionary school in Āinakea, c. 1908. George W. Baldwin, *Geography of the Hawaiian Islands* (New York: American Book Co. 1908). University of Hawaiʻi at Mānoa Library.

nineteenth century, in which the missionary social structure of a prior generation played a pivotal role. Father Elias Bond arrived in Kohala in 1841 in service of the Protestant American Board of Commissioners for Foreign Missions, and his influence extended well beyond the church during his forty-three years of work. Bond organized schools and assumed responsibility as postmaster, land surveyor, teacher, and doctor. Kamehameha IV referred to Bond as the "King of Kohala" because of his dominant role in the region.[10] Like missionaries throughout Hawaiʻi whose descendants became major land and sugar plantation owners, Bond had a hand in initiating the industry in Kohala.

As the plantations established themselves, they took over Bond's role in administering social services, including education, health care, and sale of provisions to their employees. They also segregated company housing by nationality of the workers. Shiro Takata, a third-generation Japanese resident and owner of the region's largest grocery store, told me about their pervasive influence during his childhood. "The bosses of the plantations decided

**OPPOSITE PAGE:** Kamehameha sculpture at the edge of a sugar cane field. Date unknown, prior to 1912. Bond Memorial Public Library, photo duplication by Timark Hamilton.

everything. They didn't ask 'boo' from the community. . . . Whatever the sugar company bosses decided was accepted by the community. . . . When the statue was put here, they did that themselves too."

The local population became radically diversified as the sugar industry developed. Imported diseases decimated the Native population, which declined from an estimated 8,000 in 1832 to 1,670 in 1890.[11] During the second half of the nineteenth century, most of the remaining Native Hawaiians lost their traditional access to the land. As the indigenous population diminished, immigrants from China, Japan, Portugal, Puerto Rico, Korea, Okinawa, and the Philippines arrived as sugar plantation labor. A smaller number of North Americans and Northern Europeans also came, serving as managers and administrators of the seven plantations and mills in the region.

Father Bond arrived in Kohala in 1841 to convert Native Hawaiians and immigrant laborers to Christianity, but despite his tireless efforts, Buddhism and Native Hawaiian traditions persisted. To varying degrees in these early years, immigrants recreated their home cultures while merging with the new plantation culture. North Kohala's first three Buddhist temples were constructed in 1903, 1909, and 1912.[12] Between 1846 and 1855, Father Bond oversaw construction of Kohala's first permanent Christian church. He helped start the Kohala Foreign Church (otherwise known as the "haole church") in 1868 and a Chinese congregational church in 1877. Bond also initiated a Japanese congregation that led to the construction of a Japanese church in 1896. Alongside these institutions, the elite spent their time at the small British Kohala Club, a private men's facility, which, contrary to the otherwise influential missionary ethic, allowed its members to smoke, drink, play card games, and shoot billiards.[13]

Sugar production and trade expanded during the late nineteenth and early twentieth centuries, but the Second World War changed the region's fortune. Out of security concerns, in 1941 the U.S. government closed Māhukona Harbor, which had linked the region to international sugar trade. It never reopened, and North Kohala was once again isolated from the rest of the world. In the postwar years, sugar production increased elsewhere in the Pacific, further depressing the marketability of the Hawaiian product and affecting employment in the region. By 1960, the population was 50 percent of its 1920s plantation-era peak.[14] With the waning of its labor force and economic role, the plantation lost its paternalist control over the community. Increasingly, the government took over the task of providing basic social services, and shopkeepers opened small stores and markets.

Today's local culture in North Kohala is made up of descendants of the international labor force brought in by the missionaries. Despite its remote location on the tip of an island in the middle of the Pacific Ocean, the local population descends from immigrants from many parts of the world. The region, like much of Hawai'i, has a multicultural mix that would challenge the most hybrid inner-city neighborhood anywhere. Many people in the community have little knowledge of indigenous cultural traditions. Yet the sculpture is now the center of many community activities. It receives gifts throughout the year from people of Hawaiian, Asian, and European lineage in the form of flowers and *pōhaku* (stone) offerings.

The mix of cultures embedded in the sculpture signals tensions between incongruous pasts that continue into the present. Although the social and political landscape in North Kohala has dramatically changed since the sculpture's nineteenth-century origins, dissonance between Hawaiian, Western, and more recent immigrant traditions still exists in the region. One of the goals of the participatory conservation project was to use the sculpture's hybrid nature as a window into these tensions. I hoped to learn how they continue in today's cultural surroundings.

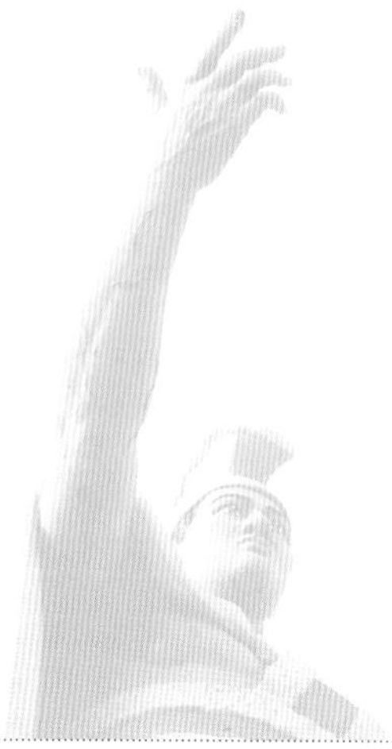

# 4 *Return to Kohala*

I RETURNED TO NORTH KOHALA once again on September 3, 1999. The local project committee suggested that we announce our plans at the annual ukulele and hula festival. This annual event with its celebration of musicians and hula artists attracts local residents whom I was told would not attend a public meeting about the sculpture. We hoped to get the whole region talking about the sculpture, its conservation, and its meaning for the next eighteen months.

I arrived a day early to explore the area as a tourist. Like countless others before me, I flew to Kona and rented a car. I drove north along the two-lane Queen Ka'ahumanu highway that hugs the coast, through an austere landscape of black lava fields decorated with struggling bougainvillea bushes. I drove slowly enough to read some of the white coral graffiti along the highway, with stones that spell out the names of prior visitors, tributes of love, and occasional obscenities.

The dry lava desert receded as I traveled up the coast, to be gradually replaced by a landscape of rocky shorelines, grassy plains, and rolling hills. At the tip of a peninsula, the district of North Kohala is isolated from the rest of the island by ocean on three sides and the extinct, 5,500-foot Kohala volcano on the fourth. The region is the oldest part of the island. It formed approximately 450,000 years ago during a series of violent eruptions of the Kohala volcano. Ridges and gulches reach down from the mountain to create a variety of microclimates with extreme variation in temperature and rainfall.

On this journey, I was better equipped to read the cultural as well as physical landscape along the road. I passed new housing developments crawling up the coast from the heavily touristed Kailua-Kona region. Lush vegetation framed entrance gates to exclusive resorts. I drove by the towering Puʻukoholā Heiau, a reconstructed stone temple where, early in his campaign to conquer other local chiefs, Kamehameha offered a human sacrifice. As I approached North Kohala, I began to see clusters of sugarcane still growing like weeds between aging plantation labor houses.

The intense sun and daily rains have been unkind to some of the wood plantation structures. In the current struggling economy, paint is peeling from many of these structures, and some are collapsing into the landscape. The moisture-laden ʻĀpaʻapaʻa trade winds blow across open areas from the windward side and carry airborne chlorides that combine with moisture to corrode metal sculptures.

When I reached the town of Hāwī (population 938), where the annual Kamehameha Day parade starts, I saw renovated plantation storefronts and a scattering of Buddhist temples, Christian churches, and a few contemporary meditation retreats. After about two hours of driving, I finally pulled into Kapaʻau. I parked my car and gazed at Kamehameha's outstretched arm that points to a coffee and ice cream shop across the road. Starving, I went in for a "Kamehameha Wrap" and placed myself at an outdoor table. From there I watched a slow stream of tourists who stopped, took pictures in front of the imposing figure, and got back in their cars to finish the seven-mile drive to the end of the highway. With a population of 1,159, there are no stoplights in Kapaʻau. Aside from the periodic carload of tourists, most people I saw were locals going about their errands. They stopped to speak with each other and to visit the Bond Memorial Library next to the coffee shop. Dress is casual. Everyone wears old T-shirts, shorts, and sandals, or an occasional *aloha* shirt.

After lunch, I walked over to the old courthouse behind the sculpture I had peered into on my first visit. Volunteers from the Kohala Senior Citizens Club occupied chairs on the lanai. They gave me a pamphlet about historic North Kohala and talked with great pride about the town and its history. I stayed for a while, gazing at the photographs of World War II veterans mounted on the walls. I listened as tourists asked questions, and the *kūpuna talked story*—a Hawaiian term for relaxed story telling. They spoke of old plantation days, Kamehameha Day celebrations, and the dramatic shipwreck and rescue that led to placing the sculpture in North Kohala.

The courthouse itself speaks of the imposed U.S. culture that awkwardly merged over time with the local culture. Constructed between 1889 and 1893, it is one of the earliest courthouses built on the islands. Its basic New England design is wood clapboard and gabled roof, with deep lanai wrapping around two sides of the structure. After its renovation in the 1970s, it housed the Kohala Senior Citizens Club, a County Office of Aging, and the Hawaiian Civic Club.

The landscape around the courthouse also reveals a layering of history and culture. In the 1980s the Senior Citizens Club built a wood and glass display case on the lawn to display typed notes and images interpreting the sculpture's history and the life of Kamehameha. The intense ultraviolet light of the tropical sun made most of the documents practically illegible. As I did on my first trip, I walked around to look at the strange mix of historic artifacts on the lawn, including large stones carved for the Hawaiian game of *kōnane* and a bronze plaque memorializing local men, many of Asian descent, who died during the war.

As a tourist for the day, I dutifully drove to the end of the highway through the small pockets of plantation settlements and old cane fields. I parked my car at the end of the road and gazed across the densely green

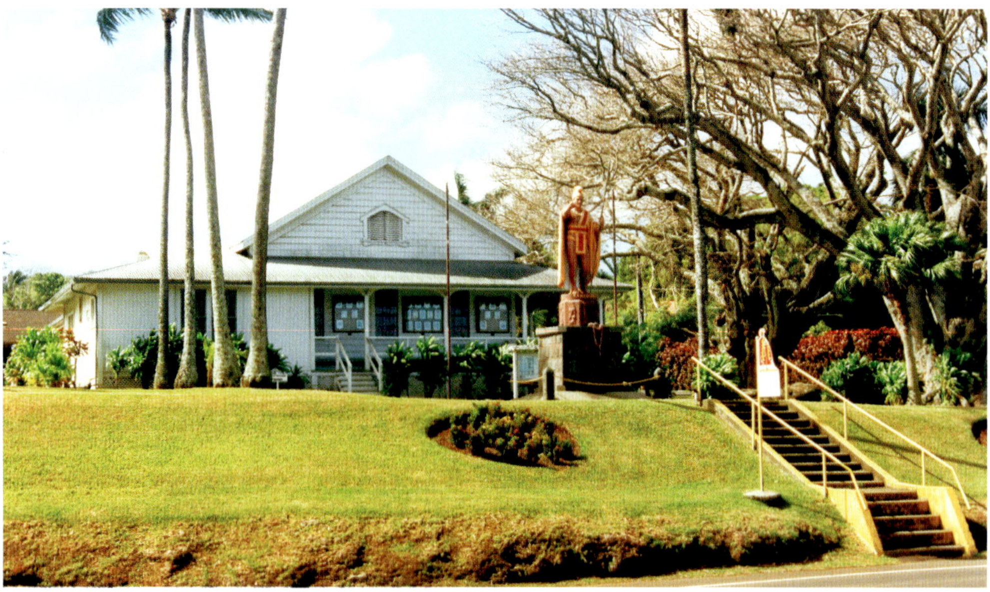

The North Kohala courthouse. Constructed between 1889 and 1893.

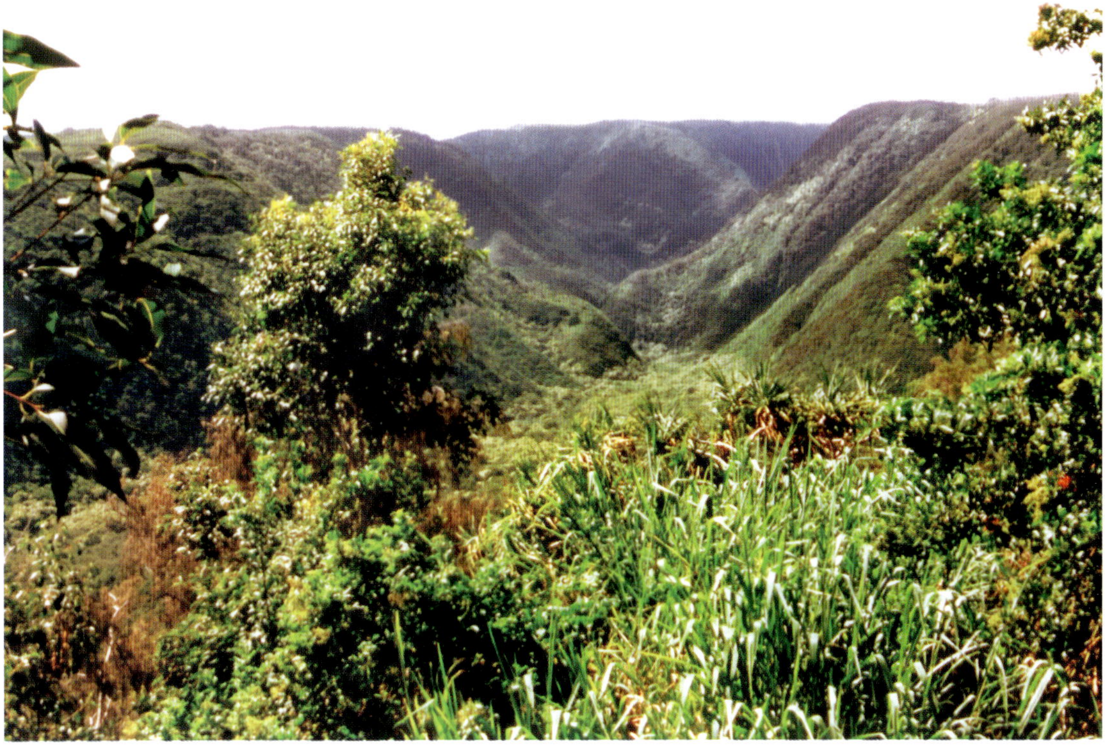

Pololū Mountains with Awini Ridge, where Kamehameha spent the first five years of his life.

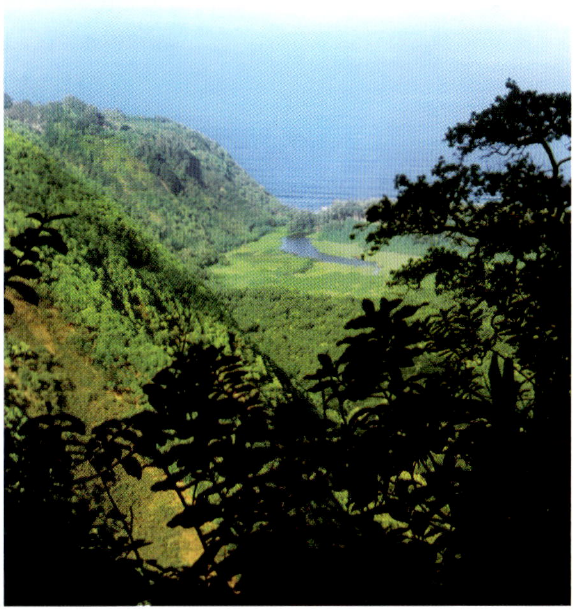

Pololū Valley in North Kohala.

Pololū Valley gorge to the Awini Ridge, where Kamehameha spent his early childhood in hiding. An ancient Hawaiian trail led me down from the parking lot along the jagged Hāmākua sea cliffs through an ironwood grove to an extraordinary black sand beach.

Exhausted from the flight, the drive, and a walk on the beach, I drove back toward Kapa'au and located Nani Svendsen's guesthouse, where I was to stay. Marilyn Cristofori and Lei Ahsing from the Hawai'i Alliance for Arts Education in Honolulu were staying there too. Nani's family had lived on the property for seven generations. As I learned later, she was a strong community advocate for all things Hawaiian. She ran the guesthouse, a flower business, and a *lo'i* (taro patch), where young people from drug abuse programs came to work the fields. Nani was someone who could get things done, and she became a valuable member of our team. With open arms and a wide smile, she greeted me with a hug and showed me to my room. Marilyn and Lei were there with groceries from the Takata Market, ready to cook a large dinner for project organizers in our multiroom suite.

This was the first time most of us had met. In addition to all her other connections, Nani was a member of the Kamehameha Day Celebration Committee. Three others arrived, and we started to cook as a group, Hawaiian style. These were people I would come to know intimately over the next few years. In their own ways, they each became my cultural guides: Raylene Ha'alelea Lancaster, who represented the Halau 'O Ha'alelea hula group and the Kohala Hawaiian Civic Club, Sharon Hayden of the Kamehameha Day Celebration Committee and the Halau 'O Ha'alelea hula group, and Kealoha Sugiyama, whom I had already met at the sculpture. He represented the Kohala Senior Citizens Club and the Kohala Hawaiian Civic Club.

Over dinner and conversation that lasted well into the night, we talked about our project and cast out ideas and concerns about using conservation as a way to get people thinking about Kamehameha and relationships to the Hawaiian past. In later conversations, I learned of their suspicions about me—who was this guy from the mainland? Will he be able to slow down, listen, and do things Kohala style? Apparently they weren't so sure, and they decided among themselves that I needed a lot of coaching.

The next day we set up a booth at the ukulele and hula festival, handed out hastily made flyers, and answered questions from surprised people who had never thought about removing the paint from the sculpture. I was delighted to see how many people stopped by and lingered, wanting to know more about the sculpture's history and why we would even think about removing the paint. I stayed several more days, driving around, hanging out at local cafes and restaurants, and talking to people about the region and the sculpture.

My next trip to North Kohala was in February 2000. By this time our plans had developed and we were ready to start our activities. This time we held a public meeting at the local high school. Raylene, Sharon, Nani, and Kealoha gathered a larger group who wanted to hear about our plans. We spoke about art projects designed to stimulate wide interest. This was the insight of Marilyn and Lei from the Hawai'i Alliance for Arts Education. As public art and education activists, they saw art production as a way to get people involved in serious social and political concerns.

Marilyn and Lei asked John Keola Lake to join us from O'ahu to initiate the community arts element of our project. John was a *kumu hula* (hula teacher) who serves as the *kahuna nui* (high priest) of the local Pu'ukohalā Heiau stone temple. He also participated in resurrecting *hula ki'i,* a nearly extinct form of hula. Literally translated as "image dance," puppets interact with humans in *hula ki'i* performances to narrate stories and legends.[1] It was almost stamped out by missionaries and their converts in past times, but *hula ki'i* is now being revived as part of a larger focus on early Hawaiian traditions. I learned that in earlier times, puppets and their human counterparts chanted, danced, and acted out ribald and slapstick skits. They were full of reference to legends and innuendo about current scandals. No wonder the missionaries found them non-Christian, just as they found traditional hula and other forms of Hawaiian culture.

In the spirit of *hula ki'i,* John wrote a script for North Kohala in which two birds sit on top of the sculpture's shoulders and discuss the figure's history through song and chanting. Children and elders interact with the birds as the story unfolds. The plan was to conduct workshops for people to make coconut puppets that they would use in community performances. Several newspapers wrote up our project, and a local television station interviewed me about the sculpture and the possibility of removing the paint. Our public campaign was off the ground.

Meanwhile, the local committee decided that I needed some deep immersion if I was going to understand the place I had come to. Raylene told me it was time for me to experience a North Kohala that few outsiders know. She took me to one of Kamehameha's personal *lo'i* that was still cultivated by locals. Here she explained the connection that Hawaiians have to their *'āina*

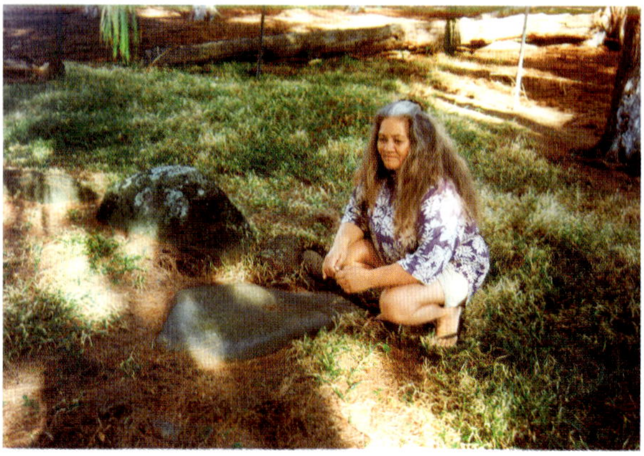

Raylene Ha'alelea Lancaster at Hale o Kā'ili, the site of Kamehameha's family *heiau.*

(land) and to the taro plant that sustained them. Raylene is also *kahu* (guardian) of the Hale o Kā'ili Heiau, Kamehameha's family *heiau* (temple), where he kept the *ki'i* (image) of the war god Kuka'ilimoku.[2] Raylene brought a small group of us down a dirt road off the highway to the *heiau* where we looked around, then sat and quietly listened. Gradually she began to talk about her work in caring for the temple and protecting the *pōhaku* that continue to speak to her. Although she asked me not to pass on some of the work that she does, I was struck by the deep connection she experiences with the land and the stones. She spoke of the *kuleana* (responsibility) she carries as her duty to honor Kamehameha's land. This was my first introduction to a deep spiritual world that many in Hawai'i inhabit.

I also spent time with John on this trip, and he told me about his life growing up in a time when most elders had not been taught the Hawaiian language or much of Hawai'i's traditional culture. Yet there were elders in his family and elsewhere that kept the culture alive through oral tradition, hula, and other practices. He described rituals, festivals, and his work at the Pu'ukoholā Heiau stone temple, as well as the Royal Order of Kamehameha. I was surprised to learn that he was a practicing Catholic and did not see any incompatibility between his Hawaiian cultural values and his belief in a Christian God.

It was then Kealoha's turn. He decided that I should know what locals know about Kamehameha's early life in North Kohala, and I had to learn it by visiting key places and learning their names. Kealoha took me to Kamehameha's birthplace at the beach near his home, and he described the story of Kamehameha's dramatic birth and narrow escape from death.[3] He recounted Hawaiian legends that foretold Kamehameha's life as a chief who would one day come to power and unite the islands. The sign of his birth would be a comet, and indeed there was a fiery light in the sky on the night of Kamehameha's birth—thought by some to be Halley's Comet, since it was visible in 1758. Threatened by this auspicious beginning of Kamehameha's life, the reigning chief, Alapa'i, ordered the child killed. The journey his caretaker Nae'ole made with the infant to the Pololū Valley, where Kamehameha spent the first five years of his life in hiding, is marked in memory by place names.

As Kealoha drove me slowly along the highway toward the sculpture, he related the story through names of neighborhoods and towns. The area near Kamehameha's birthplace is called Kokoiki. Translated to "little blood," it refers to the discharge from Kamehameha's mother as she gave birth under extreme duress. Several years earlier, Kealoha engineered the renaming of his own street to Kokoiki. Hō'ea (to arrive) is the name of the birthplace near the Mo'okini Heiau, a *luakini* (sacrificial stone temple). The town of Hāwī is said to be the place where, hidden from warriors sent to kill him, the baby's cries of hunger almost revealed his presence. Hāwī means to breathe + life + squeal. The town of Kapa'au (barkcloth + swim), where the sculpture is installed, is where Nae'ole forded a stream with the barkcloth-swathed infant. Other similarly named locations in the region include Hala'ula (error + blood), where warriors realized the severe consequences if they failed to find the infant, Makapala (ripe + eye), where the warriors had red and swollen eyes from lack of sleep, and Āpuakōhau (disloyal + dragged + beat), where local people were beaten and their houses were burned for not disclosing the whereabouts of the infant.

I spoke to others about this amazing story, and I learned that Nae'ole's journey with the infant is often told and is deeply etched in public memory. Retired high school history teacher Fred Cachola often recounts Kamehameha's birth legend during the annual Kamehameha Day celebrations. To some, it parallels biblical stories of the infant Moses hidden in the bulrushes, and Herod's efforts to kill the infant Jesus. No one in the community mentioned it, but in classical mythology, Zeus was hidden by his mother in a cave on Mount Ida on Crete so his father, Chronos, would not eat him.

Although Fred spends most of his time on O'ahu, he is from Kohala and remains deeply attached to the community. His story is typical. He left the region for O'ahu because there were few job opportunities in Kohala. As a historian, he works tirelessly even in retirement to promote an understanding of local history from a Hawaiian perspective. Fred told me more about Kamehameha's life, elaborating on what I had read.

It seems that Nae'ole oversaw Kamehameha's first five years in a small mountain village that no longer exists, over the visible ridge at the end of the highway. He was then returned to Alapa'i, the ruling chief of Hawai'i who had originally ordered him killed. His new guardian, Kekuhaupi'o, oversaw his training in warfare and court diplomacy. Kamehameha was present with other *ali'i* when Captain Cook first came to Hawai'i, and he met with him in 1779. He became the guardian of the Hawaiian war god Kuka'ilimoku in 1782. When his cousin, an early rival, was slain, Kamehameha began a long process of defeating other local chiefs. He became the *ali'i nui* (leading chief) on the island after he constructed the Pu'ukoholā Heiau in 1791 and offered his final rival as a sacrifice to Kuka'ilimoku.

Kamehameha's life is known through oral history and legend. Some people told me that he lifted the Naha stone, now in front of the public library in Hilo. Legend had it that the man who lifted it would become the chief to unite all of the Hawaiian Islands. Indeed, by amassing a large fleet of war canoes and soldiers, he launched a campaign in 1795 to defeat other islands, and he successfully campaigned against Maui and Moloka'i. He finally conquered O'ahu after dramatic battles in which his combatants were forced off Pali's cliff and fell a thousand feet to their deaths. Once again he sacrificed the *ali'i nui* to the god Kuka'ilimoku. He was then ruler of all islands except Kaua'i and Ni'ihau. Kamehameha amassed a large fleet of canoes and European schooners equipped with cannons, but in the end he negotiated a peaceful victory with the *ali'i nui* of Kaua'i.

Establishing Hawai'i's first kingdom in 1810 involved arranging Hawaiian and European customs to create island-wide tax and legal systems. Kamehameha also promoted trade with Europe and the United States. Despite his violent climb to power, he ruled peacefully until his death in 1819. He is known by those who honor him as Kamehameha the Great, and by some detractors as the Napoleon of the Pacific.

Various people helped me understand the depth of Kamehameha's connection to the land and the people of North Kohala—including his many descendants. Most of these descendants come from generations of mixed marriages between families of sugar plantation laborers brought in from the far corners of the world. It was unclear to me, in a community with so many first and last names that reference Hawaiian, Asian, and European ancestry, just who was Native Hawaiian. As I learned early on, asking this question brings up complex issues of racial identity.

Fifty percent Native Hawaiian blood is the criterion for obtaining benefits from many government and nongovernment programs. People argue that this is unfair given the low economic status of many other people who identify themselves as Native Hawaiian. Some suggest that everyone should have Native rights if any of their ancestors inhabited the archipelago at the time of Cook's arrival. According to the 2000 U.S. Census Bureau, 1,028 people out of a total of 6,038 in North Kohala self-identify as Native Hawaiian.[4]

I spoke with archaeologists in Honolulu[5] about early immigrants to the region. They think that Polynesians first settled the Kohala peninsula around 800 AD, which squares with dates provided by Adrienne Kaeppler of 800 or 900 AD for establishing Hawaiian culture in Hawai'i.[6] They were already skilled fishermen and agriculturalists when they arrived. They developed a highly structured society with differentiation between chiefs and commoners, along with elaborate systems of *kapu* (taboo), taxation, and redistribution of goods. This political economy was in place when Kamehameha was born. Land-use units called *ahupua'a* existed throughout the islands.[7] These units, extending in pie-shaped wedges from the mountains down to the ocean, were under the control of local chiefs and functioned largely as self-sufficient economies. Within the *ahupua'a,* people exchanged fish from the sea for crops grown inland. The concept of privately owned land was completely foreign in Hawai'i before Cook arrived.

As I began spending time in North Kohala, I interviewed people systematically about the Native Hawaiian past, the present, and their relationships to the sculpture. As detailed elsewhere,[8] I interviewed forty people in all, a deliberate mix of Native Hawaiian, Asian, and Caucasian residents. I selected elders, activists, teachers, students, local business people, and *keiki o ka 'āina* (young people born in the region) to get a good sampling of opinions and experience. These interviews were more structured than the many casual conversations about the same topics I had in the course of my work. At first, some people were cautious about being recorded, but as the project unfolded, I became "the guy restoring the statue," and people were more at ease speaking with me. They often recommended others I should speak with, and several times people with strong opinions approached me and asked to be interviewed. These structured conversations became less structured, over meals and at project activities, as the project continued.

My strongest impression was of the racial mix in the local population. The Native Hawaiians, Buddhists, and Christians that trace ancestry to China, Europe, Japan, Korea, Okinawa, the Philippines, and Puerto Rico can exist all in a single family. The Native Hawaiian population itself is now a minority. Very few are full-blooded. Even those who identify as Hawaiian at least partially come from somewhere else, as evidenced by people's first and last names. Many malihini (newcomer) Caucasians take on Hawaiian names and play active roles in protecting Hawaiian culture. This gave me insight into the complex, multicultural fabric of a community in a postmissionary, postplantation era. Related to this diversity was the question of who gets to decide a conservation treatment when the sculpture itself combines elements of different cultures. This question was left open at the beginning of the project. Leaders of the local groups would decide who would decide.

I frequently began my interviews by asking about the sculpture, and then moved on to Kamehameha and the Native Hawaiian past. We often shifted quickly to problems confronting people today, and much of this was about land rights and development. An increasing amount of land along the ocean is owned privately, and some newcomers prevent locals from access to the beach. Some residents, when discussing local rights, commented on how ancient customs continue. One elder I spoke with about this was Libby Paaula, who is half Hawaiian and half Chinese. Recalling the traditional *ahupuaʻa* land units, she suggested, "If the rights go down to the beach, it would be okay. You could go down to the beach with your family for a month or two, whatever, then go back up. The people in the mountains want to share with the people on the ocean, but they can't." These views echo sentiments that exist across the islands, fed by resentment that missionaries, immigrants, and more recent haole newcomers have diluted and destroyed much of what was good about the Hawaiian past.

A "Renaissance" of Hawaiian culture began in the late 1960s with aims of reviving traditions, including hula, music, outrigger canoe racing, star-navigated voyaging, surfing, lei making, feather work, taro planting, genealogical research, mythology, and legend.[9] In a more radical form, Honolulu-based indigenous rights groups oppose any person or institution with mainland roots governing Hawaiian institutions or jurisdictions. They regard the very existence of Hawaiʻi as a U.S. state as an illegitimate imposition coming from—in the words of a prominent activist-scholar—the "American foreign government."[10] They demand repatriation of lands and governmental autonomy. Cultural aspects of the Hawaiian Renaissance are visible everywhere in North Kohala, but only a few people I spoke with expressed the political forcefulness of activists I met in Honolulu.

I was curious about the problem of romanticizing and commodifying the Hawaiian past, as embodied by luau and hula presented to tourists. Fixing notions of an "authentic" Hawaiian past serves a variety of interests, from tourism to indigenous pride. Some scholars debate the danger of constructing the past as symbols for these and other purposes without recognizing that culture in the islands is continuously changing and inherently in conflict.[11] How the past is constructed in peoples' minds is relevant to the Kamehameha sculpture project for pragmatic reasons, since the decision about its appearance inevitably valorizes one interpretation over another.

My questions about the past came easily to most, since Hawaiians take the past seriously. As characterized by one Native Hawaiian scholar, "[t]he Hawaiian stands firmly in the present, with his back to the future and his eyes fixed upon the past, seeking historical answers for present day dilemmas. Such an orientation is to the Hawaiian an eminently practical one, for the future is always unknown whereas the past is rich in glory and knowledge."[12] As another contemporary Native Hawaiian scholar explains, "[i]n our language, the past (*ka wā mamua*) is the time in front or before; the future (*ka wā mahope*) is the time that comes after."[13]

Some people spoke about the high stakes of control over how the past is represented, through the sculpture, for instance. Fred Cachola was clear on the issue:

> The people who control the present control the past, and the people who control the past control the future. . . . Hawaiians, our ancient *kūpuna* [ancestors] knew that too. That's why they controlled their genealogy. They married carefully, mated carefully . . . how they behaved, everything they did, how they took care of their ancestors' bones . . . they were masters at that. Somehow we lost some of that, and we have to get it back. One inch at a time. For every inch we get back towards not only controlling our destiny but controlling our past, the better we are going to be in the present.

Local "nationalists" argue for a return of the Hawaiian monarchy to manage the land. Libby Paaula's husband, Sonny Paaula, age seventy-two and "almost all Hawaiian with a little bit of Chinese," confided that many local Native Hawaiians are reluctant to express their concerns to outsiders. He envisions a *lāhui* that incorporates *mālama ʻāina,* prior land use practices that include social order. "The reason for maintaining the monarchy is the land. If we had a sovereign, it would be maintained actively. If he wants to repatriate back to the Hawaiian kingdom, he can. If he wants to maintain American citizenship he can. I would like to have it be like a nation. Separate from the U.S. but a monarchy. Like Britain." A number of individuals express ambivalence: while wanting a monarchy, they also want a democracy.

Many see the plight of contemporary Native Hawaiians as rooted in the past injustices. As expressed by Raylene's son, Michael Lancaster, Native residents are at the bottom of the occupational ladder, with disproportionate problems of unemployment, teen pregnancy, family violence, and drug abuse. He explained that the epidemic drug is primarily "ice" (crystal methamphetamine) but local people also use heroin, cocaine, and a lot of marijuana. Restoring the integrity of indigenous culture would provide a source of pride and thus act as an antidote to current social problems. Native Hawaiian influence over the conservation project would be, in a concrete way, a mechanism to further this goal. Some people expressed this view and early on developed the position that Native Hawaiians should control the conservation project.

The question of land rights and development was also on everyone's mind. This is because of the recent sell-off of plantation property to private individuals and developers who are rapidly changing the landscape. In 1973 the Kohala Sugar Company, a consolidated conglomerate of all prior plantations, finally closed operations. People I spoke with described the period after this closure as the "postplantation era," in which former plantation workers sought employment elsewhere. The population was already in decline by 1975. Many in the postwar era joined the economic boom in Honolulu. In more recent years another wave of immigration began. Attracted by amenities of climate and culture, Caucasian malihini from the U.S. mainland trickled in as long-time residents left. They joined prior immigrants from earlier generations that had merged ethnic identities through mixed marriages. Names, facial features, skin color, argot, and local cuisine all reflect the result.

North Kohala was changing fast, with a recent population surge, shifts in employment, and striking alterations in the built environment. When the Kohala Sugar Company plantation closed, 90 percent of North Kohala was owned by its parent company, Castle and Cooke, one of the remaining big five corporations in Hawai'i largely controlled by descendants of missionary families. In the early 1990s, a Japanese development company called Chalon purchased the 19,000-acre land mass and began selling off chunks for residential and commercial development. After decades of population decline since the 1920s and stabilization toward the end of the plantation era, the local population almost doubled between 1980 and 2000, from 3,249 to 6,038[14] as the influx of newcomers outpaced the outmigration of locals.

Led by the influx of haole newcomers, a new economy began to take hold in the last years of the twentieth century. In sharp contrast to the heritage of sugar, these businesses now include ecotourism, galleries, and bookstores. But there were competing thoughts on how to manage change and who should have the voice of authority. Much of this reflects classic debate over the value of growth that takes place across the United States and elsewhere in the world.

Tourism is the growing behemoth throughout the islands. In neighboring South Kohala it takes the form of large luxury hotels and golf resorts disconnected physically and socially from their cultural context. Such development has not occurred in North Kohala; there is only one small hotel and two guesthouses in the district. But just thirty miles away are internationally acclaimed five-star luxury resorts, with tropical gardens, lush lawns, and golf courses carved into arid lava flows:

> The Hyatt Regency Waikoloa . . . built at a cost of $360 million, has three towers, two fantasy swimming pools with waterfalls and slides, and a network of canals plied by Venetian style launches. Guests may also get about the resort by mini bullet trains that glide silently from the lobbies of the towers to deliver guests to the beach, the restaurants and the shops.[15]

But tourists are also advised to "[m]ix in a little sightseeing of intriguing ancient Hawaiian temples. . . . Remnants of the ancient Hawaiian civilization are everywhere."[16] During one of my visits, an article appeared in the travel section of the *New York Times*:

> The King Kamehameha statue in the town of Kapaau had seemed an appropriate place to launch our outing. . . . The hike was the perfect complement to the mountain kayak cruise that we had taken in 1998, through the [plantation] flumes of the mountain waterway system. Both adventures offer access to what was once the most remote region of the Big Island.[17]

Partly in response to these new types of tourism, but also to new kinds of people settling in the area from the mainland, the appearance of Kapaʻau and Hāwī has changed significantly since my first visit in 1996. In 1999, the formerly dilapidated Nanbu Hotel across the street from the sculpture reopened after a major renovation. It is painted in lively colors and houses five "new economy" businesses: the Nanbu Courtyard Café, the Nanbu Art Gallery, Elements Jewelry & Crafts, a center for Chinese traditional medicine, and the Kohala Book Shop, with the largest collection of rare and used Hawaiian books anywhere in the islands, although since 2009 it has operated only on line. Other businesses in these old plantation structures include tourist gift

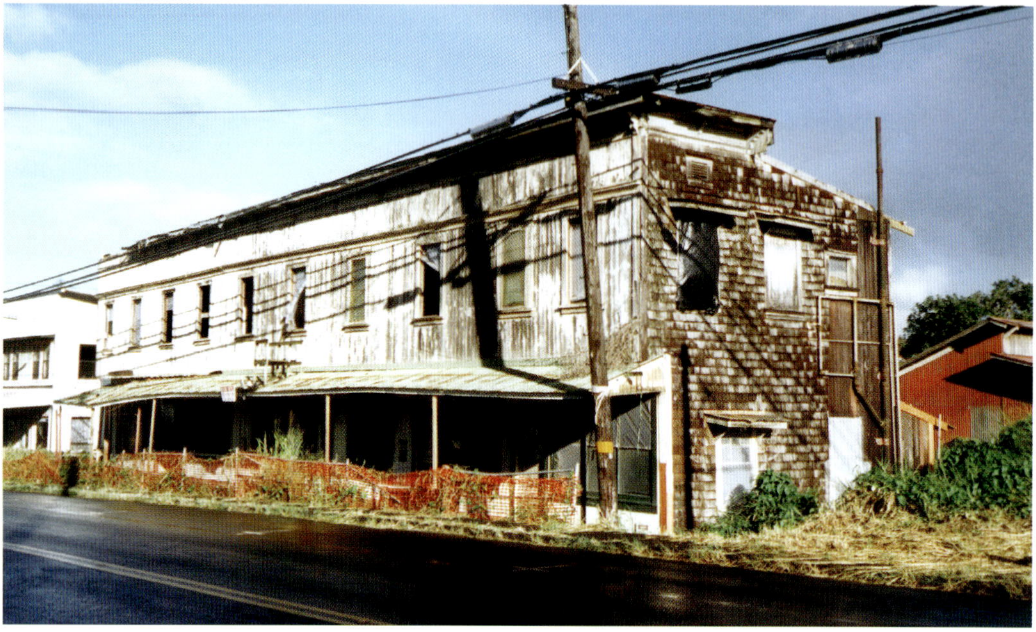

Nanbu Hotel, Kapa'au, before restoration. 1997. Tom Quinlan.

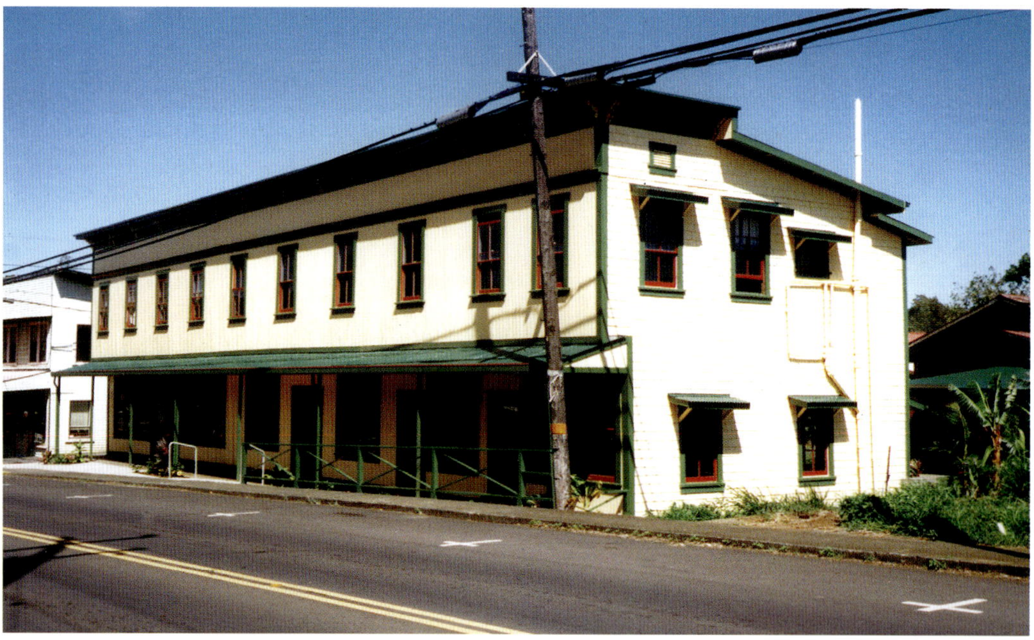

Nanbu Hotel, Kapa'au, after restoration. 1999. Tom Quinlan.

shops, cafés, a florist shop, and additional art galleries. The upscale Bamboo restaurant in a renovated hotel features a Hawaiian craft shop, Polynesian fusion cuisine, and staff that breaks to sing and dance hula to live music from local musicians.

Developers and historic preservation entrepreneurs use tax credit schemes for adaptive reuse of historic buildings. Programs initiated in North Kohala include a historic inventory of sites, a heritage corridor, a Main Street program through the National Trust for Historic Preservation, and a Merchants Association. Tourists stop and take pictures, mainly of the sculpture but increasingly of nearby old commercial buildings, Buddhist temples, New England–style churches, industrial ruins of sugar processing facilities, and as yet undeveloped (and largely unsurveyed) archaeological sites. The region's cultural diversity and eclectic architectural past are now an economic resource. There is a significant difference between marketing sugar cane and marketing heritage, as North Kohala's historic character and the place itself are treated as commodities.

In North Kohala, as in many other places, people who argue for development say that it creates jobs. Many old-timers who experienced postplantation unemployment, the flight of younger generations, and long commutes to low-wage jobs in other parts of the island welcome what they see as new economic opportunities. Henry Dulan, whose parents came from the Philippines to work in the sugar industry, is himself retired from a plantation career and postwar union organizing. He told me that "the mainland guys come here retired and say they don't want development. But I'm worried about my grandchildren. They can go to Honolulu, but not all of them have that kind of education. If they can work at a golf course, hey, why not?" For others, the fact that people may want to come to North Kohala and spend a lot of money for real estate or in business is a source of pride as well as jobs.

Some do not like the changes that development and tourism bring. Old-timer Mike Isaacs, who is half Hawaiian and half Chinese, German, "a little English," and "a little Portuguese," argued that tourism provides the wrong kind of employment. "I am totally against tourism. . . . Because tourism doesn't provide meaningful work, good pay, or good advancement. The locals end up working two or three jobs—both parents, just to keep their heads above water." Anthony Anjo, a migrant from Oʻahu with Chinese, Portuguese, Irish, and Hawaiian ancestry, expressed a vehement anger at haole entrepreneurs. He asserted that business owners come to profit on increased tourism and land speculation. "There are a bunch of asshole haoles here. . . . The merchants are trying to turn this place to their advantage." Similar anger came from Mike Isaacs: "The rift is getting wider in the community between the locals and the Caucasians because they are the ones buying and speculating. It's ripping Kohala apart."

Numbers of haole newcomers are themselves critical of further development. Having come to North Kohala in retreat from the bustle of their former lives, they fear inundation, even if it is by people motivated by the same goals as their own. Some residents see these antigrowth newcomers as hypocritical, including entrepreneurs with a stake in new growth. Shiro Takata has concerns about newcomers who quickly identify as "local" and position themselves against development. "Their projects are 'anti,' anti-water, anti-this. Sometimes I wonder, where is their energy to say, 'we are going to make Kohala a better school' or 'we are going to make the Kohala kids better.' I want a balance."

Some people argue for low-impact, "Hawaiian style" development, which translates to eco-awareness and gentle respect for land and tradition. The building complex at Father Bond's old estate is undergoing a gradual restoration by a haole owner, who offers meditation sessions in the facility. A mainland-based Buddhist foundation purchased a large tract of land with plans to develop a spiritual retreat center. Some suggest eco-tourist day trips from South Kohala rather than local construction of resorts. Others initiate agricultural businesses like raising indigenous plants for landscaping, as well as researching and propagating plants with healing properties and planting crops that prosper elsewhere on the island, such as premium coffee beans and macadamia nuts. These are ways to "keep Kohala Kohala."

In part to help figure out what it might mean to "keep Kohala Kohala," in July 2000 the local community sponsored a five-day "Kohala Millennium Reunion." Fred Cachola described this as a meeting that brought together old-timers, newcomers, and those who have left the region, in order to "share Kohala's cultural and historical traditions . . . and to help the people of Kohala to determine and express their preferred futures." The event included a "future visioning day," an exercise being taken up in various U.S. communities, with active development debates in which individuals voice preferences and try to map out possible futures for their locality. People in North Kohala are ambivalent about growth and the kind of growth they most desire. They commonly acknowledge the advantage of more jobs and physical improvements to the community while at the same time they worry that valued old ways of life and landscape will be lost.

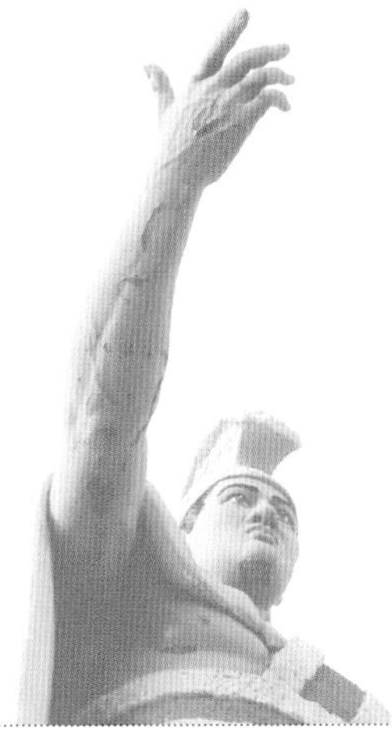

# 5 *Local Style*

I WANTED TO LEARN HOW people in North Kohala conceive of their community, including how individuals define groups and how they think about participation privileges. This was directly relevant to the questions of how to conserve the sculpture and whose opinions should count in determining its conservation. The historic migrations, economic developments, and cultural shifts that have occurred over the nineteenth and twentieth centuries provide for a rich array of potential identities and cultural affiliations that could well be in play. People do indeed struggle to define what it means to be "authentic" in today's North Kohala. I found that people take different positions as to who should count in defining the community and participating in its public life.

Native Hawaiians, and particularly descendants of Kamehameha, occupy a unique position in the social landscape. There are numerous Kamehameha descendants in the region, and people speak with intense pride about their connection to the "Native Son" who united the Hawaiian Islands. Each year in the Kamehameha Day parade, a special float carries Kamehameha descendants. I learned that this pride in family connections extends to any link with the Hawaiian *ali'i* and signifies a cultural system of identity in Hawai'i that places central importance on genealogy. People talk about their family coming from one area or another and the connections their families have to other families that have been in the region for a long time. This respect for lineage, hierarchy, and connection to land persists from precontact times and came up in conversations about local *kūpuna* (elders). For instance, many in the community pointed to Marie Solomon as the most respected *kupuna,* not only because she was a descendant of Kamehameha, but because her family came from and is buried in the area where Kamehameha lived for much of his young life.

Reference to land was a theme that surfaced constantly in my discussions about Native Hawaiian status. Although people everywhere attach symbolic meaning to the local landscape, the Hawaiian version is especially strong. The phrase *aloha ʻāina* (love of the land) came up repeatedly. All the people I spoke with, across race and social location, refer to the land and the local region in Eden-like terms, as unique and distinct. Indigenous people also know it as bound up with spiritual forces, as seen in Kamehameha's biography. A key issue I learned is the spiritual connection held to the *ʻāina* and the deep loss still felt from the mid-nineteenth-century *māhele* land transfer from indigenous populations. The Department of Hawaiian Home Lands now oversees a painfully slow and cumbersome program to provide dispossessed Native Hawaiians with homesteading land grants, just as developers increasingly challenge these land rights in the courts. The bulk of the land to be distributed was originally given to the state by Kamehameha. As part of its mission, the department provides homestead leases to Native Hawaiians with a Native blood quantum level of 50 percent. Despite legal rights to occupation, access to this "crown" land remains out of reach of most Hawaiian descendants and is at the center of the Hawaiian sovereignty movement. Although the sovereignty movement is stronger and more strident on Oʻahu, it does have advocates in North Kohala.

In addition to Hawaiian lineage and connection to the land, I learned about other criteria in North Kohala for determining who counts. Among them are possessing an *aloha* spirit, being local, and age status: *kūpuna* and *keiki* (children). These categories all came up in conversation while discussing who should participate in the conservation project and who in the community should make conservation decisions.

Closely related to the value placed on Native Hawaiian ancestry and connections to the land is an embrace of "Hawaiian values."[1] Possessing these values, often expressed as the spirit of *aloha,* can trump other distinctions such as ethnicity. In a broad sense, having *aloha* includes knowledge of Hawaiian cultural ways and practicing them through welcoming others, giving to the community, and respecting the local ecology as well as nature's symbolic meanings. Having this spirit matters and is valued above other criteria in the minds of many.

Raylene describes herself as a hapa Hawaiian, 50 percent Hawaiian. She plays a central role in North Kohala Native Hawaiian cultural matters. In addition to being custodian of Kamehameha's family stone temple, she runs an esteemed hula school that welcomes both newcomer haoles and local old-timers. She reflects on the fact that some Native Hawaiians argue for cultural authority. "Some brothers and sisters of my lineage say 'we are the blood line, and our land was taken away.' I say, 'Yes, but what are we going to do about that now? Do what was done to you, or understand what is *pono*, and go forth from there?'"

When I asked whether anyone could become Hawaiian, Raylene alluded to some of her *hālau* members who say, "'I am not a Hawaiian but I have a Hawaiian heart.' I pose the question back to them, 'What's wrong with the heart that you have? I am honored that you admire my culture, but why do you assume that your heart is any less?'"

Perhaps a reason for inclusiveness among many Native Hawaiians, including those who could promote their rights above others, is that they must also deal with other parts of their mixed heritage. Nani Svendsen, whose guest-house I stayed in during most of my visits, is one-fourth Hawaiian, one-fourth British, and half Okinawan. Her husband is Scandinavian. She describes some complexities of her hybrid life. "The Okinawans in the community say, 'We need to help each other. We have to stick together.' They see that side of me." In reflecting on one of our public discussions at the high school in which some-one described Native Hawaiian as the "host" culture, she asked, "Do I say I am Hawaiian first because I live in Hawai'i? I am also half Okinawan." Basing identity on an inclusive *aloha* spirit rather than family origin is a uniquely Hawaiian solution to the quandary arising in many parts of the world about multiple identities within one individual.[2]

When thinking of how Hawaiian values and *aloha* spirit can take root among haole residents, Raylene refers to people like Sharon Hayden, who moved to the region from New York in 1971. Sharon became a leader in the conservation project, is now a mainstay of community activities, and was one of my closest contacts. She practices hula and chanting, and exhibits a wealth of knowledge about Hawaiian language and cultural values. "Sharon is not Hawaiian, yet she values what Hawaiians value. The truth is there are many

Hawaiians who carry the blood line that don't have the same value system that Sharon knows." As Sharon puts it, "[f]or thirty years I've been hearing people say negative haole remarks. But then they say, 'We don't mean you, you are not a haole.' But in fact I am, and I honor that. I have a heritage too." Sharon gives the questions of local identity, racism, and *aloha* considerable thought:

> No one honors Hawaiians more than me, but it's about spirit. Race is not culture. Because you have that blood, it doesn't make you adhere to the tenets of that culture. To me, it's not about that any more. We've got to get over that crap. Racism is always wrong. Racism puts people in little *pukas* [holes]. By living in anger, you are not being Hawaiian; you are participating in the death of your own culture. For God's sake, don't go there. You are special enough to have Hawaiian blood. Don't let it die by your own hands because you are not having *aloha* anymore. Queen Lili'uokalani said, "A Native Hawaiian is anyone born here," and she also said that she forgave everyone that ever did her wrong. Without forgiveness there is no *aloha* and without *aloha* there is no Hawai'i.

Sharon thinks there is a selection process that keeps certain people in the community and lets others go. She gets close to Raymond Williams' concept of the "structure of feeling" in a place, which is difficult to articulate.[3] Sharon explains, "There are people that are drawn here. Destiny. And then there are people that don't belong here, and they find out. . . . When outsiders come they feel a healing sense because you are still so close to the earth. Like the concept of *aloha 'āina*. It's a two-way street, you love this land and it loves you back . . . it's absolutely felt."

Mary Winter, another long-term haole resident, from New York via Berkeley, speaks of her attachment not just to the people of North Kohala and their way of life, but to the earth itself. "The land, the spirit, the *'āina* is strong. Hiking back into the valleys is what grounded me and put me in touch with spiritual forces here. That's what made me feel at home."

Even some of the short-term visitors appear drawn by the same *aloha* forces. One day, while taking paint samples from the surface of the sculpture, I spoke with a long-haired, middle-aged Caucasian man after he finished meditating on an adjacent picnic table. He told me that he comes to North Kohala from the mainland every year or so, "because of the power fields that are well known all over the world." In part for "medicinal" reasons, he likes to sit and soak up the energy, meditate, and clear his thoughts in the park adjacent to the Kamehameha sculpture, which, he told me, has particularly strong energy levels.

Perhaps even more important than ethnicity or having *aloha,* I learned that "being local" matters for local participation. People in North Kohala express a strong dichotomy between locals and outsiders. Besides those from the mainland and other parts of the world, malihini includes people from other parts of the island, other islands, and particularly people from Honolulu. The local/nonlocal divide may also include those who left North Kohala. In a letter to the local newspaper *Kohala Mountain News,* one resident argued against those who left staying involved in local matters. "I, for one, do not want the future of my family's home decided by people who left here for greener pastures."

People speak of a "local style" that plays a defining role in imagining their community. Residents whose ancestors come from many parts of the world define themselves by the specifics of routine conduct, including how they go about their regular errands as they stop to speak with friends at various hangouts. As I heard from locals and nonlocals alike, North Kohala has a "laid-back," unhurried life. Dress is consistently casual except on Sunday morning, when large numbers of people go to church. Punctuality is less valued than on the mainland or in Honolulu, and people do not necessarily "get to the point" in conversation. This was something I had to learn and grow accustomed to to gain trust and develop relationships that permitted long conversations about the region. It did not come easily.

Language is studded with Hawaiian words and pidgin English. The Hawaiian form of pidgin developed throughout the islands during the plantation era by combining words and phrases from English, Hawaiian, Japanese, Portuguese, and Chinese. It not only facilitated communication to aid the plantation bosses, but it also helped establish a common identity among plantation workers.[4] It persists today and helps assert local identity. Conversation frequently includes past events incorporated into contemporary accounts, including mundane exchanges of gossip or news of family elsewhere. People in North Kohala repeatedly use the term *'ohana* (family) to characterize their community. They affectionately and respectfully refer to older nonfamily members as "auntie" and "uncle" in a way that extends the sense of local family.

When I asked if a newcomer could eventually become a "local," answers varied. Some old-timers say "never," others say in thirty to fifty years. Some Native Hawaiian activists and scholars argue that haoles can never become

Hawaiian. "It is not their genealogy [that prevents it], but the ideologies that are nested in their culture that limit the haole understanding and acceptance of many things that Hawaiians take for granted."[5] Even Raylene has doubts about her full acceptance as a local because she was raised in California and moved to North Kohala in 1993 at age forty-nine. "I continue to walk light here in Kohala, because I wasn't born here. I have no immediate family here. I have ancestors from this area, but to this generation of *kūpuna* I am still an outsider."

It seems that some haoles can have stronger claims to localness than newcomer Native Hawaiians. Boyd Bond is a fourth-generation descendant of Father Bond, the first missionary in the region. He lives in an old weathered plantation house and makes his living as a tour guide for small groups interested in local history and ecology. He frequently lapses into Hawaiian pidgin and readily talks story about local lore and Hawaiian legend. He also holds a critical perspective on the effects of missionary culture and recent haole immigration to the region.

Many haole newcomers, lacking Boyd's deep roots and detailed knowledge, must work hard to be accepted by locals. They adopt local style and avoid tourist looks and tourist traps. They distinguish themselves with insiders' cultural knowledge and use Hawaiian words in routine talk such as "aloha" instead of "hello" and "good-bye," and "*mahalo nui loa*" (thank you very much). Some adopt Hawaiian names and reference Hawaiian belief systems in their daily talk. For instance, when the Kilauea volcano erupts outside of Hilo, it is because "Pele (goddess of volcanoes) is angry." Others use the Hawaiian pidgin they hear around them. In an article posted in the *Kohala Mountain News,* one newcomer wrote, "If you are da kine that never say nothing, please speak up. If you are da kine that loves to hear the sound of your own voice . . . please zippa da lip."

Further complicating matters, haoles like Sharon often play leading roles in support of Hawaiian traditions. Putting it a bit more starkly than others, third-generation Japanese grocer Shiro Takata suggests that "if it wasn't for the influx of haoles, the local people wouldn't have anything . . . they react to a project, they don't go for a project, . . . Without the haoles, Hāwī town would be just deserted. Haoles speak better, they accept criticism better, they forgive faster, they accept being praised, and say thank you. They speak positive things." Sonny Paaula is more circumspect, but implies the same thing. "The newcomer is more interested in the community. If I moved to a new community I would like to know the culture, the rules, the do's and don'ts."

Some eager newcomers immediately confront unexpected barriers to their community participation. I spoke with one newcomer with a master's degree in regional planning who moved to North Kohala to work as a private consultant and to help nonprofit organizations build organizational capacity. She learned quickly that writing advocacy articles in the local paper and taking positions on local issues was not always well received. Some people "were offended when they thought I was here to push my own agenda." She reports that

> The Hawaiian system is, you close your mouth and open your eyes to learn things. If you come to a meeting, you sit in the back and you keep your mouth shut, and you listen. White, Western-educated people who come to this area will presume that they know better or that they know more than people who have lived here for generations. Haoles interrupt, talk over them, are arrogant, or find ways to put people down. In the plantation era, the whites controlled the power, so there's echoes of that re-establishing itself.

The participatory exuberance of some haoles may offend old-timers, perhaps discouraging them from participation themselves. The result can be contradictory, since the newcomer betrays the *aloha* spirit in pursuing it. This becomes another reason why old-timers have mixed feelings toward haoles and their role in the public life of North Kohala.

At the same time, there is some local appreciation for the more culturally sensitive haole residents who act as "bridges." As locals describe them, the bridges' *kuleana* is to translate local culture and make newcomers aware of local concerns. Bridges step in and teach newcomers about the region's multicultural past and present. Sharon, a prominent "bridge" in North Kohala, explains her role:

> We refer to "veneers" coming into our community. It would be easy for them to be unaware of where they had arrived. The words we use are a "rich tapestry of culture" because that's really what is here. We are passionately driven to make sure that new people arriving didn't think they were arriving to a blank slate because the sugar plantation died, and it was something to be created. There was something already here that needs to be respected."

Some versions of what is local are self-consciously multicultural, as evidenced in an event called the "Taste of Kohala," organized twice in the recent past. The event is a community fair that features dance, educational displays, and booths where visitors sample food representing the plantation cultures: Korean, Chinese, Japanese, Filipino, Puerto Rican, Okinawan, and Hawaiian. The idea is to teach newcomers about the cultural mix of the community and the variations that exist there. Of special significance to the Kamehameha sculpture project is the overwhelming presence of newcomers at town meetings, public festivals, and community hearings. Paradoxically, most Hawaiian and other non-Caucasian old-timers with strong feelings about the community do not participate in this public life.

*Kūpuna* and *keiki o ka ʻāina* are given special status in traditional Hawaiian culture. As part of the concern for the decline of traditional ways, there is a desire to reinstate the special deference to elders and children. Our local project organizers commented that both are too often left out of contemporary community life and that we should consciously integrate them into the conservation project. I was surprised that some young Hawaiian activists are against consulting elders because their views were formed in a post-missionary era when Hawaiian values were discouraged. Most elders were raised as Christians and taught to abandon the Hawaiian language. Raylene takes a nuanced position: "Sometimes they forget the filters through which they see things. Most *kūpuna* have not had a very fulfilling experience of being Hawaiian. It's good to try to discern the filters through which they are speaking."

Sharon adds that one has to actively seek out elders for their opinions. "In our community, the Hawaiians are not speaking. We have to go after them and say, 'Please Auntie, tell me what you feel.'" Some attribute this to the lingering effects of the strict social hierarchy of plantation life. Nani explains, "You have the major percentage that don't voice themselves . . . they feel intimidated to be in a group situation. They might say the wrong things, or not say it correctly. To sit next to a white person who is articulate intimidates them. . . . In the plantation days when there was a foreman . . . you just followed directions . . . the plantation did all the thinking."

In her efforts to give old-timers a voice in community life, Emma Glory, of Hawaiian, German, and Welsh ancestry and president of the Senior Citizens Group during our project, provides a similar explanation: "With our senior group in my experience they are not very responsive. It's that plantation mentality. They just let the supervisor do this kind of business. They are not that vocal and they are afraid that they will say something wrong that won't agree with the others. They are very skeptical and nervous."

Despite these barriers, some older Native Hawaiians do engage in public life. Marie Solomon was considered the most respected *kupuna* in the region and became a critical decision maker in the project team. Hawaiian activist Stephanie Cabinis supported Marie's position in one of our discussions. "I'll go along with what *kupuna* Solomon says because her family and my Na'ihe family came from and are buried in the Ahupua'a Wai'apuka, the area of King Kamehameha I's pond and an area of his favorite swimming hole. For those that question her insight, I ask whether or not they can compare her life and her family's past in living in Ahupua'a Wai'apuka. And are they born and raised in Kohala?"

Making children count takes the form of programs that transfer Native Hawaiian knowledge to the young and instill pride in their Hawaiian heritage, as a response to problems of drug use and teen pregnancy. In a locally celebrated North Kohala Elementary School program that connects across the generations, older Native Hawaiians talk story to children about the past and about Native Hawaiian culture. There are other school programs, such as a Hawaiian Academy in the high school and Hawaiian Studies classes. Again, the hope is that injecting local pride might help alleviate problems like drug use and enhance high school graduation rates, currently only at about 70 percent. The great majority leave the region as teenagers and young adults, whether they graduate from high school or not. The recurrent suggestion to involve *keiki* in the conservation project stems from these concerns as well as from local awareness that future decisions about representing the past will be in their hands.

The sculpture of King Kamehameha is arguably the strongest reminder of North Kohala's fused and layered identity. With some knowledge of the community and who counts in North Kohala, I had a better understanding of the diverse voices and concerns as they emerged in the public process of deciding how the sculpture should look.

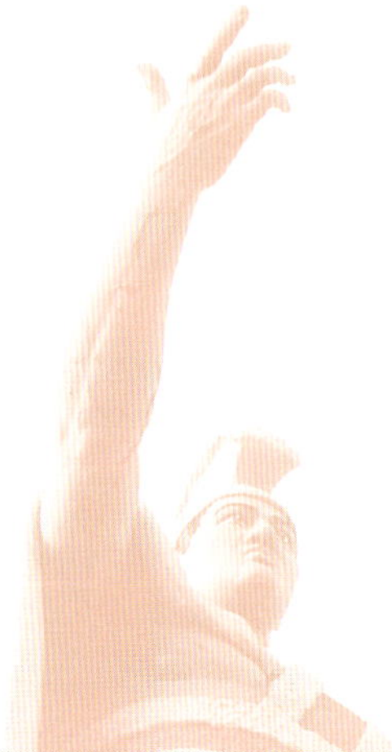

# 6 *How People Think about Their Sculpture*

AS I CAME TO KNOW people in North Kohala and understand the history that brought so many different people together from distant places, I also learned of the sculpture's place in their lives. Listening to old-timers and newcomers talk about the sculpture gave me a picture of how people think about themselves in relation to the past, and to Native Hawaiian culture. I learned that the powerful figure of Kamehameha not only carries meaning but also performs an active role in the spiritual, political, and economic life of the region. Having some sense of the relationships between the sculpture and the people who surround it helped me understand their opinions about how to conserve it.

My initial conversations were the first time many people had reason to voice any thoughts one way or the other about the sculpture's appearance. As the co-owner of Kohala Book Shop across the street from the sculpture told me after a long discussion, "I don't think anyone really gave it much thought until this came along." The conservation project gave people a concrete reason to think through their relationship with the sculpture. Project activities, including public meetings and public art projects, provided a platform for new and sometimes revised reflections. Similarly, new information from my material and archival analysis challenged preconceived notions about the physical history of the sculpture.

With or without my intervention, community residents differed in the intensity of their views about their heritage and community issues. The fate of the sculpture was no different. There was wide variation, ranging from anger to apathy. Perhaps most crucially, there was variation in the way people categorized the sculpture in terms of its function in the community. They spoke of it as a spiritual embodiment, a political resource, a cultural marker, an economic resource, and, increasingly, as an object needing care.

Many Native Hawaiians and other residents of North Kohala describe the sculpture in spiritual terms. *Kaona* in Hawaiian means hidden, subsurface meanings. In our conversations, it did not take long for many to move beyond the sculpture's materiality to these subsurface meanings and to the concept of *mana. Mana* translates to "supernatural or divine power";[1] it connotes the complex cultural system of *kapu* and its strict ordering of the world, with privileged access to knowledge and power. The Kamehameha sculpture as a receptacle of *mana* emerged both in private conversations and in public forums.

People also referred to "precontact" *ki'i* (figurative sculptures) made prior to Cook's arrival on the islands in Hawai'i. Although scholars debate their specific functions and the rituals associated with them,[2] some Native Hawaiians I spoke with conveyed oral traditions that descend through generations about their meaning and use. These sculptures were images of *akua* (spirits, divinities) and manifestations of natural phenomena. Some were freestanding monumental temple sculptures, some were *akua kā'ai* (mounted on top of supports), and some were *āumakua* sculptures (family or personal gods, deified ancestors). Their *mana* reportedly accumulated through prayers and offerings that followed carefully scripted *kapu.*[3]

I spoke on several occasions with Edward Halealoha Ayau, a Honolulu burial rights activist and descendant of Kamehameha. He is a strong advocate of repatriating all human remains in museums and archives for reburial following strict Hawaiian protocols. He was both criticized and praised in the media during the period of our project for borrowing several *ki'i* from the Bishop Museum's collection and, against the museum's wishes, reburying them in an undisclosed location. I asked him how *mana* came to inhabit early Hawaiian carved images. He responded, "The question is—how do you invite the spirit into it? The elaborate carving of *ki'i* and prayer grabs spirits'

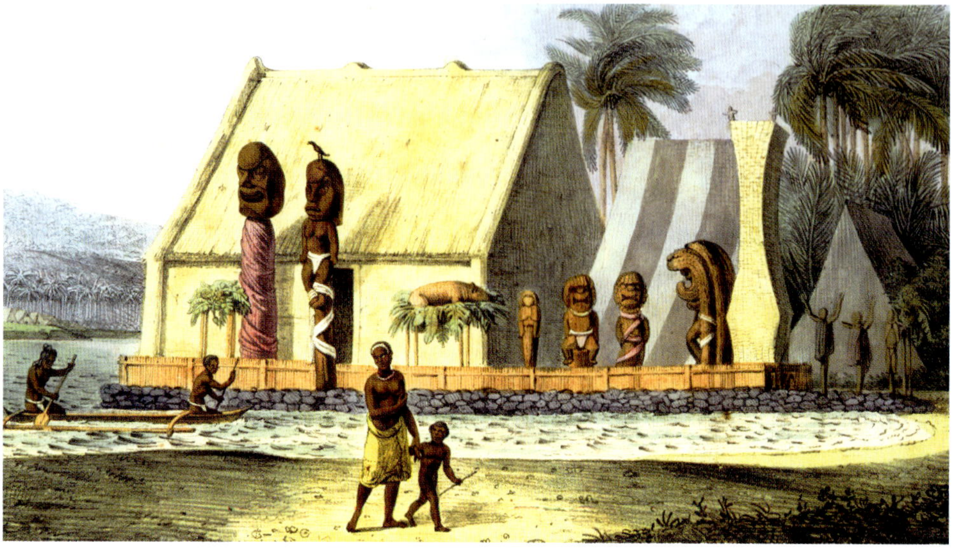

Monumental temple images in front of Ahueha Heiau, Kamehameha's personal *heiau* in Kailua, Kona. Hand-colored lithograph from original watercolor by Louis Choris, 1816. Bishop Museum Archives. Bishop Museum.

attention to inhabit. That's why there's a protocol. That's why chiefs had feathered *kāhilis* [feathered standards] and took their gods to war. You are attracting the *mana* of the spirits."

Precontact *ki'i* had abstract human features but never represented portraits of individual chiefs. John Keola Lake told me that in traditional Hawaiian culture it wasn't considered man's design to capture the likeness of other men. To capture a human image in a sculpture would be stealing its *mana,* or power. *Kālai ki'i,* specially trained image carvers, created *ki'i* under prescribed circumstances. The strict protocol for cutting down a tree for a new *ki'i* included chanting and at times even human sacrifice.[4] The images themselves were only exposed at certain times of the year and only seen by people of high rank and special access.

Because the sculpture was Hawai'i's first heroic-scale image created in the Western tradition, I wondered if some people thought that it contradicted Native Hawaiian spiritual values. No one I spoke with seemed concerned about this, especially when I explained that in my research I found no formal *kapu* established during fabrication and installation. In other words, it was not originally a spiritual object. A frequent question I asked to those who referred to *mana* was whether the sculpture could contain it, like precontact *ki'i.*

The answer was often "yes." To Ayau, a facsimile of Kamehameha is a very strong *ki'i,* even if it wasn't consecrated or made in the Hawaiian tradition. He explained, "The *ki'i,* or image of Kamehameha, can be thought of as a receptacle. It can accumulate *mana* from the artist but also from all those who made offerings to it since it was created."

Indeed, *ho'okupu* (offerings) are almost always present on the sculpture's pedestal in the form of food, flowers, ribbons, and *pōhaku.* Raylene described this modern day *ki'i* as a "go-between for people and the divine." She agreed that giving *ho'okupu* to the sculpture increases its *mana:*

> Many people have come and offered lei, given chants to it. We today, on Kamehameha Day or whenever called upon, place lei. We are placing our *mana* there. It's our acknowledgment of that person [Kamehameha] who gathered our people so they could live in peace. For those of us that come and act this way, then it is. For those that come and act as if it is a statue, then it is.

Others told me of offerings they personally make to the figure. Hilton Nalani Cabrera is a hula instructor who joined our project team first in community activities and later as an assistant in the conservation project. As a Kamehameha descendant with deep spiritual connections and respect for genealogy, he recalled his own childhood: "From a young kid I always danced or presented gifts to the *mo'i* (king), the Kamehameha statue."

On Kamehameha Day 1996, John Keola Lake, in his role as the *kahuna nui* of Pu'ukoholā Heiau, led a group of approximately three hundred people on a midnight march from the Mo'okini Heiau, where Kamehameha was born, to the base of the sculpture. The march culminated in sunrise chanting, offerings, and celebrations.[5] Many local participants now refer to this march as an important spiritual occasion and awakening for the community.

Spiritual understandings of the sculpture and notions of embodiment change over time, from generation to generation. Old-timers describe the fear and respect that their grandparents instilled in them. As Valerie Anjo, Navas Santiago, and Sadie Rodenhurst each recall:

> My grandmother always told us that the statue was very sacred, even though it was a symbol, and made by a white man. She always told us that no woman was allowed to climb up on the statue because it was *kapu.*

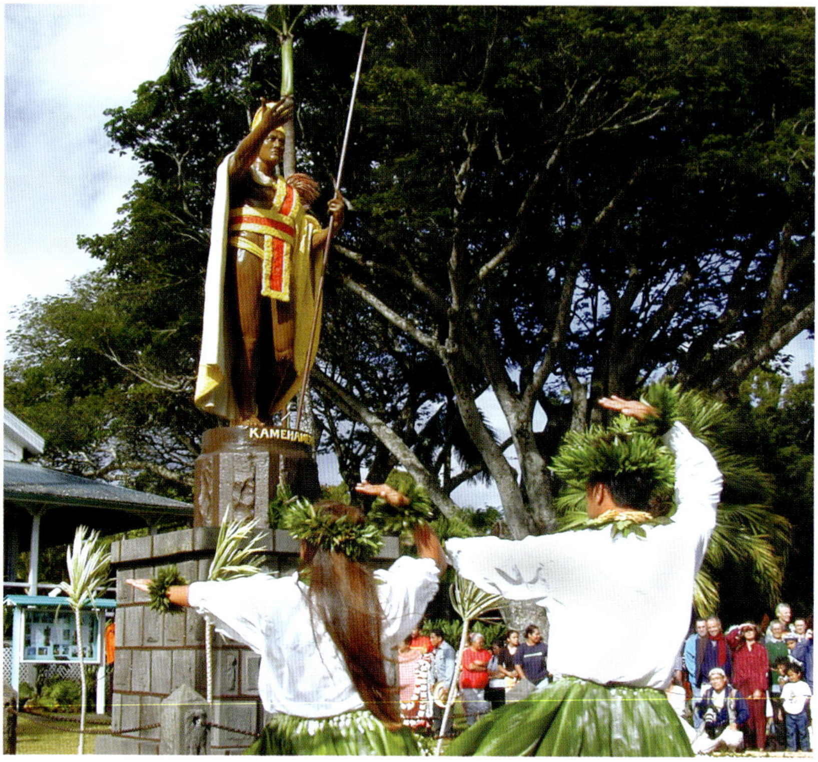


Hula offering to Kamehameha by Hilton Nalani Cabrera and his sister, Cheryl Cabrera.

And if you had your monthly period you wouldn't go around him or near him; it was also *kapu.*

When my grandmother comes to the Kapa'au store, she brings me along. When I come to the statue, I was scared of him. I didn't look at him. We came on the down side, and you think I am gonna look at the statue? Oh no, I looked on the other side. I was afraid of the statue. People used to tell them that he wanted to have five ["children," in reference to the hand gesture]. I was afraid he would take me. I never touched the statue until I was a man. Many of us were afraid of him.

We were young kids at the time. They said, "Don't say anything bad when you are in front of the statue. Don't swear." There were certain ways to be in front of the statue. I never asked why, but they all believe in the spirit, the Hawaiians.

Not all Native Hawaiians believe that the sculpture has *mana.* The majority I spoke with regard the idea as being inconsistent with their "Christian" values. Marie Solomon, one of the most respected *kupuna,* flatly told me, "It has no *mana.*" But for her as well as for others, a deep respect gives the object extraordinary capacities. While those who feared the figure's power as children no longer have concerns about touching him, each feels a strong deference toward Kamehameha and the "spirit" they say the sculpture embodies. They feel that an aura descends on him from prior generations. The sculpture carries a sense of *kuleana* to the king's descendants. Audrey Veloria explained, "They are on his *ʻāina.* Their *mana* and their responsibility of being Hawaiian is to be the keepers and to be the teachers, to keep it going. I believe he speaks to them and relates to them."

I asked as many people as I could about the degree to which the sculpture is an embodiment of Kamehameha. Some described a certain mimesis, in which the sculpture stands in for Kamehameha. Most people I spoke with, including the self-described secular, use the personal pronoun "he" when describing it, and several referred to him as part of the community *ʻohana.* Raylene suggested, "For many, he's great grandpa. When they talk to the statue, they're talking to their ancestor."

People greet him as they drive by on their daily errands. At ninety-five, Albert Solomon (a distant relative of Marie Solomon) recalled, "All my life until now, if I go down there, I pass the statue and say '*aloha mai no mōʻī nui*' (greetings to the great king). I've always respected the statue, like my great grandparents respected it." Emma Glory also described a more secular relationship: "Maybe I'm a Christian and I don't think too much about spirits, but when I am standing in front of the statue I think of all his accomplishments. How hard he fought to unite the Islands. I think, 'Thank you,' and I put on lei." Henry Dulan commented in a similar vein: "I'm not going to worship him, but I respect him as a warrior. It's good to recognize him as king of the Hawaiians." Kealoha Sugiyama also spoke of his accomplishments: "When we view Kamehameha the Great and we look at the statue, we go beyond the metal form, to what he did for the Hawaiian kingdom, his unification of all the islands, preparing us for the coming of the foreigners."

In addition to being a spiritual object and standing in for a local chief who became Hawaiʻi's first king, the sculpture also functions as a political resource.

The image is featured in the logo of the Kamehameha Schools.

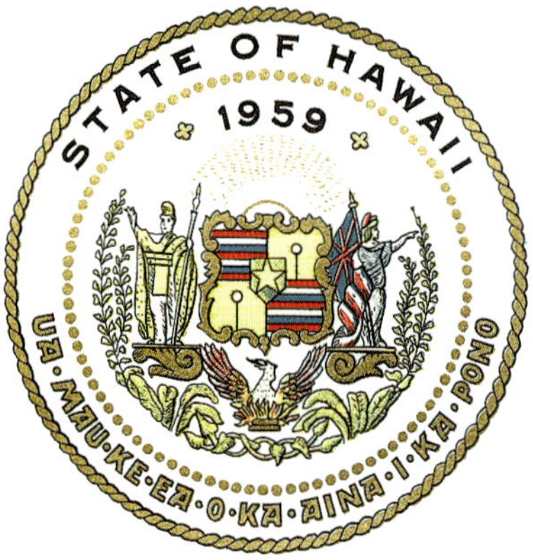


Appropriated for contemporary political use, the sculpture's image appears on the official state seal.

It circulates widely as a symbol of official state authority. It is on the state seal, official stationery, and other legal documents. The Kamehameha Schools also incorporate the image into their logo.

When Hawai'i became the fiftieth state in 1959, state officials ordered a cast of the Honolulu replica as one of the two sculptures the state was permitted to place in Statuary Hall inside the U.S. Capitol building in Washington, D.C.[6] Selecting the Kamehameha sculpture to represent the state in Washington, D.C., did not happen without public debate. As described by one commentator, "Honolulu newspaper columns have recently been heated up over charges that he was a Hawaiian Hitler and a pagan savage. Hawaiians have not taken kindly to such remarks, calling them ill-mannered obscenities. There can be little doubt of the king's great historical importance, or that he is an authentic hero in the eyes of his people."[7]

When I asked about the sculpture's role in local and state politics, I learned that its political significance is even more complex today than its originators envisioned. Walter Murray Gibson and King Kalākaua's efforts to stir Hawaiian nationalism through linkage to European royalty and empire

**OPPOSITE PAGE:** Replica of the Kamehameha sculpture given by the state of Hawai'i in 1969 to the federal government, installed in the U.S. Capitol building, Washington, D.C. Architect of the Capitol.

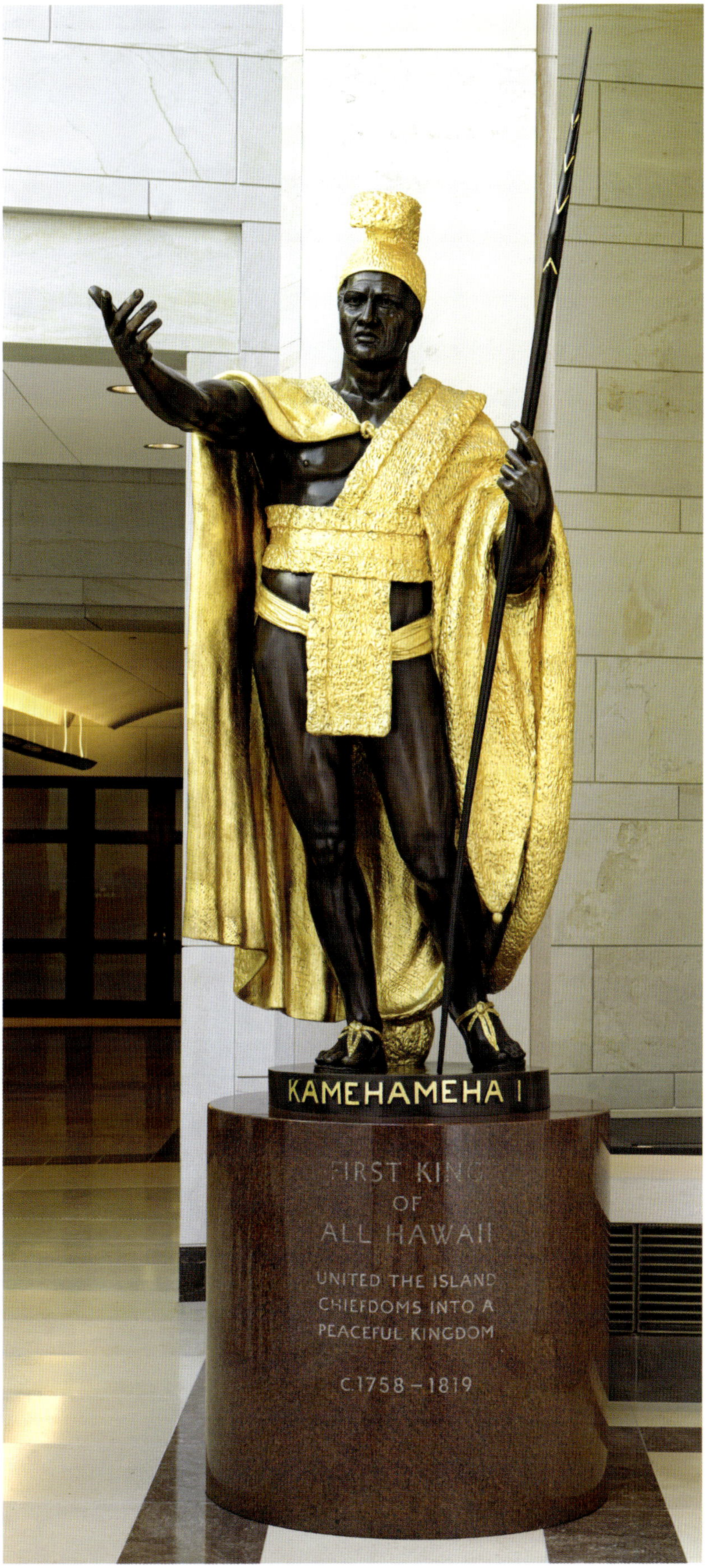
KAMEHAMEHA I
FIRST KING
OF
ALL HAWAII
UNITED THE ISLAND
CHIEFDOMS INTO A
PEACEFUL KINGDOM
C.1758–1819

have little resonance today in North Kohala. Sharon was the only person in my conversations who mentioned its original purpose to commemorate the "discovery" of the islands by Captain Cook. This original meaning was largely lost, or perhaps intentionally buried just five years after its commission, when the sculpture functioned as an emblem for King Kalākaua's coronation. Instead, my questions evoked tensions that reflected historical events that occurred soon after its installation, starting with the U.S. aggression, Queen Liliʻuokalani's imprisonment, and the following military coup. I occasionally heard comments that the sculpture reflects and reinforces U.S. dominance in Hawaiian culture.

On the other hand, everyone seemed aware of the sculpture's creation by an American sculptor living in Europe. This cut two ways. For some it was a source of pride, evidence that skilled and important people from such a distance honored their local chief. But for others, it carried the weight of U.S. incursion. Local activist Anthony Anjo told me that the sculpture was a gift, but a false one:

> They gave a statue as a false gift, like the wooden horse. I don't respect and revere the statue as some other people do, because of the motives behind it. These Europeans that came to Hawaiʻi thought that Hawaiians were a bunch of simpletons. "Yeah, we will give them a statue, make them happy, of their king." But behind the scenes they didn't give a damn about the Hawaiians. "We'll just do this to create good will." But the good and the will was for them, and look what happened—we now have statehood.

Historian Fred Cachola points to the interests of the haole legislators in 1878. "Look at who was in the legislature at that time: they were leaning towards the West, trying to undo all the Hawaiian things around them. The statue is symbolic of the people with money who controlled, and determined to make Hawaiʻi part of the U.S." Anthony took this sentiment about U.S. imperialism further: "There's too much Western influence in this sculpture. Towards the end of Kamehameha's life he wasn't thinking of statues being made to eulogize him. Maybe he was thinking, 'What have I done? What have I let out of the box? My people are dying left and right and what's going to happen?'"

A few people told me that Kamehameha shouldn't be regarded as a hero at all. They see him not as brave unifier of the Islands but as a conqueror guilty of bloody invasions and war. Kamehameha killed and sacrificed his own cousin, Keoua, in 1791, early in his military campaigns.[8] His epithet as the "Napoleon of the Pacific" signals instead a ruthless usurper who broke *kapu* by killing his cousin to attain power. Referring to the loss of thousands of lives in his conquest of other islands, one newcomer expressed dismay at local celebrations of Kamehameha, wishing that "there was a cultural figure they could memorialize that wasn't such a fierce, bloody warrior."

But such complaints about Kamehameha's violent tactics were rare. Much more common was a reverence for Kamehameha that took one form or another. At age twenty-seven, Raylene's son Mike Lancaster found more relevance in the places Kamehameha lived, worked, and worshiped. As an act of spiritual service, he spent months in an isolated valley, living under an open canopy while planting taro to resurrect Kamehameha's personal *lo'i* (taro patch). His comments reflected his own preference for restoring a historical site rather than conserving a sculpture. "The statue is like a relic. I used to get kind of upset because they protect the statue, yet the places where he did a lot are not protected. I used to be a little bitter about it."

The sculpture's use as a symbol for the state rarely came up in our conversations. This may be because the image on the state seal is copied from the gilt Honolulu cast, but it may also be due to a local notion that the king is not state property, but part of North Kohala's local history and *'ohana*. Many residents have never seen the Honolulu cast, and few have seen the Washington, D.C., copy. Yet the sculpture does have value as an extension of local government power. The captain of the North Kohala Police Department always kept a collage above his desk that juxtaposes Kamehameha with images of the police. The sculpture is also used as the centerpiece for the display of the U.S. and state flags mounted on either side of its plinth.

In 1997, these flags became the focus of heated disagreement. Kealoha, who had volunteered his time to repaint the sculpture, replaced the flags with *kāhili* for Kamehameha Day celebrations, which evoked an angry reaction on the part of some old-timers. According to Kealoha, one commented, "I am an American, and I think the flag should be up 365 days a year." As Emma Glory, president of the Senior Citizens Group, remembered it:

> Boy, was there trouble. "You aren't going to take the flags down!" "The nerve of you to hang *kāhilis* up there." The community was angry—all of the GIs and the veterans. "That's where the American flag belongs." I got up and said, "You know, this is our Kamehameha statue. He was born

> here, raised here, we sing songs about him. What's wrong with pulling the flag down once a year and putting up *kāhilis?*" They were going to call Senator Inouye. It was mostly the veterans that took offense that the flag was lowered.

People told me about another aspect of the sculpture that troubled them: the hand gesture, which suggested control and authority, the opposite idea of welcoming and warmth. I carried around a photograph of the sculpture, and when I spoke to people about its meaning and use in the community I asked why he held out his right hand. This was often an icebreaker, sometimes leading to humorous responses. Indeed, most people had a ready answer. More than half gave variations of the *aloha* theme, such as high school student Jasmine Ono's reflection: "He is telling people to come." A newcomer who came to the region for spiritual attachment to the land described the gesture as a "welcome and sharing of energy." Four people qualified this interpretation with warnings such as "Welcome but don't fuck with me." A similar variation was that "He is saying to his enemies, 'Come, challenge me.' 'I come with peace, but if you are looking for trouble, I can fight, I can spear you.'"

Still others read the hand gesture with more direct political interpretations. Joe Chang, an old-timer of Chinese ancestry, mentioned land reparations to Hawaiian people. "Kamehameha is asking the white man give me back my land." This was echoed by old-timers hanging out at the Soda Fountain restaurant, who all agreed that "he's asking for land back." David Roy of the Royal Order of Kamehameha provided another perspective:

> We don't like the attitude of his holding his palm out like that. It's like he is giving something away. That's what they've been doing all their lives, giving things away. They've given land away, and all kinds of things. Now they don't even have a kingdom. The Westerner has the impression of "*aloha*"—yeah, you come here and you can get everything you want. And they expect us to perform that way.

Interpreting the gesture also brings out a streak of off-color humor. "He wants paper—to clean his behind." At times my question evoked disparaging remarks against Native Hawaiians. "I could tell you a joke. The joke is he's Hawaiian, so he's got his hand out." "He's asking for money. He's begging."

Whether as a symbol of the state or of the status of Native Hawaiians, the sculpture evokes strong political imagery among those who see it and live with it on a daily basis. Yet it also plays a more neutral role as a marker of local identity, tradition, and collective life. It creates a place for public events. By far its most important cultural use is in annual celebrations on Kamehameha Day, June 11, a two-day civic festival involving much of the local population. From my reading, I learned that June 11 was designated a public holiday in memory of Kamehameha I by Royal proclamation of Kamehameha V on December 22, 1871. The first celebration in Honolulu was held on June 11, 1872, and included sporting events, with a grand prize of a Kamehameha plate made in San Francisco. Over the years, the celebration changed in form and venue, and it is now a significant cultural celebration for residents of Honolulu and a tourist draw for the state.

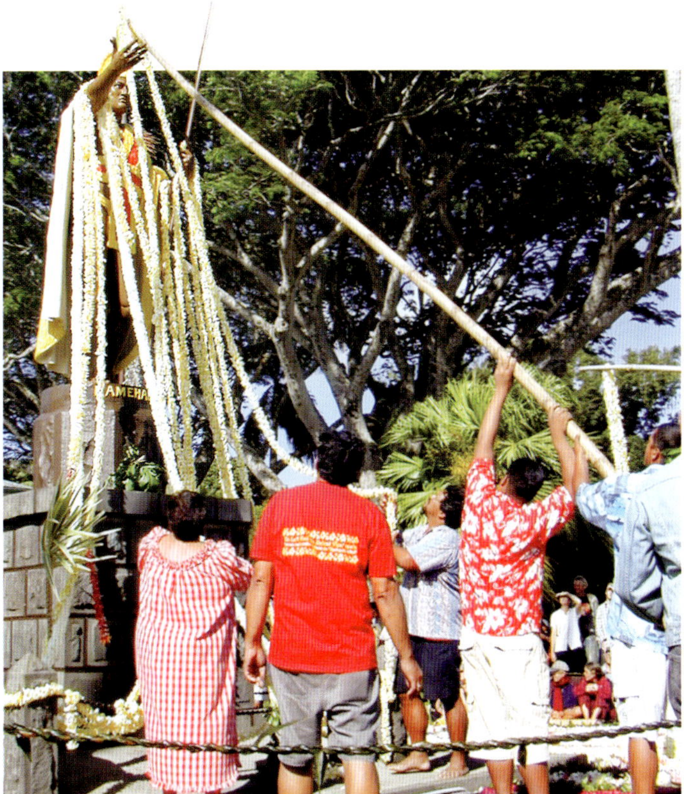

Lei offerings from groups and individuals brought to the sculpture through ceremony.

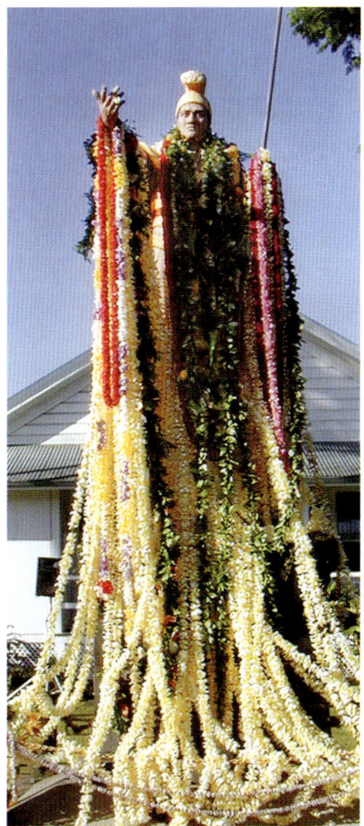

Lei offerings on Kamehameha Day.

The North Kohala celebration includes spiritual elements such as sunrise chanting conducted by priests and others from the nearby Puʻukoholā Heiau stone temple, the Royal Order of Kamehameha, and other Native Hawaiian groups. Celebrations on the lawn around the sculpture include hula, singing, chanting, slack key guitar playing, and *kūpuna* talking story about Kamehameha and the significance of Kamehameha Day. In an address to those gathered at the old courthouse on Kamehameha Day 2001, Marie Solomon explained that the celebration is for three things: Kapaʻau, the *mōʻī*, and the *kiʻi*. People representing each island and many cultural groups bring long lei as gifts to the sculpture. Students from the high school Hawaiian Studies class place these lei around the figure's neck at sunrise.

A parade begins in Hāwī and culminates just beyond the sculpture in Kapaʻau. Many people in the parade stop and give *hoʻokupu* to appointed children, who carry them up the steps and place them on top of the stone plinth. Floats made by churches, businesses, and other sponsors roll past, along with a convertible containing descendants of Kamehameha. The parade also includes *pāʻū* queens representing all eight islands and other *pāʻū* riders. These women horseback riders wear long skirts that mark past intersections of Hawaiian, missionary, and cowboy cultures. Festivities terminate at a nearby public park, where thousands gather for a day of picnics and entertainment, with rock music as well as more Hawaiian-style singing and dancing. Kamehameha Day celebrations also include educational and craft displays in the high school gym. Displays include lei making, poi (taro root) pounding, *lauhala* (Pandanas leaf) weaving, woodcarving, *lomi-lomi* (massage), and Hawaiian games such as *ʻulu maika*.

My conversations with old-timers often evoked thoughts about Kamehameha Day celebrations that extend far back into local memory. Kindy Sproat was the region's most respected Hawaiian falsetto singer and storyteller. During one of our many conversations about the way North Kohala used to be, he recalled childhood activities on Kamehameha Day in front of the sculpture. "Back in the late '30s, all the kids from the Makapala School brought flowers. We would play tug-of-war and practice throwing spears." Old-timer Navas Santiago had similar memories. "People would come, you know, Hawaiian style, with their beautiful music, and singing. People would just gather around the statue. A lot of nice music and hula hula." Emma Glory also had similar memories. "I can just see Daddy with his black pants, his shirt with the little cape—telling stories about the king and his accomplishments. Sing and praise and have a good time, and eat-*luau*. Roast a pig."

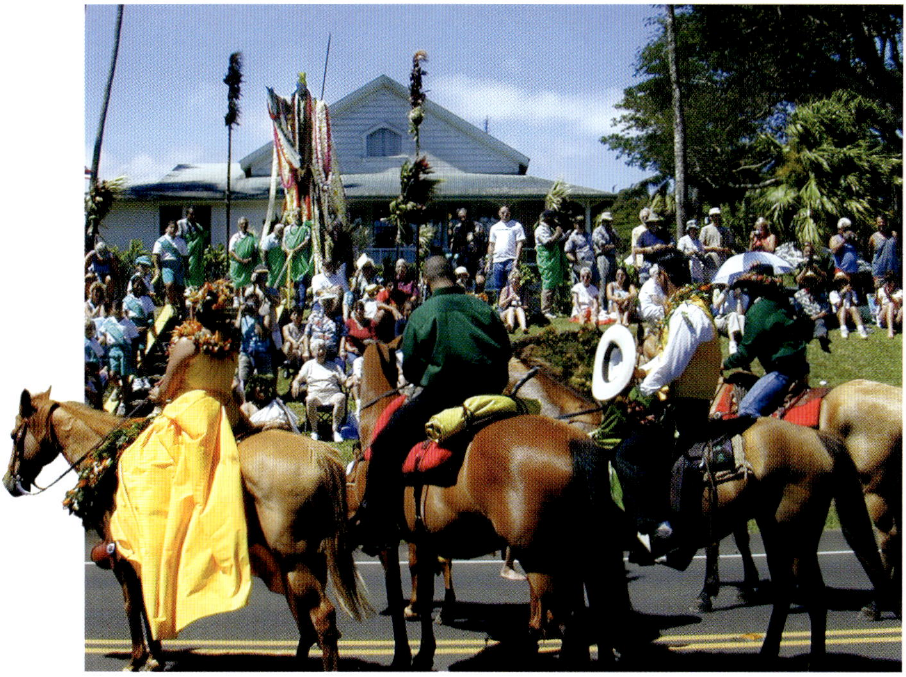

*Pā'ū* and Hawaiian cowboy riders stop to make *ho'okupu* to the Kamehameha sculpture on Kamehameha Day, June 11, 2001.

The parades in front of the sculpture began in the 1940s, when the Hawaiian legislature first provided funding for local celebrations. The plantations donated trucks, and volunteers decorated them as "floats." The celebrations always began with lei draping. Audrey Veloria recalled stories from Marie Solomon: "Auntie Marie tells us that as they came they would carry the lei and chant in Hawaiian who they were, and they would wish an appreciation to the king, then it would be lifted on the 'y' stick and put over his neck. In the old custom they would identify who you are and say why you've come [in the chant], and leave your gift. 'I am Audrey, and I am coming from the family of _______ and I present this to you this day we will remember you and here's the lei.'"

Enthusiasm for the celebrations evidently languished in the 1970s and 1980s but revitalized in 1996 with the formation of the North Kohala Kamehameha Day Celebration Committee, a group that made conscious use of the sculpture as the symbolic and geographic core of its efforts. The committee members, all long-term residents, are volunteers from Native Hawaiian, Asian, and Caucasian descent: "bridges."

The sculpture's role remains open-ended, following no clear pattern as to whether it is a spiritual thing or a political thing or a civic thing. All the diverse activities around it actively create local culture in a way that involves constant negotiation and unclear resolutions. For some in the community, Kamehameha Day is sacred. Members of the Royal Order of Kamehameha continue a tradition of practicing secret rituals that began with King Kamehameha V in 1865. They conduct these rituals privately before the public ceremonies begin. For others, it is more akin to the kind of holiday celebration one would find in a typical U.S. small town. They look forward to gathering with friends and family for the parade, hula, and ukulele performances.

The sculpture serves as a focal point in the landscape, a marker for giving directions to strangers, an object for reminiscing about past events in the community, and a place for both formal and informal gatherings. People arrange to meet each other at the picnic tables around the sculpture. According to Audrey Veloria, "When *kūpuna* want to share stories, they say 'meet me by the statue.' They feel that's where they can tell their stories and have them received calmly." As a kindergarten teacher who moved to North Kohala from Honolulu in 1970, she thinks of the king as a venerated family patriarch. "Like a child that never knew its grandpa, I come and I feel his presence and I hear his stories and I feel good, peaceful." She describes traditions that continue in the community, perhaps stemming from ancient spiritual traditions of gift giving. "If someone did well in an athletic fête they would offer him a lei. If they get married they take a picture there. It's a way to pay respect to Kohala's king." The sculpture provides a way for continuity with Hawaiian traditions of showing thanks for good fortune.

People take photographs at the sculpture. Photograph albums contain images of family members, cousins, and friends standing in front of it after weddings, graduation ceremonies, and other important events. It is thus continually reproduced as part of family documentation and remembrance. Over its history, a continuous stream of photographs in the media has documented private and public events associated with the various casts of the sculpture, especially the one in Honolulu, but also the North Kohala version. All these copies and reproductions further multiply perceptions of the sculpture. These images come back, no doubt to influence the perceptions and feelings of those who live and work nearby.

Local residents use the sculpture consciously as a didactic resource. For "bridges" and others, events like Kamehameha Day provide an opportunity to teach newcomers and outsiders about local culture and to "preserve" and recreate parts of the past for the future. Educators are aware of the opportunities made possible by the day-to-day presence of the sculpture. Following traditional means of transmitting knowledge in Hawaiian culture, the artifact serves as a base for talking story. Volunteers and tourist guides use it to communicate the history of the region to visitors, and old-timers use it to pass on their knowledge. Teachers from kindergarten through high school bring classes on field trips to the site to teach Hawaiian history, Kamehameha's connection to North Kohala, and events from contact with Captain Cook to annexation and statehood. Tourists learn about Kamehameha and the sculpture from the collage of photographs, printed literature, and typewritten text in the exhibit case assembled by the Senior Citizens Group on the front lawn just behind the sculpture. Community organizations use the image in their T-shirt logos.

Old-timers like Navas Santiago tell many versions of the remarkable story of the Kamehameha sculpture's journey to Kohala. As with any oral tradition that is told and retold, there are variations of the sculpture's history:

> I will tell you the story of the statue. It was made in Italy. On the way coming to the Hawaiian Islands, the statue got into trouble and the ship that they were bringing it on and the statue went into the water, the sea. They got him out, but one of the arms was broken. They brought him to Honolulu. The man who built the statue in Italy came down and had it repaired, and from there, they brought him to Kohala.

At age ninety-six, Albert Solomon freely told stories to visitors of the local Kamuela Museum that he founded. He told me how he carried on the spiritual lineage of his Hawaiian great grandmother and grandmother as well as the mixed heritage from the other side of his family. "I am quarter Hawaiian, I've got one-eighth Yaki Indian, one-eighth Spanish, one-eighth Jew, one-eighth Turk, one-eighth Syrian, and one-eighth Arabian." His story of recovering the sculpture after the shipwreck reveals the extent to which local knowledge can vary from newspaper reports of the time:

> On their way out they hit high seas, and it washed overboard. It fell in the deep ocean, so they figured it was lost forever. So they took Baker's profile to make the Honolulu one.

> Russian fishermen went out in ships and the tide dropped low down, fifteen feet. They saw the big hand sticking out. They thought he was a sea monster of some kind, but it was a human hand. They spun around and sized him up good, but they were scared so they reported to the Russian officials what they had seen. They figured they were seeing things, been out on the high seas, so the fishermen never said nothing, because you can't open your mouth in Russia, they put you in a firing squad. So they waited until the next month of May. They got hold of a diver, and they went back there, and the hand was gone. The diver went down and sure enough he came up reporting that there was a statue down there, so they hoisted him up, and one hand was ripped off, but the hand was there. It was ripped off tight from dragging in the ocean.

The reference to the Baker half-brother photographs to create the second cast, the involvement of Russian fishermen, the extent of time that it was under the sea, and the bronze hand appearing at low tide are all at variance with nineteenth-century documents, yet they add drama to Solomon's core story of the shipwreck and recovery. As images and stories are reproduced and reconstructed, locals continue oral traditions and maintain North Kohala as a particular place with a unique substantive history. Through the sculpture, the community "performs" its culture in ways that actively connect the Hawaiian past with the present.[9]

People also use the sculpture for economic gain. As a commodity, the image does well. Both the local and statewide tourist industries market Hawai'i through the image. It appears on travel guides and countless brochures and postcards found everywhere in Honolulu, North Kohala, and elsewhere on the Islands. Garment makers silk-screen images of the sculpture on T-shirts and incorporate it into "*aloha*" shirt designs. It finds its way into art worlds as an inspiration for folk art. Mass-produced, carved wood copies of the gilt image line shelves in local shops, and older knockoffs for the tourist industry recycle in "Hawaiiana" shops. Local goods tend to feature the painted version of the sculpture, whereas in Honolulu and elsewhere, the gilt version dominates.

A Japanese corporation commissioned an oversized replica of the gilt sculpture for their "Princeville" resort on the island of Kaua'i to serve as an emblem of the Royal Hawaiian past. In 1993, residents of the island of Kaua'i

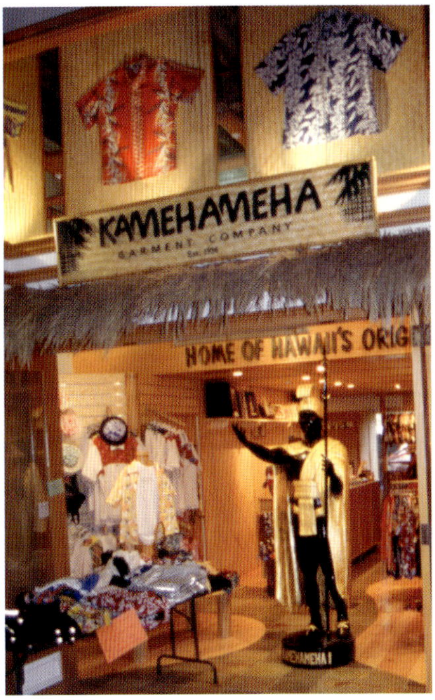


Aloha shirt store in Honolulu.

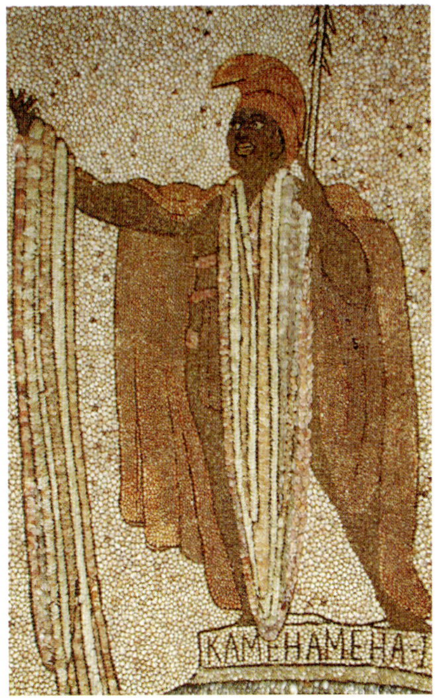


Folk art incorporating shells into the design of the Kamehameha sculpture. Mounted in the office of the State Parks Service, Honolulu. Courtesy of Hawai'i State Parks.

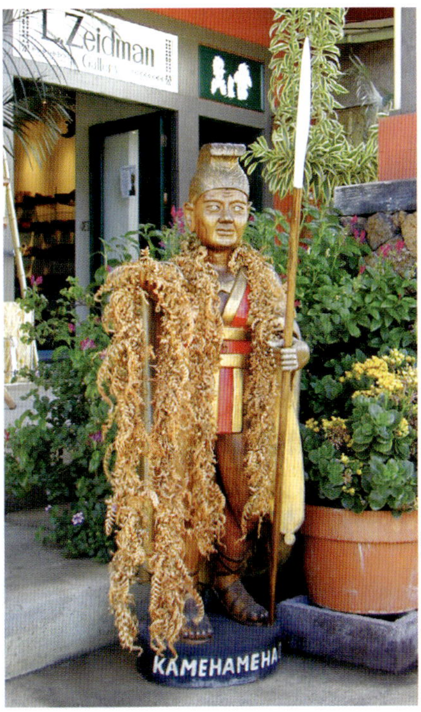


Hand-carved reproduction of the sculpture from the Philippines, on sale in front of a "Hawaiiana" shop in Hāwī.

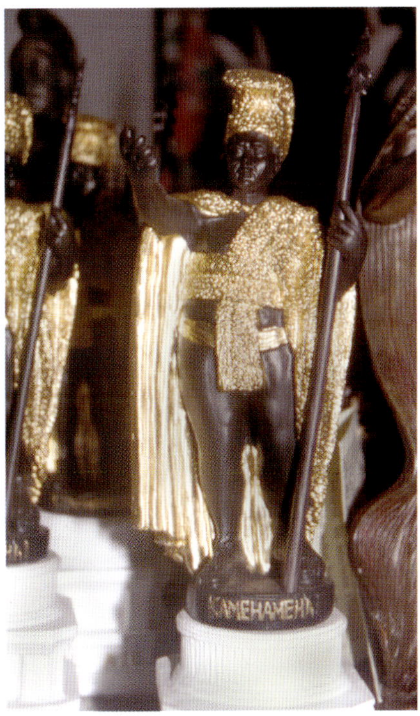


Mass-produced, carved wood reproductions of the sculpture on sale with other souvenirs in tourist shop in Kapa'au.

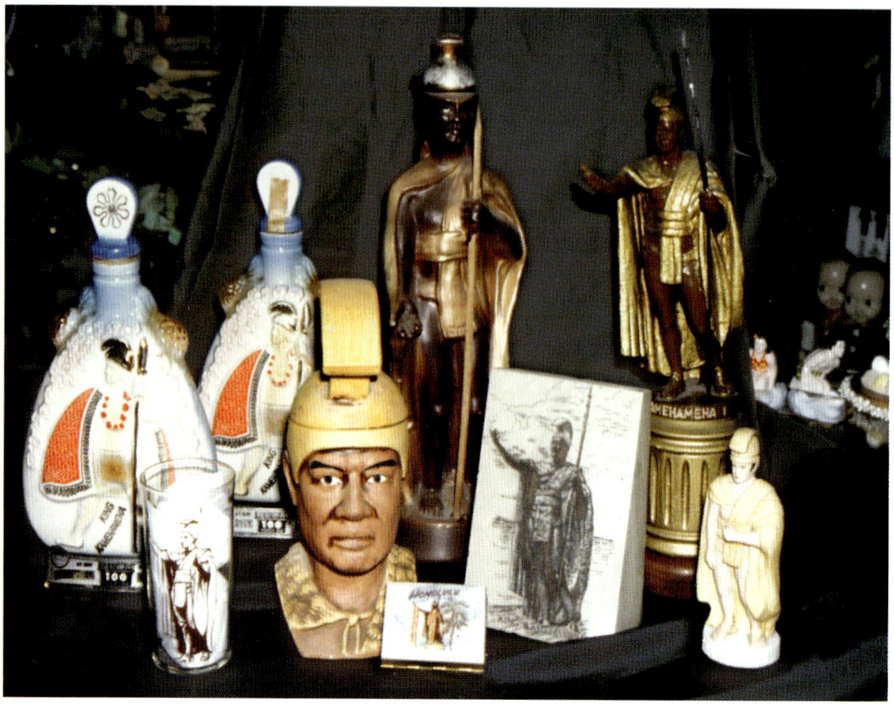

Reproductions of the image on tourist items from the past are now recycled and purchased by collectors of "Hawaiiana." Photograph by author of items for sale in Bailey's Antiques and Aloha Shirts, Honolulu.

protested the installation of the oversized replica because Kamehameha had failed to conquer the island by force. According to Terry Plunkett and Lucas Kekuna, the Japanese corporation gave in and placed their $125,000 bronze in storage. Several years later the Hilo chapter of the Kamehameha Schools Alumni Association convinced the Japanese owners of Princeville to donate the bronze to their city on the Big Island of Hawai'i. They paid for the shipment from Kaua'i to Hilo and installed it in 1997. This fourth cast of the Kamehameha sculpture now resides in Hilo on the island of Hawai'i and serves as a tourist draw as well as a source of local pride.

The local retail district pivots on the sculpture and its location, and the closer a business is to the sculpture, the better. From its mounted pedestal in front of the courthouse, Kamehameha's dramatic hand gesture—whatever it is doing—directs attention to the Rainbow Café and the Ackerman Gallery

**OPPOSITE PAGE:** Kamehameha I sculpture in Hilo, Hawai'i. Artist: R. Sandrin. 1993.

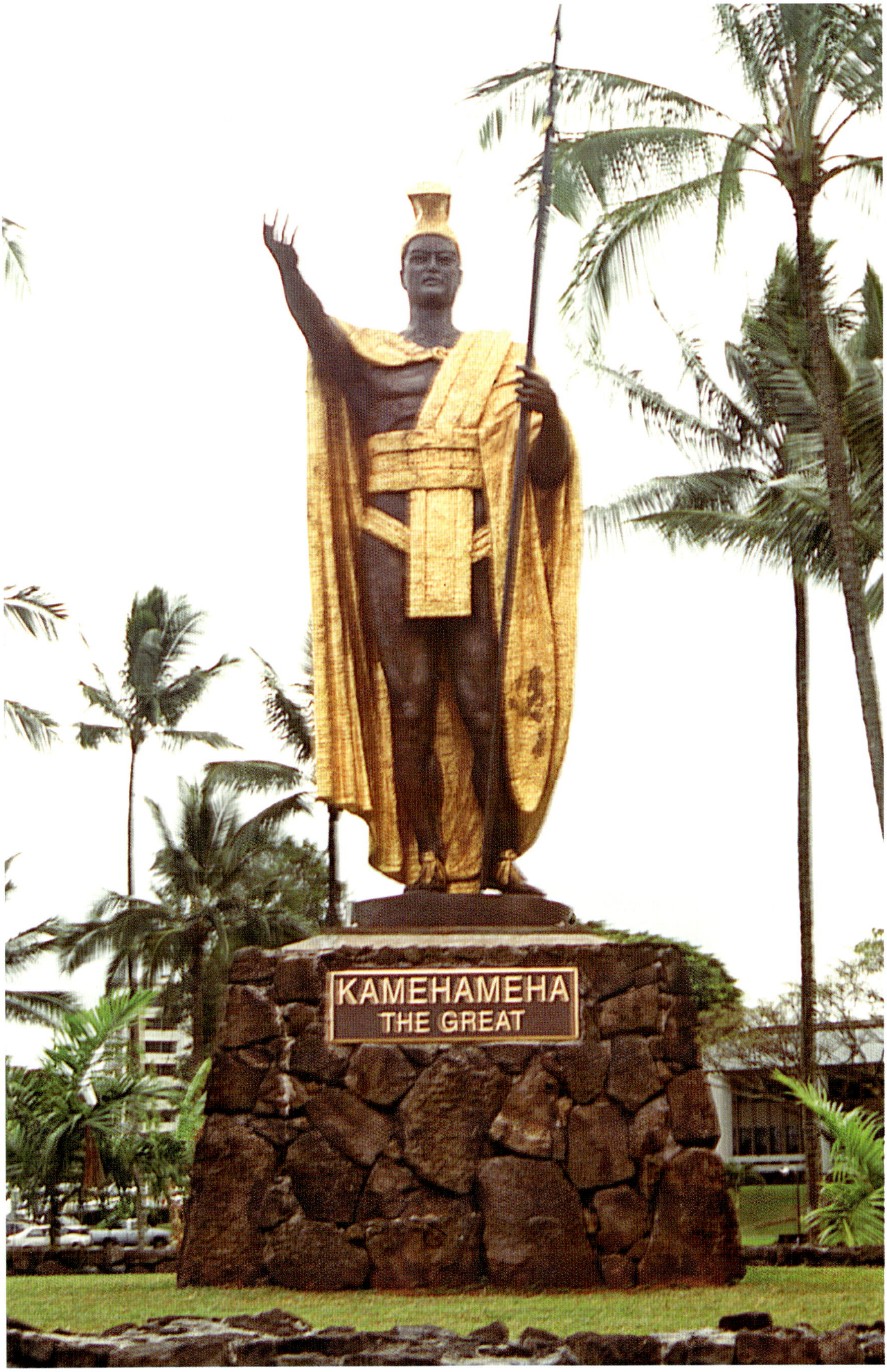
KAMEHAMEHA
THE GREAT

just across the street. Looking back on the days in 1985 when he established his café at that location, then-newcomer Dan Rich recalled, "I figured I had a captive audience. I actually utilized as little advertising as I could because that's very expensive, and I figured I had the best advertising already because every magazine advertises the king and where it is."

Jen Davis moved to the region and purchased the café from Rich. She featured the "Kamehameha Wrap" that I ate on my very first day in Kapa'au. Given the café's proximate location, I got to know Jen as well as her menu. She agreed with Rich: "Being able to say that the business is across the street from the statue has been helpful. In fact, in my advertising, I say, 'across from the King Kamehameha statue, North Kohala.' I was interested in this location because people would stop here anyway, and I was right. Everyday I say 'Thank you, king!' He is pointing right to my café! They stop and get out, then they have some ice cream." Another set of newcomers who purchased

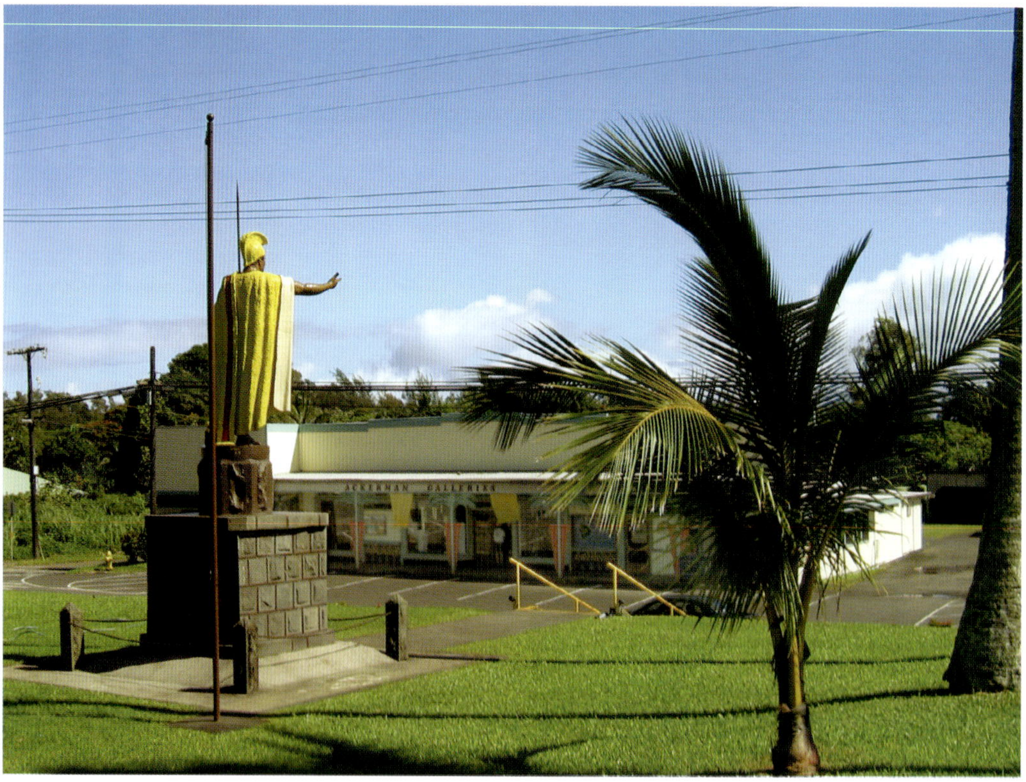


The sculpture points across the street to the Rainbow Café and the Ackerman Gallery.

the café from Jen in 2004 repeated the same sentiment to me. To Diana Soler, "he's saying 'Go right over there!'" The staff at the Ackerman Gallery report that they get about 70 percent more business than their other location down the street because of the foot traffic from the sculpture.

There is heated discussion among the leadership of the North Kohala Merchants Association about how to market local culture. One point of contention is whether to allow stores to be open on Kamehameha Day. Some merchants want to open their stores because of the tourist draw to watch the parade. One member complained that the Kamehameha Day Celebration Committee is run by "a bunch of aging hippies." On the other side, Anthony Anjo expresses anger and distrust of the Merchants Association. "The merchants are going to use this (conservation) project, because their whole agenda is to bring more business here."

Representatives from the North Kohala Kamehameha Day Celebration Committee were less strident in their opposition, but they resisted "commercializing" a state holiday. They also feared nonlocal business interests, which, in return for financial sponsorship, had their logos and messages permeate the holiday event. Sharon spoke of the "O'ahu-centric" nature of state funding for holiday celebrations. Worried about losing "control to Honolulu, even for Kamehameha Day," she explained, "We don't accept money given from the state because then you have to advertise Hawaiian Airlines, and you have to do all these things that would take us to the 'commercial' where we don't want to go." Raylene agreed. "Look into your heart, not your wallet, and tell me what is the focus of the day? Can't we raise money the other 364 days of the year and keep this day to pay our respects and to educate?" Her intention is to "lead the Kamehameha Day Committee back to clearness of focus and intent."

But as usual in North Kohala, the "sides" overlap and individuals tend to accept tourism just as they invoke the traditions of local distinctiveness. Navas Santiago, a second-generation Puerto Rican immigrant who "grew up on the plantations" and retired from the Kohala Sugar Company in 1971, proudly told me, "Tourists come from all over the world. Why? They want to see the Kamehameha statue. From all over the world!" Whatever kind of conservation treatment it might undergo or just how it might be perceived on other grounds, the sculpture's durability is seen as part of the commercial vitality of the region.

For a smaller number of government officials and neighbors, the sculpture is an object needing an entirely different kind of attention. Located on a street populated by residents and visitors, it generates mundane concerns about safety. Visitors use an uneven stairway that does not meet contemporary codes, much less Americans with Disabilities Act standards. The stairs are on the district's major highway, and there is no sidewalk. The captain of the North Kohala Police Department and the supervisor of building and construction maintenance told me they are concerned about tourists who park on the other side of the highway and walk distractedly across the road. Tourists often look through their camera lens while crossing the street. Jen Davis of Jen's Kohala Café suggested a crosswalk in front of the sculpture even though it is in the middle of the block, because "95 percent of the people walk across the street right in front of the statue. Every once in a while you hear an 'rrr' as a car slams on the brakes. It's an accident waiting to happen."

In contrast to its commercial utility, some business owners complain that tourists use their parking spaces while visiting the sculpture—apparently not coming into their stores. Others complain there is insufficient parking for tour buses, inadequate signage, and not enough lighting at night. Officials explained to me that they are working to remedy all these various problems, seeking government financing from different levels of jurisdiction.

Apart from these commonplace issues, care of the sculpture itself is a problem that local officials have more difficulty dealing with, in part because of jurisdictional complications. The state may or may not own the sculpture, and it is on county land. I could not trace early records of its maintenance. I found no references to maintaining the sculpture prior to the mid-1960s in the state and county archives, historical journals, and newspapers. According to one old-timer, the sugar company bosses took care of everything during the plantation era, including the sculpture. "They regularly had it cleaned and painted." At some point in the years following the Second World War, the County Department of Public Works in Hilo assumed responsibility for its care. In 1973, through a government reorganization, the county work crew was transferred to the state. The same crew continued caring for the sculpture as they had done before, through the local Building Maintenance Department.

I found Joe Chang, the government employee in charge of painting the sculpture for most of the period from 1968 through 1988. He lit up when I asked about his maintenance methods during those years. Some of these methods seemed aggressive compared to techniques used today by art con-

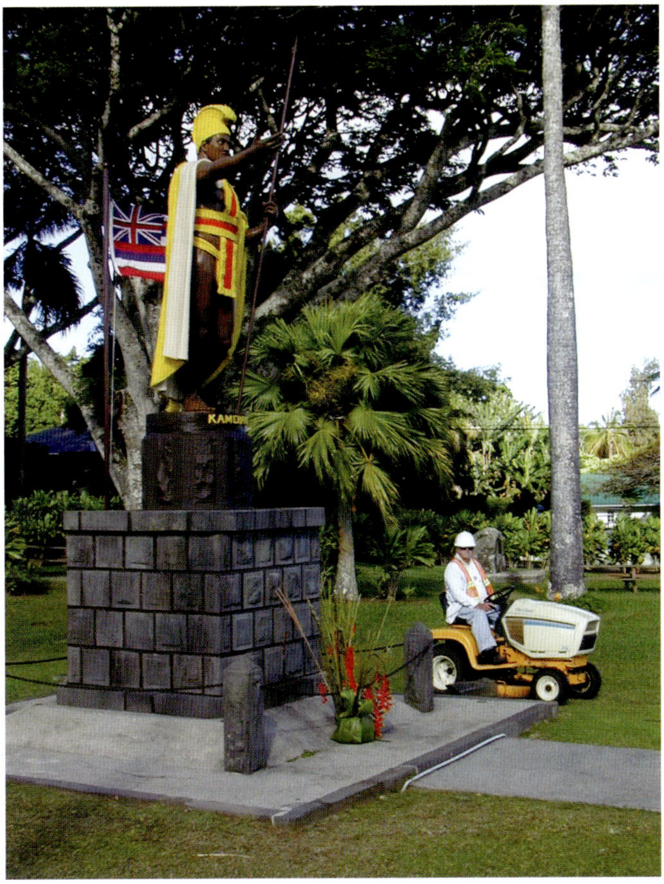

The Hawai'i County maintenance crew cares for landscaping around the sculpture since it is installed on county land. The State Department of Accounting and General Services cares for the sculpture since it is owned by the state.

servators. "We used wire brushes every year, and a power washer. Strong stream of water, and detergent. We spread detergent on him, and blast him off with a power washer. Just like we did the buildings." In their regular painting campaigns, the highway crews used house paint. Chang clearly cared and thought considerably about his charge. At one point he even added eyeballs to the deep sockets on the face:

> The eyes were hollow. Made out of bronze material. He looked like a zombie, like a skeleton, so I got brass balls from a poison can, a check valve, about a half-inch diameter. I glued the eyeballs in with epoxy. It will

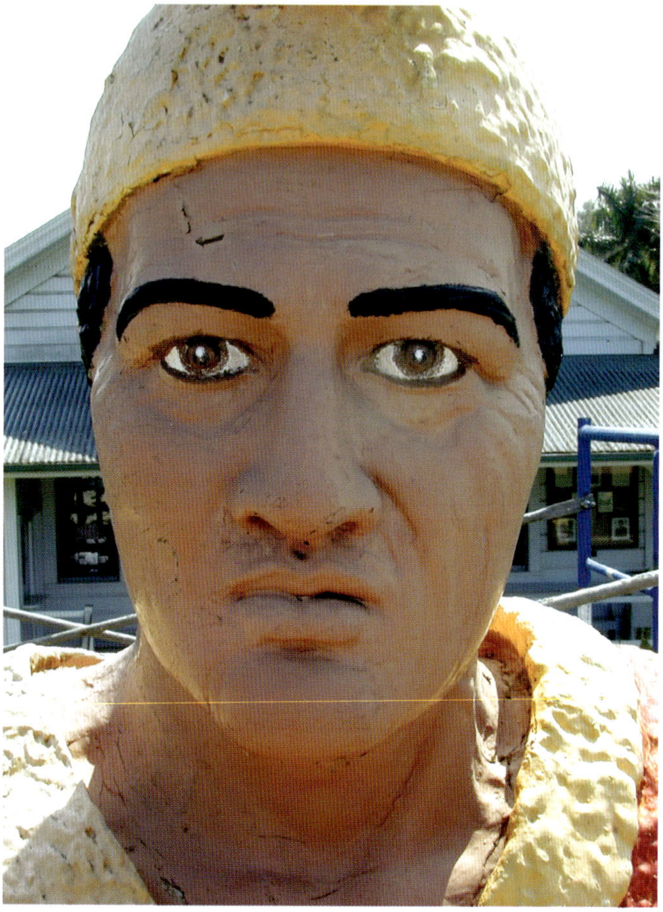

Detail of the face on the Kamehameha sculpture with eyeballs added in the late 1970s by Joe Chang. The brass spheres are from a can of poison he purchased at a local hardware store and adhered with epoxy resin.

> last forever. Then painted on top of them, with red, and white in the iris, and red lines. He looked realistic. I painted the fingernails pink, like mine. And pink toenails.

He also reported that his crew gave particular attention to skin color:

> The painter looked around on the school ground and he picked out a Filipino girl with nice copper-colored skin that would match with the king's skin. Not real dark. She was about middle, this girl had a nice color, and she wasn't a Hawaiian.

Another state official described the process, without knowing the work was carried out by the state for many years:

> They request money from DAGS [Department of Accounting and General Services] each year for paint, they are given the paint, and they paint it themselves. And then I guess because they started a tradition, traditions begin. One doesn't know how it started, but it continues.
>
> It always bothered me that you have all this paint going on the statue. It never comes off, it's not removed. Its not taken off, its not scraped off. Its just layer upon layer upon layer. Nobody is concerned about what kind of paint is going on, and nobody cares. I'm sure you've got oil-based, lead-based, water-based, whatever. Of course the water base over the oil base ends up peeling, and it looks terrible.

The local maintenance office stopped painting it in 1992 due to a lack of funds from the state. After that, the sculpture received no care from the state or county. The state agency that maintains and administers most public art in Hawai'i is the Art in Public Places Division of the State Foundation on Culture and the Arts. Although part of their mission is to "preserve and display works of art expressive of the character of the Hawaiian Islands," they curiously choose to maintain the Honolulu cast and not the North Kohala cast. Many local residents presume this is because they do not support painting the sculpture. They refer to the state's decision to maintain the Honolulu cast as yet another instance of "O'ahu-centric" state policy. Whatever its motivation, the distancing of state agencies from caring for the sculpture creates a strange twist on its political symbolism, since the state's abandonment forces a local care program that fosters a process of local ownership.

On several occasions since 1992, volunteers stepped up to the plate. As Raylene proclaimed, "If nobody else is, we're going to do it." The volunteers have to deal not only with challenges from the natural environment, but more random social events. Vandals attacked its base with blue spray paint in the mid-1990s. When it became apparent that no official was going to remove the graffiti, Sharon took the project on. "I used several things to get it off. When one thing didn't work, I used another. Chemicals from a hardware store, paint stripper, you name it, I tried it. We never found out who did it."

When Kealoha volunteered to paint the sculpture in 1996, he used a vinyl house paint that the Department of Accounting and General Services provided. He also told me that he paid particular attention to the eyes: "I gave him eyeliner, and white spots to make reflections." He described adding the red paint to the *kāʻei* right after sunset, because he knew there would be complaints. Indeed, some people I spoke with four years later were still angry about his choice of paint color.

This anger communicates passionate concerns about how the sculpture looks. It also tells of a jockeying for control over who makes decisions in North Kohala about public issues. With all the ways that local residents use and derive meaning from the sculpture, it was clear to me that any conservation action would inevitably serve the interests of some elements of the community and not others. If I made it attractive to outsiders, it would enhance its value as a tourist commodity. Gilding it would further its royal-European associations. If I painted it, I would honor a locally minted tradition that conflicts with the intent of its makers. We were about to test a process that would make all these opinions public. Somehow we would come to a local style of deciding how to decide.

# 7 *The Community Takes Sides*

OUR FIRST TASK WAS TO get people thinking about the sculpture in a new way—not just as a spiritual, educational, political, and economic object, but as a "conservation object." By now, I knew the difficulties of getting older folks, including respected *kūpuna,* involved in public activities. We had to spark interest in the *keiki* as a first step, since their participation would lead to family discussion, parent involvement, and grandparent approval. Nani agreed. "It's the kids at a young age that can steer their parents. That's where you can get people to participate—through kids." John Keola Lake added, "The heart and soul is the young people. The young people involve parents. When the parents get involved . . . then it's community based."

The idea was to create projects for kids that would make adults talk about the sculpture. Public art and arts education were our tools. With funding for art materials provided by our grants, four teachers coordinated art projects to start people thinking about the sculpture. I began speaking about the project to students and local groups, always with John, Raylene, or others who could chant and dance the story of the sculpture, at times with our coconut hula puppets. We spoke to more than five hundred students at the Kohala Elementary School, the Kamehameha Preschool, the Kohala Middle School art class, and the Kohala High School.

John Keola Lake enacts the history of the sculpture through *ki'i* (puppets) with a fourth grade class, Kohala Elementary School. Hawai'i Alliance for Arts Education.

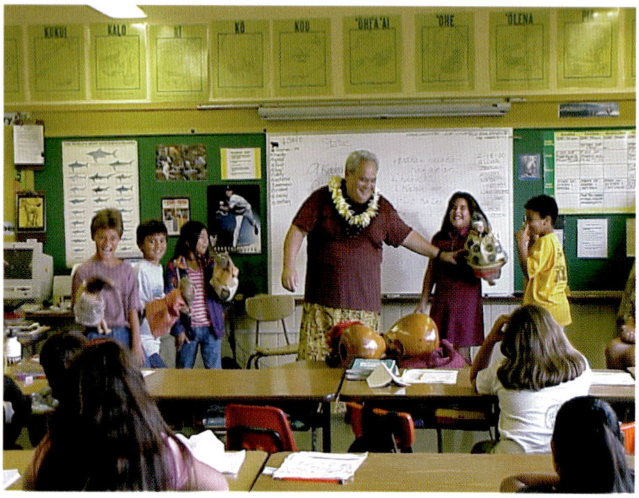

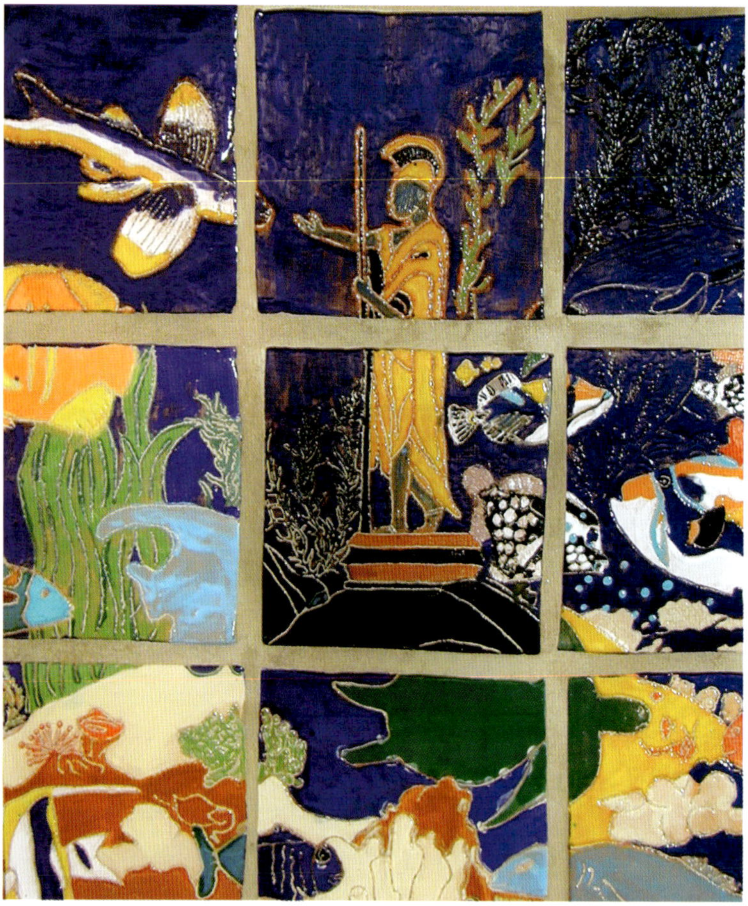

Tile mural by the Kohala Middle School art class depicting the sculpture after the shipwreck under the sea. Installed at the Kohala Hospital, June 2001.

After describing my research findings and the problem of gilding versus painting the sculpture, I asked student classes to raise hands in a vote for gold or paint. Hands always went up tentatively as students watched their classmates, and classes of younger students often voted almost unanimously for either gold or paint. In these initial student polls, unanimous opinions one way or another were more a result of group pressure than the reflective opinions we hoped to develop over time through discussion among families.

One art class created a tile mural depicting the sculpture at the bottom of the sea. They installed the tiles at the Kohala Hospital for Kamehameha Day in June 2001. Another class made a timeline relating moments in Kamehameha's life to other world events. Still another class made copies of known works of art featuring the sculpture. Hawaiian Academy students at the North Kohala High School wrote a song about the sculpture, and Hawaiian Studies students held sessions on its history and the technology of bronze casting. Many classes took field trips to the sculpture to discuss its history, social significance, and conservation.

One way or another, the project provided a platform for teachers and youth leaders to enliven discussions of local and Hawaiian history, a version of what teacher Margaret Hoy referred to as "project-based learning." Speaking of pedagogic opportunity more generally, high school teacher Randee Golden explained, "Teachers need things that are real. They jumped on the project."

Local Girl Scout Troop 999 carved soap images of the sculpture and prepared two display boards for the cultural festival on Kamehameha Day 2001. The first was a map showing the sculpture's route from its initial design in Florence to reinstallation in Kapaʻau. The second was a collection of newspaper articles written about the project. John joined with Raylene's *hula hālau* to conduct puppet-making workshops for performances of the *hula kiʻi* he wrote. In the end, approximately fifty adults and several dozen children participated in *hula kiʻi* activities.

Teacher Randee Golden, who created a puppet and participated in the *hula kiʻi* performances, described her personal experience:

> For me, making the *kiʻi* was a very special process. There was an immediate connection with *ka mōʻī* and his statue. We knew we were making dancers for our *hoʻokupu* to Kamehameha. Learning the hula connected us directly, as it seemed to also do for the preschoolers who shared their dance.

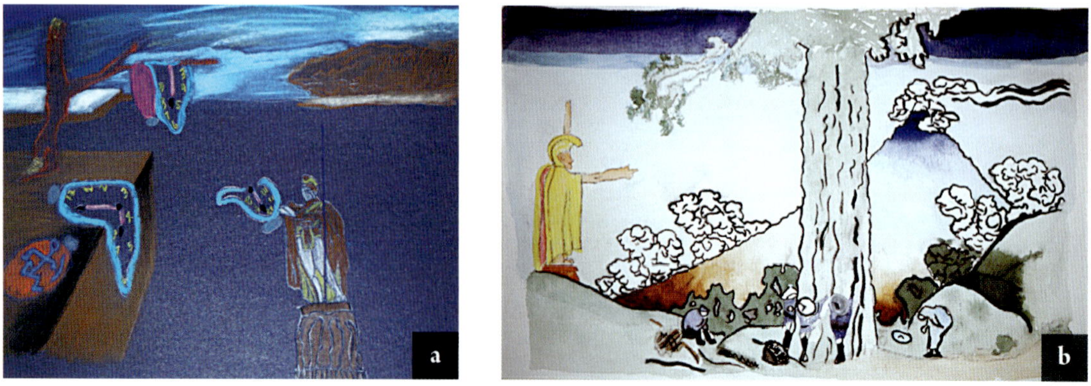

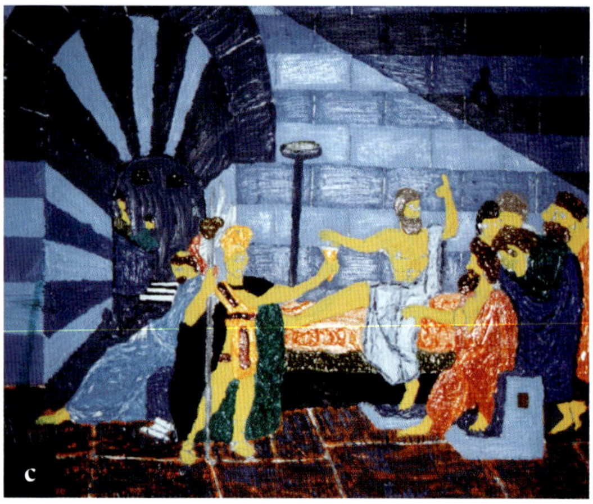

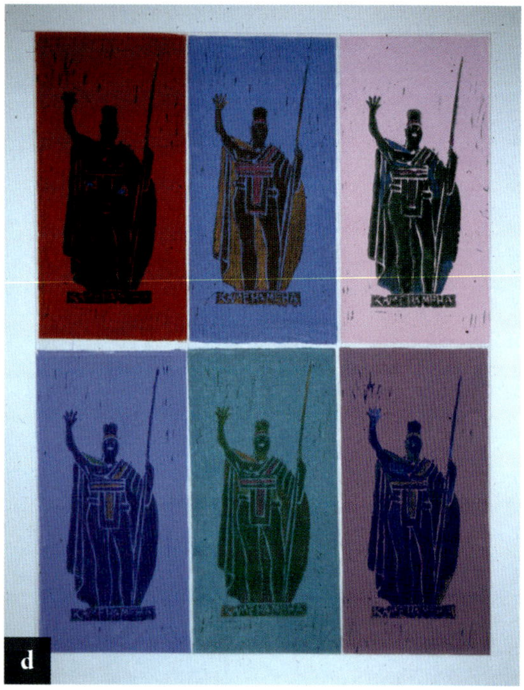

Kamehameha sculpture inserted into (a) a Salvador Dali landscape, (b) a Japanese landscape, (c) the "Death of Socrates," and (d) an Andy Warhol image, by students in the Kohala High School art class.

In addition to working with *keiki,* we worked with the media. At first, the project leaders wrote articles in the *Kohala Mountain News.* As the project proceeded, newspapers, television programs, and radio stations from other parts of the Islands covered our activities. At the onset of our efforts, the *Honolulu Star-Bulletin* got it somewhat wrong, but set the tone for dialogue with a strong editorial point of view. "The statue of King Kamehameha I on the Big Island will be restored, but it's not been decided whether to go with the original bronze or to repaint it. Our view: Bronze is better." Articles with less editorial

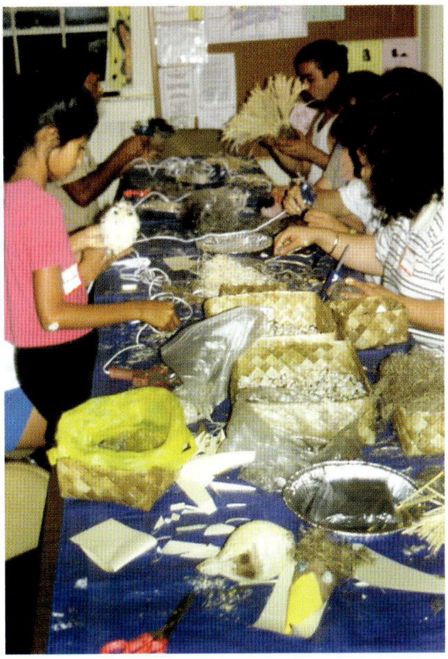

*Hula ki'i* puppet-making workshop conducted by John Keola Lake and artists from the Hawai'i Alliance for Arts Education and the Halau 'O Ha'alelea *hula hālau*. Hawai'i Alliance for Arts Education.

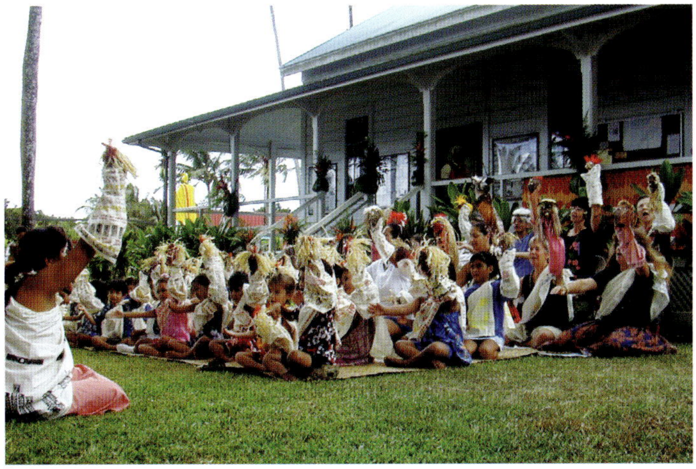

*Hula ki'i* performance depicting the history of the sculpture through dialogue, song, dance, and chanting. Performed by the Halau 'O Ha'alelea *hula halau* and children from the community.

edge emphasized the participatory process.[1] The local-access television station in North Kohala featured the project on two occasions. Letters to the editor and articles commenting on the project regularly appeared in the *Kohala Mountain News.* Media coverage helped make the project possible. It not only communicated the condition of the sculpture, but the coverage drew attention to the project's participatory aspects and legitimized its goals, making them worthy of public discussion.

We only held a few public meetings, since we knew that most people who attend them are newcomers rather than old-timers. Instead, we addressed local groups, such as the Senior Citizens Group, during their regularly scheduled meetings. Some project participants took on the responsibility of talking to those not otherwise reached, particularly respected elders, on a one-to-one basis at their homes. If the public meetings and the media blitz did not spread the news, the "coconut wireless" did. Boyd Bond commented, "People are talking about it everywhere, within extended families and in public spaces and community group meetings."

The Merchants Association debated the issue at one of their meetings. According to Herb Yim, director of the Kohala Hospital, who became interested in the project through the tile mural, "some said gold and some said paint, but I'll tell you one thing, the Hawaiians there felt that the discussion is a great teaching tool." The Senior Citizens Group held an informal poll by asking members to raise their hands during a meeting in March 2000. Gold had a slight margin: thirty-one voted for gold, twenty-seven for paint, and a number abstained. According to group president Emma Glory, some said they needed more information before deciding. Gold also gained an edge among members of the Ka'ahumanu Society, where a majority among the twenty-one attendees voted for gold leaf. Dora Lincoln, who was initially angered that the Ka'ahumanu Society was not involved with the project, said, "We want it to be the way it came here. It shouldn't be changed to something different." After she contacted me through another elder to let me know about "her angry protest," we invited the Ka'ahumanu Society to become the fifth local coordinating organization that guided the public process.

During the June 2000 Kamehameha Day celebration, project leaders spoke at public gatherings and distributed approximately two hundred opinion ballots and flyers, which were in effect straw votes, on gold versus paint. Hundreds of people stopped by the project booth at the cultural festival in the high school gym. Of the 102 ballots returned, 50 were for gold, 46 for paint, with six undecided. It seemed that the pro-gold camp continued its slight edge.

As the project unfolded, I told people what I had found in the Honolulu archives and what I had learned from material analysis. My conversations with local residents led to further contacts as word got around about my interest in the history and community relationships with the sculpture. People showed me old family photographs taken at the sculpture site and told me stories passed down from grandparents. Elders increasingly took interest in the problem of the sculpture's care, and at times contacted me through friends and younger family members to arrange conversations. The sculpture gradually became a conservation object in addition to its other meanings and uses.

The knowledge I brought from the archives and my material analysis began to fuse with local knowledge. Prior notions were altered as residents learned more about the sculpture's technical history. From watching iron and copper alloys corrode in Kohala's subtropical marine environment, many already had a basic understanding of metal degradation—that it is a destructive oxidation process involving moisture and is stimulated by atmospheric pollutants such as sulfuric acid generated by volcanic activity. Some even knew that chlorides, either blown from the ocean or retained in the sculpture from the shipwreck, accelerate metal corrosion.

After submersion in the ocean, exposure in the Falklands' Port Stanley, and shipment to Honolulu, the sculpture was undoubtedly corroded under the paint, a clear threat to its physical longevity. I took samples from spots of pale green powdery corrosion that I tentatively identified as bronze disease. Left untreated, bronze disease can extensively pit the surface of a copper alloy sculpture. Given a sufficient quantity of chlorides with direct access to the metal, bronze disease can convert an entire sculpture into powdery green corrosion over time. The presence of trihydroxychlorides was confirmed in the corrosion crust by environmental scanning electron microscopy at the J. Paul Getty Museum by David Scott, senior scientist in the Museum Research Laboratory.

This confirmation was a turning point in our deliberations. Stripping the paint and chemically treating aggressive corrosion was no longer a matter of elective surgery. It was necessary. Something had to be done, and I reported this to individuals and groups at public meetings. My diagnosis was greeted without opposition or controversy. After paint removal, we could assess other technical concerns on the metal surface, including "stress corrosion" and open cracks caused by the shipwreck, the recovery, or subsequent earthquakes.

In addition to the corrosion, the thick layer of paint was peeling and faded. I explained to people at our meetings that the fading was caused by opacifiers in the paint film that migrated to the surface over time, causing a "chalky" appearance. Losses in the paint were more than two inches in diameter in some areas. I also detected multiple paint layers in different colors. It was clear that Kamehameha had had different skin tones over the years and that his sandals, toenails, fingernails, and feathered garments also shifted in appearance.

The most significant mystery to solve before beginning conservation work remained: What was at the bottom of all the paint? Was it originally painted or partially gold-leafed? On February 21, 2000, five months after first announcing the project, I finally had an answer, and I reported my results to the Senior Citizens Group at their monthly meeting. John Keola Lake began our presentation with a Hawaiian chant and talking story about Kamehameha. Knowing the significance of this announcement, I came prepared with old newspaper articles, photographs, and analytic results. I carefully walked through my own research in trying to learn whether the sculpture was originally gilded at the Paris foundry. I told them that an 1880 article written after it was cast referred to it as "gold bronze," but another article reported that "the feather cloak has not been gilded."

I had taken small samples of paint from deep recesses in the drapery folds and sent them to James Martin, a scientist at the Williamstown Art Conservation Center, for chemical analysis. James used electron microscopy with energy-dispersive x-ray fluorescence spectrometry to determine whether there were traces of gold on the bottom sides of the samples. The electron microscope allowed him to view highly magnified images of the surface to see if it had the character of gold leaf. The x-ray fluorescence analysis he used is a common research tool in our field. Samples are bombarded with high-energy x-rays in order to analyze rays that are then emitted from the sample. This emitted radiation is characteristic of specific materials. He called me immediately to tell me that he had discovered gold on the underside of some of my paint samples.

To confirm this result, I sent a second set of samples to David Scott at the J. Paul Getty Museum. David used x-ray diffraction, a technique that similarly analyzes radiation diffracted off the sample. He not only confirmed that the traces of shiny material were gold, but that it was an alloy of 99.8 percent gold with traces of copper and other elements. This told me that gold foil approximately 24kt had been applied to the sculpture when it was made in 1880. We later took photographs of larger paint samples with traces of gold on the underside as we removed them during the conservation treatment.

Combining all the technical and archival evidence, I suggested to the

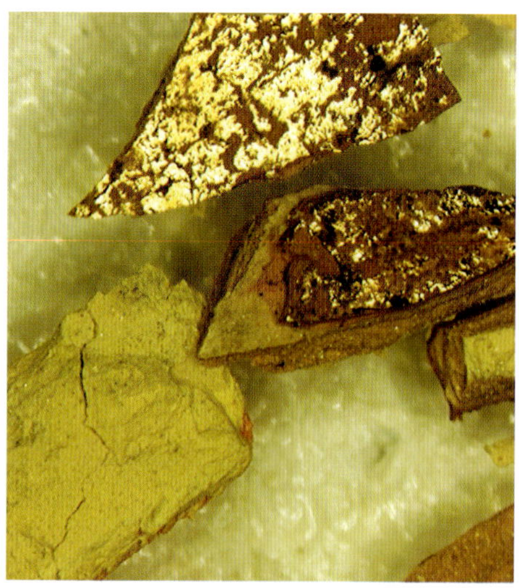

Bottom of paint sample under low-power magnification with residue of gold leaf. Orion Analytical, LLC.

Senior Citizens Group a likely chain of events. After the sculpture was pulled out of the ocean, rapidly formed green corrosion probably disfigured the surface by the time it reached Honolulu in 1883. Without funds, materials, or technical expertise to regild and chemically patinate the sculpture brown, it was most likely cleaned of loose gold and corrosion, then entirely painted brown during the hastily performed restoration in the spring of 1883. I passed around copies of early twentieth-century black and white photographs I found. The gray shading in different sections of the sculpture indicated that

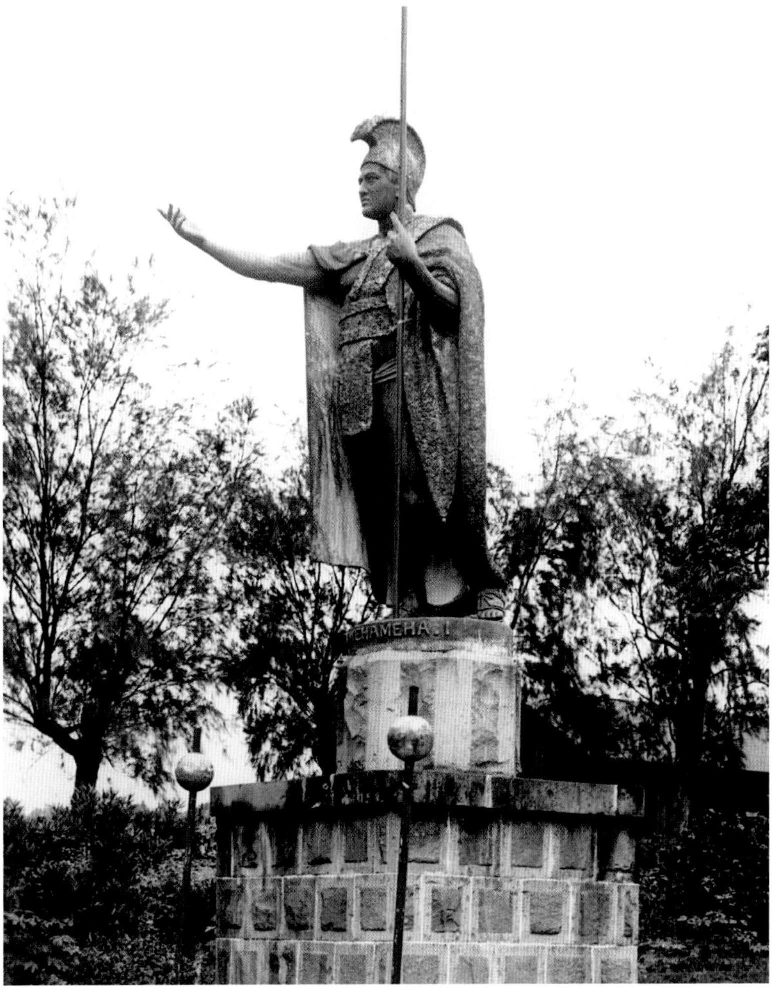

Early black-and-white photograph of the sculpture indicates a polychrome surface. The date is unknown, but comparison with other dated photographs indicates that it was taken after 1912 and before the Second World War. Hawai'i State Archives.

they were different colors, especially evident in darker skin tones and lighter garments. Oral accounts from old-timers at the meeting all confirmed that it was painted in bright colors in their earliest memories. I wasn't sure when, but at some point between 1883 and 1912, the tradition of painting it in different colors had been established.

The news that the sculpture was originally gold-leafed was a bombshell. Jaws literally dropped in the packed room of approximately sixty elders. There was an audible murmur of surprise, in part because this fact might now alter what should be done to the sculpture. Many walked outside after the meeting to see the one-inch "window" I had opened in a protected crevice by carefully peeling the paint off to expose remnants of underlying gold. This was visible proof. The revelation of gold was to prompt new ways of looking at the sculpture. A member of the Royal Order of Kamehameha later said to me, "Knowing that it was gold leaf to begin with makes you take a second gander."

Although we now knew that the sculpture had been painted, cleaned, and repainted since 1883, I was unable to specify which colors came at what period. I took a number of samples from each field of color and sent them to David Scott and James Martin, now at Orion Analytical. David used x-ray diffraction and x-ray fluorescence to determine the elemental and mineral content of the paint. James cast the samples in plastic cubes, then carefully cut them through the center and polished the sides to view the paint layers through various microscopic techniques. Using stereomicroscopy, polarized light microscopy, fluorescence microscopy, and scanning electron microscopy with energy-dispersive x-ray fluorescence spectrometry, he counted up to twenty-six layers of industrial and house paint in some of the samples.

I decided to map these color changes over history. The best way I could think of to communicate how the sculpture looked at different periods was to produce artist renderings. I sent samples and color charts to San Francisco Bay Area artist John Finger, who painted three watercolor images to indicate the changes in color over time. I showed these paintings to the Senior Citizens Group and other community groups to help demonstrate what I had learned.

The questions people asked at our presentation foreshadowed themes that played out over the following twenty-eight months of public discussion. In addition to cultural questions about what the artist wanted and why the Kohala cast is different from the Honolulu sculpture, approximately half the questions were on technical and financial matters. People wanted to know where the money for the project came from, if it would be maintained after

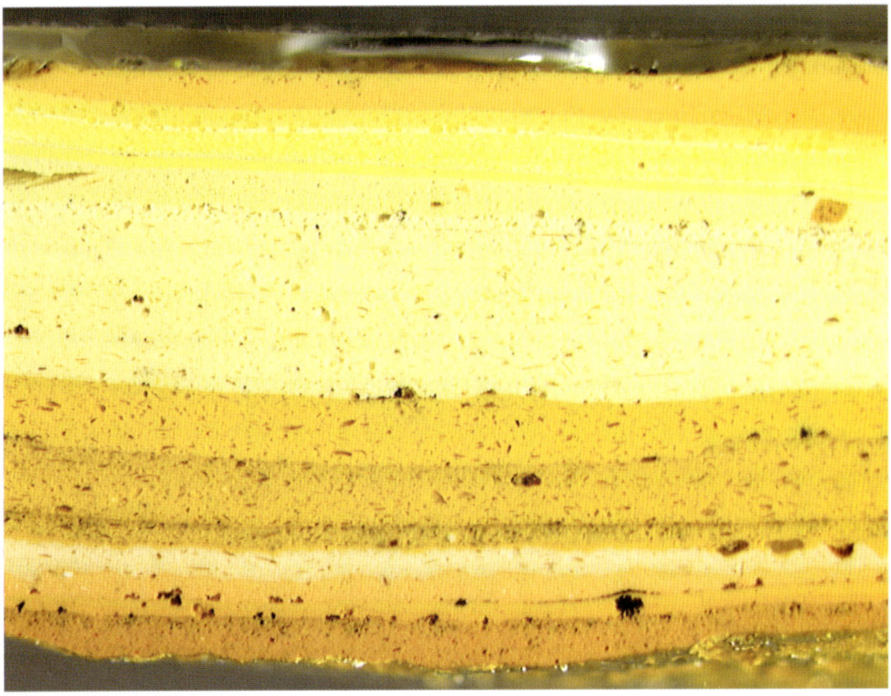

Photomicrograph of a paint cross-section from the sash. At least twenty-six layers of paint are present. Magnification 4x. Williamstown Art Conservation Center.

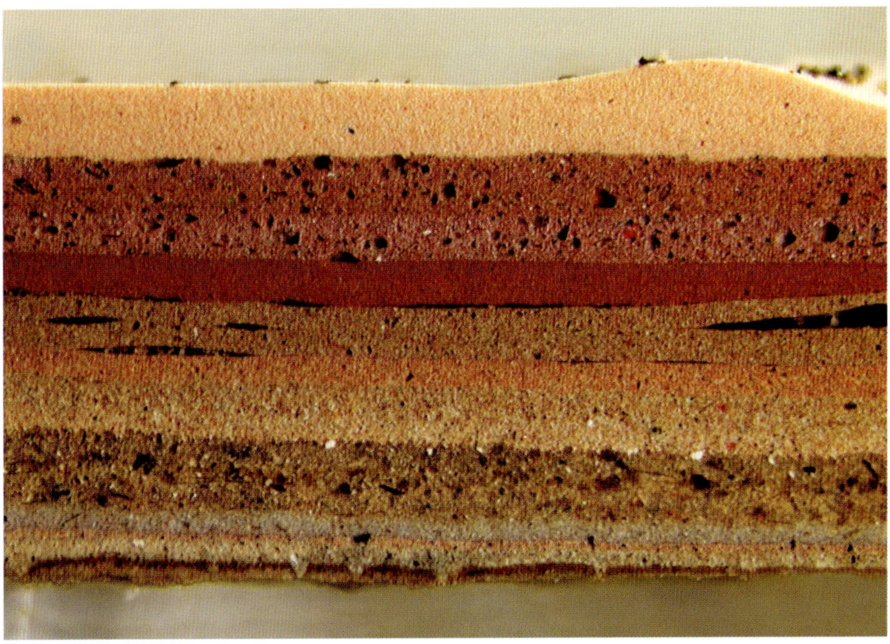

Photomicrograph of a paint cross-section from the figure's calf. At least seventeen layers are present. Magnification 10x. Williamstown Art Conservation Center.

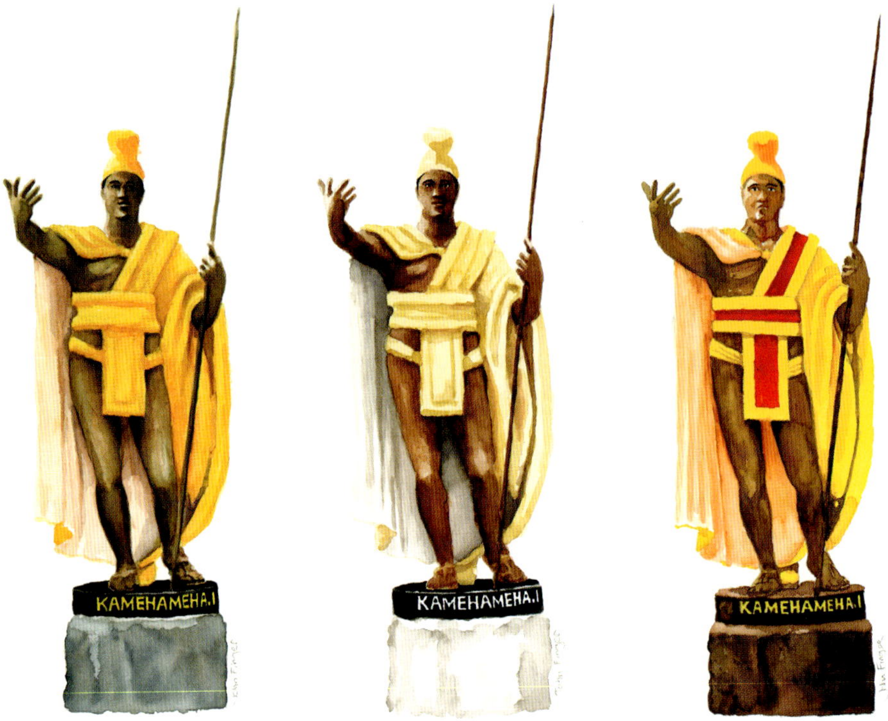


Watercolor images evoking color schemes at different points in the sculpture's history, based on cross-section analysis. Produced by artist John Finger.

this one-time effort, how long gold leaf lasts, why paint gets lighter with age, and which surface treatment better protects the metal: gold or paint.

I responded to all these questions, explaining the role of the Hawai'i Alliance for Arts Education as fiscal manager and indicating the wide support we received from federal and private granting institutions. The grant funding relaxed concern about financial cost to the community. But I could not respond to concern about money for future care and maintenance. The State Foundation for Culture and the Arts made no promises to add the sculpture to its otherwise well-managed program of caring for state-owned artworks.

As public discussion about conserving the sculpture gathered steam in classrooms, family settings, and public gatherings, a theme developed to "get it right." But just as getting it right proved difficult for the sculpture's designers when they originally fused Western and Hawaiian symbols in their sculpture, getting its conservation right brought out many deep cultural and practical concerns. Parallel to its changing colors over the years, it acquired layers of social meaning and uses that differ from anyone's "original" version—Thomas J. Gould, Walter Murray Gibson, or King Kalākaua. I spoke with Ida Otake, the mother of a high school student who had become active in the project. She told me that they discussed the conservation issue at home and concluded that the community faced a vexing problem. "The statue isn't just a statue. When you talk about the *mana,* it has different meaning for different people. It's a very personal thing and therefore it's very hard to decide how it should look."

There was an underlying persistent belief—at least for many—that in order to conserve the sculpture, some true essence, hard as that might be to decide upon, needed to be defined and recovered. In a sense, reflecting on how to conserve the sculpture was a search for its material and cultural authenticity. This search took many forms, but three themes regularly recurred: honoring the original appearance, honoring the artist's intentions, and honoring the tradition of painting it.

One of the most frequently repeated concepts was that the sculpture in North Kohala is the first cast. Although this focus on being the first did not necessarily translate to a preference either for gilding or painting, it was often used as a springboard for launching arguments about its conservation. Many people did not realize that there are now four over-lifesize casts, but everyone knew that their sculpture was the original. Local residents take pride in this knowledge. Although the Honolulu cast was authorized by the artist and came from the same molds, the North Kohala cast retains an aura of authenticity and distinction. As Albert Solomon put it, "they should respect this one. He's the boss. In Honolulu it's second-hand. This is the real McCoy."

This focus on the original can bring forth a variety of special attributes. In being the "real McCoy," it is closer to the artist's hand and retains something of the spirit of its makers, in addition to the spirit of Kamehameha. The value inherent in being the first could imply a greater financial worth and hence a value that conservation could enhance or lessen. Yet I was only asked twice about its monetary value. Perhaps because the sculpture is fixed in place, comments about its financial value were rarely voiced, in contrast to frequent discussions of financial value when people talk about conserving moveable cultural heritage. Instead, its value in being the first cast was usually expressed in cultural terms.

But appreciating its status as the original did not necessarily translate into accentuating uniqueness. Many thought all the casts should look the same: "At least make it unified. I would want it to be one color. Unified. One color." Some felt that it was confusing to tourists for each Kamehameha sculpture to look different. There was also concern that looking different might undermine originality by making it less obvious that the Kohala sculpture is indeed the first of a "set."

But again, there were arguments for maintaining a distinctive appearance, as expressed by Nani in a letter published in the *Kohala Mountain News:*

> Some of you say all the statues should look the same; to me that is equal in comparison to re-facing our quaint Nakahara Store and giving it a Wal-Mart sign. Are we not a unique community? Do we not live a unique lifestyle?

In conversation later, she extended her analogy to the threat that Kona's chain stores pose to small, family-owned businesses in Kohala. Just as she did not want homogeneity in storefronts, she did not want it in sculptures.

No issue of the conservation more captured people's imagination than the problem of whether to keep the sculpture painted or return it to its gilded foundry appearance. This simple framing provided an accessible way for people to enter the debate, and it brought forth all manner of viewpoints on authenticity, artist's intent, and cultural meanings as people took positions, changed their positions, and (sometimes) returned to former ones. However simple the choice, it served as a rich vehicle for eliciting opinions.

A general theme in the pro-gold camp was the greater art historical propriety that would follow from honoring the artist's intent. One informant argued that since the sculpture was painted in 1883 because of a lack of financial and technical resources available to regild it, it should now be gilt since the resources were available to do it right. Indeed, he said, returning the sculpture to its original condition should have been done long before. David Roy of the local Royal Order of Kamehameha was thoughtful on hearing my findings. "To think that they used layer after layer of paint on the gold leaf is incomprehensible. I don't understand it."

Community members brought many analogies to the debate. One pointed out that neither gold nor paint were part of an earlier Hawaiian tradition, thereby refuting any possible argument for paint being more traditionally Hawaiian. Roger Virtue provided an interesting view: "In my opinion, the statue should be restored to whatever the sculptor intended it to be. It's kind of like colorizing old black-and-white films. They were shot with certain shadows and views to reflect the creative viewpoint of the director. So it is with the statue. Gold may have been unknown to ancient Hawaiians, but so is the paint that is being considered."

For some, gold is symbolic of royalty and evocative of its symbolism in other civilizations and therefore suitable for a Hawaiian king. Albert Solomon said, "Gold is the world standard. It's a standard for wealth, power, and strength. And gold is formed by sunrays that go to the earth. Shame—to disrespect the statue with paint!" Richard Stevens commented, "The history of gold is the history of the pharaohs. It's the sun god that reflects the metal. Reflecting the light that powers the world, and the whole concept of *mana* fits in well with that. A power that emanates within and touches those that come in contact with it. I am stuck on this idea of reflecting his *mana,* his spirit."

Two people of Asian descent associated gold with its use in Asian cultures. Gladys Nanbu, a devout Christian who showed me the ancestral gilt *butsudan* in her living room where she still burns incense and offers food, referred to the tradition of placing gold leaf on bronze images throughout much of Asia. "I think it should be gold, like the Buddhas in Japan."

For a number of pro-gold people, the issue was simple and straightforward. For them, painting the image is distasteful, insulting, unattractive, and a blow to the dignity of Kamehameha and the people of North Kohala. "It is time to reverse over a century of obscene bad taste and restore the statue to its original condition. To continue the practice of mutilation reflects poorly on the Kohala community."

Those in the pro-paint camp had just as rich a palette of reasoning. Some wanted to preserve the lifelike appearance. The Kohala Hawaiian Civic Club president commented, "Our king looks almost lifelike in the colors, as if he is still here." Others provided similar thoughts: "The paint feels more alive than gilding." Even when challenged by a friend, Cheryl Sproat stuck to her guns. "A friend of ours who is an ethnomusicologist from the University of Hawai'i at Mānoa said the statue looks like a cartoon figure. I took another look at him and thought 'No, I like the paint.' For me it makes him look more real."

Pro-paint arguments repeatedly stressed preserving local ways, especially in the context of the community's cultural, economic, and land use challenges. "Growing up in Kohala, I always remember it being painted. We have so many changes in Kohala. The statue should remain the same!" "The local art and tradition of painting the statue is part of our pride."

Among activists like Anthony Anjo, anti-gold arguments occasionally incorporated anger against Euro-American incursion. "It's stupid to gild it in European fashion." And more moderate voices such as Fred Cachola said, "It shouldn't emit a Western value. It detracts from Kamehameha the man. He was a very humble person. He worked in his favorite taro patches. A man of the people, willing to get his hands in the dirt. Putting a gold cloak on him demeans him."

For some, the layering of paint is valued because it reflects, in physical terms, layers of local history, including changing ways of honoring Kamehameha. Nani wrote in her letter to the *Kohala Mountain News:*

> As I sit and think of a conservator arriving to repair and restore this monument, I think of all the layers that will be removed and erased, from the many hands of our Kohala people that painted the statue. Yes, all of the paint will need to be removed. Yet to never again coat it with lifelike colors, to me is an end to a unique custom, erasing Kohala's tradition. It is not a mistake that the statue had been painted all these years, it was an honor to protect our Kamehameha *'E Kahi* (The Lonely One)[2] the way we knew best with our humble cans of paint. His present colors are a history lesson to all the children, and these colors remind me of a real king who once existed rather than a gilded statue that only embellishes the world of today.

In an example that shows that sophistication can fall on either side of the argument, some argued for painting based on classical Western traditions. Margaret Hoy reported that her high school art class performed research on historical treatment of sculptures in conjunction with the conservation project. "We've looked at the early Greek and Roman statuary. At that time when those sculptures were made, they were painted."

Ironically, during our project, scholars of classical art were busy identifying original colors used on Greek and Roman sculpture such as the Augustus Caesar of Prima Porta that was used as a model for the Kamehameha sculpture.[3]

In still another basis for supporting paint, what counts is maintaining a *variety* of versions of the sculpture. The various casts should—*in combination*—honor both the original intent and the local tradition of painting. The gilt cast in Honolulu satisfies the artist's intent. That lets North Kohala off the hook and allows it to maintain its own unique tradition. With his unique vision as a trained historian and descendant of the original missionary in the region, Boyd Bond offers a response: "The [original] vision was to stand in front of the 'Iōlani Palace. Now the vision is fulfilled. It [the Kohala original] has been painted over twenty-six times, and twenty-six times they decided 'paint.'

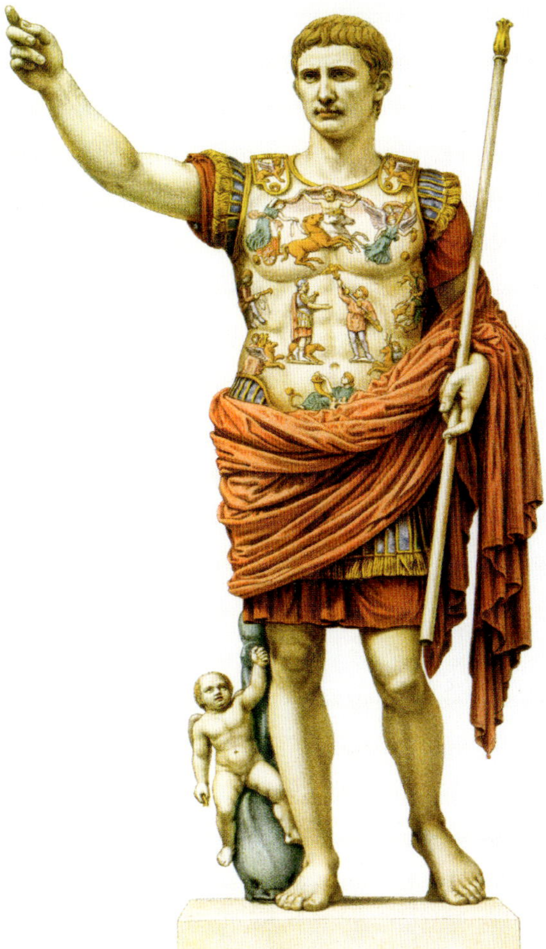

Painted reconstruction of Augustus Caesar of Prima Porta. Color reconstruction by L. Fenger, 1886. New York University Libraries.

So painting is our vision." The idea that multiple casts fulfill multiple aims undermines arguments for a single authenticity of artist's intent or authenticity of a living cultural tradition. It allows reproductions to fill in for the original.

Especially for those who raised the pro-paint argument because paint was more authentic, the question became exactly what color would be true to that authenticity. Characteristically straightforward, *kupuna* Marie Solomon voiced her concern: "The feathers should be painted red and yellow. They were the symbols of royalty." Sharon agreed: "The correctness of it being yellow and red seems really important to me. When I go to Hilo and see the other one, or I go to Honolulu, they are beautiful statues but they are not him. That's not his cape, and that's not the Sash of Līloa that has survived since the thirteenth century."

And yet the right color wasn't necessarily seen to require an exact match to the original feather garments at the Bishop Museum. Emma Glory said, "We don't like flashy things. The colors on the statue [as painted in Kohala] are bright. Would a warrior like him have worn such bright colors? I believe that Kamehameha was not a 'bright' person, didn't like gaudy colors." Navas Santiago remembers an entirely different symbolism of yellow: it signified the theme color of the Kohala Sugar Plantation. This would, in his thinking, make it appropriate for Kamehameha's cloak. "Yellow has been the color of Kohala, the plantation, all the equipment, like tractors, they used to paint them yellow. The trucks, uniforms were yellow. That's why they kept it yellow. All the signs were yellow. That was the Kohala color."

Most discussions about color focused not on feathers but on skin. Arguments moved quickly to skin tone, using distinctions that exist in Hawai'i as elsewhere. Some of those who talked about skin color did not want the figure's skin to be too light. Sam Torres said,

> If you go back to the books, Hawaiians were not brown. The old Hawaiians in those days were like the Negroes. They had dark, purple black skin. Now he is tan-complected. No way the Hawaiians were tan-complected. Now even if you look at the old Hawaiians, some are Filipino or dark colored. No way were they tan-colored.

At a school presentation about the project, a fourth-grade student commented, "It would be more Hawaiian if the skin was darker." Others did not want the skin to be too dark. I heard occasional reference to the seemingly black skin on the Honolulu sculpture. "The one in Honolulu, it makes him look black, yeah?" I didn't always admit that I was on the team that patinated the Honolulu sculpture in 1994. We patinated it brown with torches and typical chemicals, including ferric acetate, ferric nitrate, and a little potassium sulfide, yet it subsequently darkened with the application of a protective hot wax coating and continual deposits of carbon soot from nearby traffic. I heard frequent comments on dark skin tones:

> We want to put ourselves apart from that stigma [of being black]. We have our own [stigma] to carry. It's like we have our own and it's different. If it

> was a "po' boy brown" we would say "that's a Hawaiian brown." But what's a Hawaiian brown? I have a niece that looks just like you [referring to my pale complexion] and she's a quarter Hawaiian.
>
> Hawaiians are light brown color. They are not black. When you look at the [Honolulu] statue it's kind of black. It should be a little more brown.
>
> You know when you paint him [don't] make the Hawaiian look more of a black guy.
>
> People here don't like the gold or dark skin on the Honolulu or Hilo sculptures. Makes him look like a *nigger.*

Three people used the term "nigger" in conversation with me. This was jarring. Kindy Sproat, whose roots in Kohala go deep, offered an explanation for why old-timers use the term. "We all used to use the word all the time. Any black horse, cowboy dog, or cat was called 'nigger.' Anyone with dark skin was called a 'nigger.' It wasn't until I went off to the military in the war that I learned it was a tender term." He pointed out that growing up in North Kohala during the 1930s, he only saw one African American.

In traditional conservation analysis, objects that self-destruct are seen as having "inherent vice"; their material or mode of fabrication destines them to severe deterioration. A poorly fabricated sculpture with low-quality materials may not survive in an aggressive outdoor environment. Only radical reconstruction or substitution of materials would enable it to survive, but such actions are contrary to conservation ethics.

Perhaps we should think of an artwork as also having inherent vice in a cultural sense. Over time, its meaning may no longer be tolerable to new generations that surround it. For a small number of people I spoke with, the sculpture has certain culturally inherent vices. For them, the conservation project presented an opportunity to correct errors too deeply embedded to be handled with usual techniques. Those with knowledge of Native Hawaiian traditions see disrespect in a *kāʻei* that drags on the ground and is not properly tied. The hand gesture is distinctly not Hawaiian; the *ʻahu ʻula* has European tassels, and the sandals are classical. These criticisms as well as others were part of local discourse. Sharon said, "I think it is probably safe to assume that it [the clothing error] was done without any knowledge of what this cape and sash represented. Liberties were taken to put a Roman type of sandal on him, and the typical tassels of European-style heroes were added to the cloak. This tells you that the artist did what he could relate to!"

It would be hard to overestimate the hand in Hawaiian culture. Hand gestures are rich with meaning, as reflected not only in the storytelling rituals of hula, but in people's everyday interactions. Since Hawaiians did not have a written language, the hand along with the voice conveyed knowledge and history in precontact Hawai'i. By placing a spear in his left hand and giving him the open-palm gesture of his right hand, Walter Murray Gibson saw in Kamehameha a "successful warrior inviting the people to accept the peace and order he had secured." Yet eight people criticized the right-hand gesture as being non-Hawaiian, with one going so far as to suggest turning the hand around.

The sandals could also be altered. Fred Cachola suggested chiseling them off. "Why did Mr. Gould put Roman sandals on him? Of all the things on the statue, they are so foreign. It gives him a Roman feeling. Knocking off the sandals would be contrary to the legislature who approved it, but what were they thinking? The sandals say a lot about the legislators at the time. Maybe now it's time to rethink this. Take the sandals off!" Emma Glory said, "The sandals are more like Napoleon's footwear that was put on our king." And one person commented anonymously, "If the decision is to use gold leaf, please leave King Kamehameha's feet alone. No gold sandals!"

My paint sample analysis revealed that the sandals were at times painted yellow to indicate gold and at times painted various shades of brown to match the skin. They were white before Kealoha painted them brown again in 1996. "I painted them brown because they are European, not Hawaiian. I wanted them to disappear." Objects from the past can symbolize oppressive regimes or "golden eras" of indigenous traditions.[4] For some in Kohala, conservation provided an opportunity to partially reconcile, if not altogether resolve, contradictory readings of the sculpture. Physical intervention, more radical than ethically allowed in the conservation profession, could potentially clean up the ambiguity and make the sculpture more "authentic" than its makers had intended. By *reversing* artist's intent, some saw conservation's potential for re-presenting the Hawaiian past for future generations.

I was surprised by the rich set of arguments North Kohala residents posed for deciding how to conserve the sculpture. And yet no clear patterns emerged among various groups in the community. Positions on gilding, painting, and other alterations cut across categories of race, age, and length of time in the community. In fact, the hybrid nature of the sculpture and the multicultural mix in the community was, in a way, repeated in this mix of opinions. The religious and cultural strands of the Hawaiian past persist and reveal themselves, but their presence scatters across different elements of the community, sometimes intermixing within individuals who are ambivalent about how elements of their very own identity can be honored through the presence of the sculpture.

Anticipating a change in the sculpture caused people to pay attention to it in ways they had not done before. When considering the effect of the project on her own attitude and those of other locals, Nani ran a sort of thought experiment by considering the ultimate change: removing the sculpture entirely:

> For many I think they took it for granted that the statue was here. You know you pass it everyday so it's, it's there. It was always there. It will always be there, but to ask the question, "What if the commission decided to move it to Hulihe'e Palace in Kona?" They would say, "No. It belongs here. It rightfully belongs here." All of a sudden you'd have an opinion about where it belongs. You get the dialogue from them, and those who always had a bond with the statue are finding themselves even thinking more about it and his life. Then you start going back to his life, his purpose and what was he trying to do with his people.

# 8 *Decision*

WHO DECIDES AND HOW TO decide were in the hands of the local project team. They met and debated these questions behind the scenes during the months of community discussion. The question of "who decides" paralleled other concerns in the community over the status and rights of Native Hawaiians and respected *kūpuna.* A new category appeared in the discussions: "the expert," including myself as sculpture conservator and the professional administrators in Honolulu. Other local categories such as old-timers versus newcomers did not appear in discussions, although the local versus nonlocal dichotomy did.

The question of "how to decide" stirred issues of multiculturalism and authority in North Kohala, along with cultural models for decision making. The committee debated whether to ask the experts, ask only Native Hawaiians, ask all locals, negotiate a decision, or conduct a community ballot.

I attended some of these meetings. I also took the opportunity to ask people that I encountered in my own activities. Many people I spoke with thought that as a professional expert from outside the community, I should decide. Some of the comments were, "We should leave it up to you. You are the restorer. We should defer to your judgment." "This is why you are here today to be a part of this restoration. You are called to be a participant with the knowledge you bear."

Analogies to medicine and belief in science figured in some arguments. Gladys Nanbu posed the question: "If a doctor came in that invented the medication, he's the one that did the research, he's the one that did the study. We have to put our trust to you. Even if you came from wherever you came from, I don't think they should bring race into this because you have studied and researched, and I think you know and you have the knowledge. It doesn't matter if you're a haole or whatever." Some wanted to avoid local conflict. "I think that you should decide. You shouldn't ask too many people. It will get confusing. I have very strong feelings about this." A thoughtful response in this vein came from Keahi Allen, chair of the King Kamehameha Celebration Commission in Honolulu:

> The value of your research is that you are giving them the truth. A lot of their opinions are based on hearsay, and you erase that and say "This is what we discovered." Is that a bad thing to do? To erase myth and legend? No, I don't think so. You are doing it in a scientific manner. There is no question. In the layers of paint, it was this color and this color, but the original layer was gold leaf. It's so wonderful today that we have the technical capabilities of analyzing what has happened over the years. To be able to magnify it to see layers and layers of different colors, and to say "this is what it was originally because this is what we scraped it down to." I am amazed that you found gold leaf.

Some wanted the state to resume caring for the sculpture. "If you have regular caretakers come, you will always have it cared for properly. To have constant care, it must be done by workers who know the business." There are two state agencies in Honolulu that care for cultural sites and state-owned works of art: the State Historic Preservation Office of the Department of Land and Natural Resources and the State Foundation on Culture and the Arts. These agencies contract with conservators in private practice to perform condition assessments and material analysis of artworks, as well as built structures and cultural landscapes. They rely on outside technical expertise to develop "Statements of Significance," "Treatment Proposals," and specifications for contracted work. Conservation projects are either awarded as sole-source contracts or put out to bid, requiring contractors to meet professional conservation qualifications.

To learn about public participation in official state projects, I spoke with Carol Hasegawa at the State Foundation, Carol Ogata in the Historic

Preservation Office, and Ross Cordy in the Archaeological Division. Carol Hasegawa reported that her agency has no experience in public inclusion during deliberations over how to conserve a sculpture. Carol Ogata could not provide any example of public participation in architectural projects either, but strongly suggested speaking with Ross Cordy since contestation in archaeology is now the norm. Cordy explained that recent state law legislates that all development projects requiring permits must receive comment, but not approval, from the public. If no prior archaeological survey of a development site exists, the state requires that one take place. They develop a Preservation Plan. This may include public hearings in addition to consulting with local stakeholders and representatives of the island Native Hawaiian Burial Council. A number of North Kohala residents I spoke with were deeply angry with the state. They accused the agency of approving development sites that destroy Hawaiian burials without ever going through this formal process that they are bound to.

I spoke with Edward Ayau, Marie Solomon, Kehau Cachola-Abad, and other Native Hawaiian activists about their concerns with development in relation to burials and changes to sacred landscapes. They told me that *iwi* (bones) are infused with *mana* and must be left undisturbed.[1] Statewide organizations such as Hui Malama I Na Kupuna ʻO Hawaiʻi Nei (We Care For and Protect the Kūpuna of Hawaiʻi) fight to protect *iwi* and grave goods from encroaching development and archaeological excavation in Kohala.

Native Hawaiian and Caucasian scholars debate the role of archaeology in Hawaiʻi.[2] There is growing distrust of contract archaeologists who survey potential development sites to determine their archaeological significance. Mike Isaacs, an old-timer activist, told me that despite this effort, haole contract archaeologists are "in the hands of developers" and either intentionally disregard precontact remains or are not trained to recognize them, which results in the destruction of sacred sites. I also learned of additional complications that arise when Native Hawaiian caretakers refuse to identify burial sites that lie in the path of development because of the *kapu* tradition of secret burial.

Few people I spoke with about the sculpture knew the details of state contracting in conservation. Yet there was general awareness about the tensions between state and local authority over archaeological projects. Two people suggested state-local hybrid models for our project. Emma Glory said, "The group from Honolulu would offer the expertise. They could say, 'be careful with what kind of paint you are going to put on it.' It's not that we would expect them to come and do the work, but some accountability."

Audrey Veloria added, "There should be liaisons, bridges that have representatives at both ends. As long as you have people from the community and they represent the *kūpuna* in their heart when you make a decision, that will wash good."

Levels of trust in scientific authority, outside expertise, or state agencies varied. Kealoha approved of my role only after meeting with me in the presence of the sculpture. Marie Solomon eventually came to accept my role, but she later told me she was cautious and at first held back and watched. In a conversation at the end of our project, she expressed general reservations about my profession, based on her experiences at the Bishop Museum in Honolulu. "Western culture doesn't respect other cultures. That is the problem with conservators: they don't respect other cultures."

Several people were angry after hearing a rumor that I would take the sculpture off its pedestal and truck it to Kona for conservation—which was never an option. After expressing initial anger when he met me, Mike Isaacs, a contractor and farmer, later confided that he and his buddies had been talking about the project. "Who is this guy from the mainland? He shouldn't touch our statue. We will stop him from doing anything to it. It isn't right that someone from the outside should come in and do the work without first knowing the community. It would have been best to come here first, get to know the community, then have it announced by local people that you are going to do the work." After I described our public activities, he opened up and helped me connect to a number of his friends and contacts.

Sam Torres was a retired state maintenance worker who had worked on the sculpture in the past. He expressed similar thoughts when I contacted him. "Who are you to come to town as an outsider and strip the paint off the statue? Don't you realize that if you take it down to bronze it isn't going to last? It's been painted since the days of the plantation because it was damaged in the ocean. If that statue is damaged, they had better be prepared to order a new statue from overseas and bury this one. You should talk to Joe Chang, who painted it for years." His voice changed after I recounted my prior conversations with Joe Chang and told him that leaving a stripped down, unprotected surface wasn't an option. He then described how the maintenance crew used to select paint colors, and he revealed his own personal preferences for Kamehameha's skin tone.

At one point, a well-known developer contacted me to discuss the project. Under the misconception that we lacked adequate funding, he sent me an e-mail offering to finance the project. During a follow-up meeting, he made it clear that he would provide support only if the decision were to apply gold leaf. The local committee declined this offer since, in their view, it undermined the public process. I was glad to walk away from the offer, knowing how many in the community feel about newcomer real estate developers. Committee members taught me to be careful about whom I associated with, since word travels fast in North Kohala.

Throughout the process of researching and participating in community activities, I was aware of my presence as an outsider and as a central participant in the project. At times I struggled with this. I had decided from the beginning that I would not voice my opinion on the gold versus paint issue, nor would I weigh in on who should decide or how to decide. Instead, I would play the role of outside technical expert and distance myself from cultural discussions about the sculpture's spiritual, economic, political, and other social meanings. I would provide information on historical coatings and current condition. Yet as my research and participation progressed, new issues presented themselves. I learned about the racism embedded in arguments for the sculpture's commission when I read that its primary supporter referred to Kamehameha as the "barbarian conqueror" who "made the white men his friends." Along with its origins to commemorate Captain Cook's "discovery" of the Hawaiian Islands, this information, buried in the state archives, could have critical implications for how local residents understand their sculpture.

I spoke with project members about my role and the historical information I was uncovering. Not unexpectedly, I received mixed advice. Several strongly advised me to keep the more sensitive information to myself, thinking it would be irresponsible to announce it to a community that so intensely loves its sculpture. One person suggested, "Don't bring up the ugly origins of the sculpture," while another commented, "It's not your role to stir up angry feelings in our community." A third person recommended a middle course: "Adopt a 'don't ask, don't tell' policy. If people ask, then tell."

I mentioned this dilemma to Ian Hodder, an archaeologist I know from my work in Turkey as field conservator at a site near his and from my subsequent work at Stanford University. He has attacked positivist, or purely scientific, models of archaeology. Instead, he brings a wide variety of viewpoints from scholars and the public to his interpretations of the ancient past. His writings and my conversations with him greatly affected my approach in North Kohala. Yet he was strong in his advice to me: "It would be deceitful not to communicate everything that you learn about the sculpture."

I decided to adopt a middle road strategy, a modified "don't ask, don't tell" policy. I provided technical information in public meetings to help residents weigh the practical aspects of the decision. This included metal corrosion, aging properties of gold and paint, and costs of future maintenance. I communicated potentially divisive cultural information in conversation, but I did not announce sensitive issues in public unless asked. I wrote short articles for the *Kohala Mountain News* and was interviewed by the local-access television station, as well as by various radio programs throughout the Islands. The big news item was usually my discovery of gold under 117 years of paint. Reporters never got to the issues that troubled me most.

Not everyone in the community agreed that outside experts or Honolulu administrators should play a role in decision making. About 25 percent of the people in my early interviews said that only Native Hawaiians should decide. This typically led to conversations about indigenous Hawaiian culture in the context of economic and cultural abuse. I spoke with Shiro and Clara Takata about this. As older Japanese plantation descendants who run a local market, they have a finger on the pulse of the community. Shiro voiced a strong opinion, linking the decision to a Supreme Court ruling allowing non–Native Hawaiians to vote for the Office of Hawaiian Affairs' (OHA) Board:

> Let the Hawaiians decide. This time let the Hawaiians really decide. What in the world is he doing making it worse [referring to the local farmer who brought a "white rights" case to the Supreme Court]. This is where the Hawaiians claim they were really cheated and fooled. This place was taken over different from Nevada or California. Let the Hawaiians have Hawai'i. Most of the people born and raised in Kohala would say "that's okay." It's the influx of haoles that would say this is not right.

The bitter dispute between local haole rancher Harold "Freddy" Rice and the Office of Hawaiian Affairs that Shiro referred to ended in a legal battle before the U.S. Supreme Court in 2000.[3] At question was whether all residents should have the right to vote for trustees of the OHA, a right previously reserved for Native Hawaiians. One of the OHA's primary functions is administering a $300 million trust to provide economic, social, health, and education aid to Hawaiian residents with Native blood. Rice won the landmark case, fueling resentment among those who argue that Native Hawaiians should control the money generated from "crown" lands.

Well aware of parallel legal battles over land and voting rights of Native

Hawaiians, many brought them up in discussing the Native Hawaiian role in our project. Retired Hawaiian school teacher Earl Veloria:

> I would like to see the decision based on feelings gathered from Hawaiians. A lot of people see that statue as an artwork, a masterpiece, but the Hawaiian people see something different. Other people pay attention to the statue, they have a feeling of ownership, but it won't make them the true decision makers for it. It should be the Hawaiian community.

Reflecting empathy that is characteristic of many Caucasians in Hawai'i, a number of newcomer and long-term haole residents also endorsed a Native Hawaiian decision. Richard Stevens said, "It's the people of Hawaiian descent that really count here. This is their man. He's ours, too. We've given our hearts to this place. But it's really the Hawaiians.'"

Among those advocating a Native Hawaiian decision, approximately half suggested consulting local *kūpuna,* who carry the voice of Native lineage. Valerie Anjo said, "I think you should go to the elders, the *kūpuna.* They've been here longer... they grew up with the statue, their fathers, and generations before them. Us, we only have knowledge of today."

Some people foresaw possible complications arising from consulting *kūpuna.* Even those of Hawaiian descent sometimes regard the practice as old-fashioned and hierarchical. It is certainly foreign to many newcomers and old-timers who are not of Hawaiian lineage. Some think of it as a double-edged sword. For those who respect *kūpuna,* there is concern that the "answers" may not be appropriate to the contemporary condition. This can create the dilemma of "disobeying" those who are strongly admired. Two thoughtful Hawaiians involved in the project voiced this concern. Fred Cachola suggested that if we consult *kūpuna* then do not accept what they come up with, it hurts everybody. John Keola Lake made a similar argument: "Once they make the decision you gotta respect it. That's the fear of the *kūpuna.*" In the end, Raylene provided a strategy that influenced the local project team's decision: to ask for their wisdom, not their technical knowledge.

> It's not right to go to *kūpuna* and ask them detailed questions. You must do your homework, answer your questions yourself, then go to them and say this is where you are here and now, this is where you would like to go. They will direct you. But you must be ready to accept what they say, follow their direction. It's not right to present them with paint chips and

> ask them what color it should be, or whether it should be gold or paint. Bring to them the decision that you have made, and ask for their *mana'o* [opinions, thoughts].

About one-third of the people I spoke with suggested a process of public negotiation, rather than consulting elders or voting. The models suggested often involved some sort of cultural fusion. Tom Quinlan, a local preservation entrepreneur, incorporates public dialogue into his design process by inviting people to talk story so that his projects can involve and benefit from alternative viewpoints. His professional facilitators also borrow from a Native American tradition involving the passing of a "talking stick" around at public meetings. "You can only talk while you are in possession of the stick."

Various Hawaiian concepts fed into the negotiation models we discussed. For instance, *'ae like* translates to "coming to an agreement." Kealoha suggested it as a process:

> Everyone sits around. The facilitator states the situation, then everyone shares their thoughts. Pros and cons. You go around again and discuss your thoughts. There must be a general consensus. Everyone must agree. . . . You continue to discuss it until everyone agrees. The facilitator asks, "Who doesn't agree? Everyone else wants it this way. Can you live with this? Can you accept it?" Keep doing this until the last person is won over.

Reaching out to old-timers was a great concern among project leaders. Some proposed projects in which high school students would perform the oral histories of their elders, including their thoughts about Kamehameha and their memories of the sculpture. The students would then bring the elders' concerns back to project leaders. Some team members paid visits to elders to solicit their opinions. Nani reported from one such visit:

> I said, "How do you feel about it?"
>
> And she said, "Well, I guess it's what the community wants, it'll be all right." And that wasn't good enough for me because I knew it meant a lot to her, but she just wasn't aware of it. And so I placed the question to her: "What if they said they were going to take the statue away from Kohala, and place it somewhere else, in a museum?"
>
> And all of a sudden there was a connection for her. A very deep-rooted connection.

And then the connection became, "No, it can't go anywhere."

But that was just to make her see that she was tied to the statue like all of us.

*Kūkā* means consultation or discussion, and *kūkā kūkā* means council, or conference. Several people advocated this general method for airing opinions. "Somewhere along the line, resolution must be drawn. It may be through *ho'oponopono.*" Literally translated, *ho'oponopono* means to put things right, or to correct. It is a process based on traditional methods of conflict resolution within extended Hawaiian families that has gained increasing popularity in the public sphere since the 1970s.[4] According to Victoria Shook, author of a widely read book on *ho'oponopono,* it is

> a highly structured process with four distinct phases: an opening phase that includes the prayer and a statement of the problem; a discussion phase in which all members involved share their thoughts and feelings in a calm manner and listen to all the others as they speak; a resolution phase that enables the exchange of confession, forgiveness, and release; and a closing phase to summarize what has transpired and to give spiritual and individual thanks for sincere participation.

Shook explains that *ho'oponopono* is a culture-specific process. The terms and concepts derive from Hawaiian beliefs and customs, and it differs from most Western doctrines of group-process facilitation in its spiritual focus, the articulation of forgiveness, and its ritualized system of controls and steps. Raylene added that if anger developed, it could become necessary. "*Ho'oponopono* could be used to allow all sides to forgive, to make things right, then a decision-making process could be invoked."

Some residents feared that ersatz "Hawaiian" methods smuggle in alien modes of decision making, including the idea of town meetings. Bruce Kaiiloa Chrisma complained, "Town meetings are a New England concept, not a Hawaiian concept." Mike Gomes described *ho'oponopono* as itself romantic and "revisionist." "Read *The Ruling Chiefs of Hawai'i*[5] to find out how Hawaiians traditionally made decisions. It's nothing but blood. They didn't ask around a circle."

Whereas asking the *kūpuna* risks losing the benefits that might come from a more open practice, working through public meetings might involve the opposite kind of danger. Transparency and public process might, ironically, exclude those most connected to North Kohala through birth or lineage, because it is mainly newcomers who attend public forums. For that reason, Sharon stated, "Town meetings don't work in North Kohala. Old-timers shouldn't be excluded as a method of communicating." Methods needed to be developed to get old-timers and others who do not ordinarily engage in the public life of the community to participate.

A small minority felt that only those who are indeed active in the community, especially in the Kamehameha Day celebrations, should decide. After my second presentation and description of the project to the Senior Citizens Group, an elderly Caucasian couple came up to me with concerns about who should decide. "Only people that go to meetings. If they don't care enough to show up at a meeting, they shouldn't have a vote." These sentiments went against the strong tide for wide involvement, at least some degree of privileging of indigenous concerns, and interest in developing mechanisms for old-timers to participate in ways they felt comfortable.

Reflecting U.S. majoritarian thinking, most people I spoke with and the majority of the local project leaders felt that all local residents should participate in the decision making. Although the arguments had many facets, including the suggestion that newcomers should not have a voice, the fundamental argument was that of a democratic culture. Everyone who lives in North Kohala counts, regardless of race or lineage. Sharon suggested, "Some of the greatest supporters of the Hawaiian culture are non-Hawaiian and our elders are a perfect example of that, as not all or even a majority of them are Hawaiian. The statue is part of the entire community . . . to discriminate would not be right."

Many argued that since Hawai'i is now part of a democracy that runs on elections and referenda, the decision should come through a public vote. In response to suggestions for district-wide balloting, some residents expressed concern about low voter turnout. In fact, although 62 percent of potential voters registered to vote in the November 2000 general elections, only 28 percent actually voted.[6] This is a low figure even by U.S. standards, considering that the 2000 election included voting for the President of the United States. Some argued that the tradition of election-style democracy is not fully embraced by a semirural population distanced from larger spheres of influence, especially in regard to plantation-oriented old-timers unused to expressing their opinions in any forum outside the home. David Roy offered his argument against voting: "Don't have a democratic vote. Talk to the *kūpuna.* This matter of a democratic approach is faulty because they would have to be guided in their decisions. They would need to have a solid base of understanding, which would come from recommendations of their leaders."

The sixteen-month process of public dialogue, community involvement, and deciding who should decide and how to decide did not always go smoothly, but there was a lively dynamic. Anthony Anjo warned me, "Your project has become a hot potato." Kealoha began to worry part of the way through. "This so called simple question of shall we gild or paint has somewhat divided our community. It kind of disturbs me that now the community is divided whereas before it was accepted that the statue was always painted." High school teacher Randee Golden argued that public tension is a necessary consequence of public process, especially in a small community where people know each other and many are related. "This community would *moku moku* [divide into factions] about everything. It's the nature of small communities. The grumbling, from my understanding, is natural." According to Hilton Nalani Cabrera, the controversy "makes the community speak. It brings out voices of the *kūpuna,* the *keikis,* of the *'ōpio* [youth], having all their voices speak. If they disagree, that's their opinion. Nothing wrong with it. They will get over it once they see what Kamehameha will look like." Or in Nani's view, "I believe that this is the right thing, and that we will all be amazed as to how much participation will be involved, how much awareness and gratitude that will be here in this community."

In ways that could not have been entirely anticipated, the actual decision making involved an intricate mix of consulting with a *kupuna,* public participation through balloting, and the voice of state authority. After lengthy deliberation on the mode of deciding, the local committee decided to hold a community-wide election. The results would be presented for approval to the Kamehameha Celebration Commission in Honolulu, since they held final authority. The leaders also agreed to seek the wisdom of a *kupuna* on their provisional decision to have a vote. They unanimously selected Marie Solomon as the *kupuna* of authority.

Marie Solomon was known to speak bluntly on issues worthy of her engagement. A descendant of Kamehameha, she was born in Makapala near the end of the highway and was schooled in her family's genealogy and local history. As a young woman, she toured the United States performing hula, and she appeared in Hollywood movies as a hula dancer and as a light-skinned African woman. She returned to North Kohala, raised a large family, and spent her later years as a Native Hawaiian activist. At the center of many networks, she was a member of the Queen Ka'ahumanu Society, Kohala Hawaiian Civic

Club, North Kohala Elementary School *Kūpuna* Program, Kohala Cultural & Historic Preservation Group, and the Maka ʻala ʻO Kohala (Eyes of Kohala, or Watching Over Kohala). She was on the board of the Hawaiʻi Island Burial Council and consulted with archaeologists on reburial and repatriation issues.

People spoke of her in reverential tones. Emma Glory said, "She is an important person in the district with the stories she tells. She has a lot of influence. She isn't yelling Hawaiian sovereignty stuff. She just says her piece and shuts up." Kealoha elaborated, "We should honor her opinion. Throughout the state, when there are Hawaiian issues, she is always called upon for her opinions, knowledge, and wisdom. She was raised by her grandmother. That was the key to Hawaiian culture. In the olden days, children were raised by their grandparents. They could instill their wisdom."

We called a meeting at Nani's guesthouse with Marie Solomon on June 13, 2000, where project leaders presented options for decision making and their preference for a district-wide ballot. She had not taken an active role in the project to date, but after months of consideration behind the scenes and hearing that the committee wanted to know her thoughts on a potential balloting process, she spoke. The room was quiet as she began with a description of a recent trip to the Bishop Museum in Honolulu, where she consulted about burial objects in storage:

> We went into a back room where all of our gods are kept, lying on their backs, for haoles to study. This is wrong. Why aren't Hawaiians taking care of these things? Saving our heritage is important. Generation after generation have lived with the statue. Many eyes have beheld it—our fathers and grandfathers. I have taken [the sculpture] for granted until now. I never thought about what if it wasn't there any more, or what if this man were to come and paint it blue. I am happy that Mrs. Ahi and the other teachers are getting the *keiki* involved. We have tried so hard to involve them in the past. This man has come in and pressed the right buttons. He is asking us.
>
> I think he [the sculpture] should be painted yellow and red, the symbols of the royalty. Why be like the Honolulu and Hilo statues? Kohala is special. We should paint him, not use gold, that's a haole thing. The statue will be as a teacher. It will have information, and anyone walking up there will know.

Everyone in the room was stunned. *Kupuna* Solomon had spoken.

Decisively. But the question posed to her was not whether to gild or to paint. It was whether to vote. After a few moments of silence, Kealoha stood up and said in half-jest, "Okay. Decided. We can all go home now." He laughed, but everyone else remained silent. After an awkward moment, I asked, "Does this mean that the question has been decided?" Everyone cautiously nodded their heads. I then added, "I can live with this, but what about the public discussion? The high school students' public dialogue isn't scheduled until November." Nani suggested that although we accept Marie's opinion, it puts a lot of weight on her shoulders since at this point the community is expecting public dialogue and a public decision. Marie Solomon responded, "Well, we could still have the vote."

After more discussion, Nani and Marie Solomon resolved that Nani would author an article in the *Kohala Mountain News* articulating the opinions that Marie Solomon had voiced. I was to write another article for the paper providing technical information. The vote would go on. Yet word traveled through informal channels that *kupuna* Solomon had voiced her opinion. Meanwhile the public forum and community activities continued. Many people I spoke with changed their preference during this period from gilding to paint, some giving reasons like those that Marie Solomon had expressed. For some, her decision influenced their own. An informal vote was taken at a Senior Citizens Group meeting several months later that reversed an earlier show of hands for gold. Emma Glory said,

> We took another vote, you know—just what would you like to see that statue finished and then it went reverse. They said they like the painting better than the gilding because there was color and the king had color on his cape and why shouldn't it be on the statue?

By the time local project leaders met on August 25, 2000, to make final plans for project activities and the ballot, the atmosphere had changed. Sharon described it: "Our underlying thought is still that 'Auntie rules.'" During October 2000 the local project team worked with staff from the Hawai'i Arts Alliance to design a poster advertising the vote, the ballot, and accompanying literature. To save time and money, each household received one ballot in their post office box, rather than one for each adult.

The high school speech club held a dialogue (as opposed to a debate) over gold versus paint as a final public event before the vote. I met with student moderator Daniel Otake and presenters Jasmine Ono and Jennifer

Withrow at the school on the day of the event. Despite some anxiety about public speaking, they had a good handle on the issues. Jasmine and Jennifer even decided to switch roles, each arguing the opposite of their own opinions. We rehearsed their arguments together, and I answered lingering questions about the cost of gold and how long it would last, as opposed to paint.

The project committee decided to expand the dialogue into a larger forum. Approximately fifty people filtered into the school cafeteria, including students, teachers, reporters, and the project video crew. They took their seats at the long tables, and a *kupuna* began chanting a formal offering. Michael Fuentes facilitated the evening, and Fern White laid the ground rules for the dialogue. Daniel then moved to the lectern in front of the room and began with a description of the conservation project and the community's choice at hand. Jennifer and Jasmine each argued their positions, questioned each other, and presented rebuttals. Afterwards, there was a panel discussion with project organizers and myself, a question-and-answer session, and finally three *kūpuna* talked story about their memories of the sculpture and its upcoming conservation. The evening ended with a communal song in which everyone sang and held hands in a circle, then we bowed our heads and a *kupuna* offered a Christian prayer.

Ballots went out in mid-November 2000, with a notice that they had to

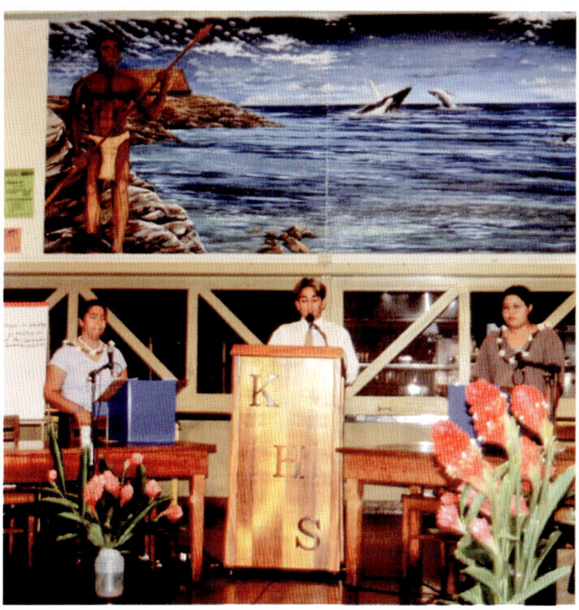


The Kohala High School Speech Club presented arguments for gold versus paint in the high school cafeteria. Presenters: Jasmine Ono and Jennifer Withrow. Moderator: Daniel Otake.

be returned within three weeks to collection boxes installed in grocery stores, the post office, and other public places. The community voted 71 percent for paint. There were five write-ins for stripping the paint and chemically patinating the entire sculpture. One person suggested painting the skin and gilding the feathered garments. The 176 ballots that were returned represented approximately 10 percent of those placed in family post office boxes.

The local decision was made. After the votes were tallied with the help of the Hawai'i Alliance for Arts Education, North Kohala's decision was presented to the state's representing agency, the King Kamehameha Celebration Committee. Keahi Allen reported back that the agency supported the local decision. The decision was made, but discussion didn't end. The primary question on many peoples' minds was not why the vote went for paint, but why the turnout was only 10 percent. Experienced activists among the group argued that getting 10 percent of a population to take an active role by marking a ballot at home and taking it to a public ballot box is an indicator of success for any public project.

Explanations for the turnout further revealed local culture. Some

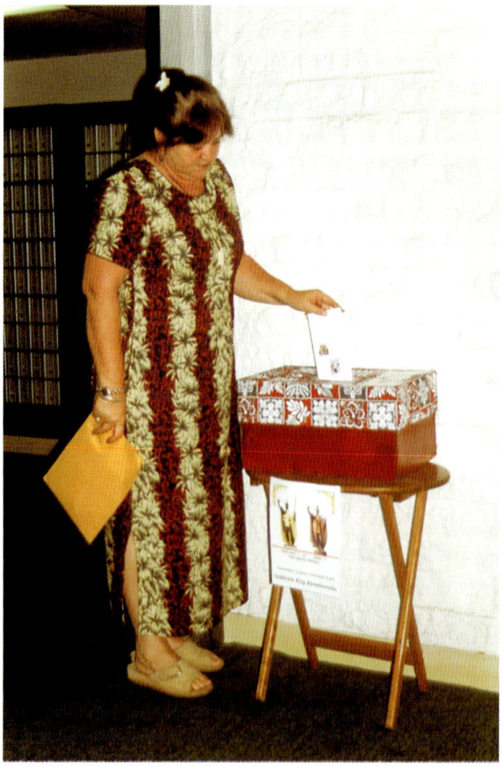

Ballot boxes placed in public places throughout North Kohala, with posters advertising the community ballot.

commented that voting is not "Hawaiian." Elders who worked on plantations do not vote because they were not socialized to participate in any public forum, whereas others in the community simply don't trust the process. One person lamented that despite our intense public activity that led to discussion among families throughout the district, the project in the end didn't break patterns of nonparticipation. "It is typical of rural Hawai'i," Randee Golden concluded. "People here work very hard and are busy with their families. They have two or three jobs, up to seven kids, and they pay rent. It's more about survival. They don't come to meetings, they don't vote. They don't have time to engage in the public process."

Sharon commented that many people felt the decision had already been made by the time the ballot occurred. "People knew the way the vote would go, so they did not feel compelled to fill out the ballot. The decision had already been made by Auntie Marie." According to Nani, "if the word had been that it was going towards gold, many more would have voted."

Regardless of the meaning of the turnout, the decision to paint moved the project forward. It gave us direction to organize the hands-on phase of conservation. Stephanie Na'ihe Cabinis, Emma Glory, Sharon Hayden, Dora Lincoln, Raylene Ha'alelea Lancaster, Daniel Otake, Kealoha Sugiyama, and Marie Solomon formed a team to advise on a host of smaller decisions during the conservation treatment. Together, this team represented the Ka'ahumanu Society, Kamehameha Day Celebration Committee, Kohala Hawaiian Civic Club, Kohala High School Speech Club, and Kohala Senior Citizens Club. Laddy Shim of the Royal Order of Kamehameha joined the team to advise on the final selection of paint colors.

Meanwhile I assembled a work crew to help me on the scaffolding. My first selection was Michael Jones, from O'ahu. I had worked with Michael on many projects in the past. A former mason and museum preparator, he runs a sculpture maintenance business in Honolulu, which meant he arrived with a truck, tools, and a vast array of contacts for equipment rentals and scaffolding sources. We work well together and had just finished reinstalling the two lead sculptures blown over and damaged at the nearby Parker Ranch. Michael set to work on my long list of supplies that could be purchased in Honolulu and shipped to Hilo with his truck on a boat.

Wanting to continue local participation in the project, I asked around for someone with sufficient strength, sensitivity, and dedication to join Michael and me on the scaffolding. Sharon and Raylene both came up with the same name: Hilton Nalani Cabrera. I knew Nalani from various project activities. A descendant of Kamehameha and a local hula instructor, he had spoken with me earlier about his relationship with the sculpture. When I visited him at his home, he knew my purpose. As he recalls the visit:

> I had a dream with a vision of Kamehameha saying someone is going to come and ask you to do something, and when he does, say "yes." I thought it was going to be lei, or dancing the hula, or a chant for Kamehameha, but no, it was the restoration of the statue. I had the dream after the last Kamehameha Day program. I woke up in a cold sweat. I didn't know what it was until Glenn came and asked me to be part of the project, and I knew that was my calling, for whatever reason I needed to be there.

Nalani maintained a close spiritual connection with the sculpture throughout the project, enriching our conversation and our decision. The team was complete, yet we needed a paint contractor who could bring equipment and expertise for the critical step of low-pressure, high-volume spray-coating the primer on the sculpture after the three of us had prepared the surface. I searched the island for the right firm for this subcontract until I found Mark Bowden. He not only had this difficult-to-find equipment and the expertise in painting outdoor metal structures, but his family has deep connections in nearby Waimea.

Before we could begin, there was one last piece of cultural research to do. Raylene Haʻalelea Lancaster asked me if I knew whether *kapu* was placed on the sculpture when it was installed in 1883. She referred to recent *heiau* conservation projects in which Native Hawaiian *kahu* and work crews performed ritual chanting, offering, and reciting of genealogies in order to lift *kapu* and temporarily "deconsecrate" the site during the physical work. Curious about this, I met with Billy Fields, a mason who practices the traditional craft of *uhau humu pōhaku* (dry-stone masonry) and is frequently contracted to construct stone burials for human remains repatriated from museums or excavated at archaeological and development sites. He also restores *heiau*. Billy described the protocol he uses, developed through advice from Pualani Kanahele of the Native Edith Kanakaʻole Foundation in Hilo. He and his crew follow strict rituals to lift and replace *kapu* at the beginning and end of his projects. For instance, his workers must all chant at least five generations of their genealogy as they ask permission to perform the work before lifting *kapu*.

Although I found no evidence in the archives that *kapu* was placed on the sculpture in 1883, I did note that media coverage of the events referred to prolonged Hawaiian chanting. No trace of ritual existed in local public memory, at least with the old-timers the project team spoke with. Raylene suggested that since *kapu* was not placed on the sculpture, we were free to do what we felt was appropriate. As the *kahuna nui* of the nearby Puʻukoholā Heiau, John Keola Lake agreed and suggested that following the same protocols used in precontact times is not always appropriate. "We no longer go back to the *heiau* and do all the things that were done, such as sacrificial killing. Seven generations of mindsets have changed since then." He further reconciled contemporary rituals of chanting and offerings with his own Catholic faith. "We are searching for how to restore precious things that are not only symbolic but useful to us today. I bring the presence of God, whether I call him Kane or the Lord Father. If there is chanting to be done, it is out of respect."

On *kupuna* Marie Solomon's recommendation, the project team decided to have a low-key blessing. They asked Raylene to offer a Hawaiian chant in a private ceremony, with no onlookers, no cameras, and no participants. She would be alone and would notify me after the blessing occurred. After settling the question, Chris Bowden, Mark's wife and co-owner of Bowden Painting, requested a Christian blessing. In an e-mail, she explained that her eighty-nine-year-old grandfather from Oʻahu was "the ordained and renowned [English and Hawaiian speaking] Kahu Samuel Makaneole Saffery, Jr. and is the current *Kahu* for the well known, Liliʻuokalani Protestant Church. His father before him, Samuel Makaneole Saffery, Sr., was the servicing *Kahu* there as well."

I forwarded the offer to the committee and they accepted, agreeing that a small family blessing was appropriate, especially since the Bowdens were now part of the project team. They requested that both the Hawaiian and the Christian blessing remain low-key, without public attention—a wish that did not come to pass.

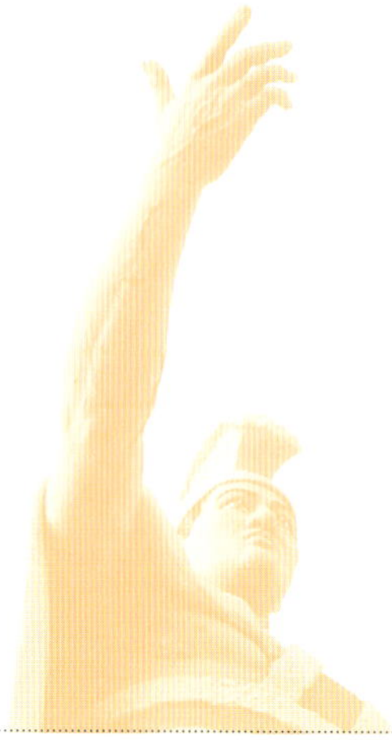

# 9 *On the Scaffolding*

I RETURNED TO NORTH KOHALA in February 2001 to finally perform the hands-on conservation work on the scaffolding. Michael Jones flew in from Honolulu and picked up his truck full of supplies at the shipping dock. We checked into Nani's guesthouse and met with Nalani to strategize our first steps. Mark Bowden's painting crew erected three sturdy scaffolding towers with adjustable planks around the sculpture, and Tuti Baker's team began videotaping our preliminary work. I also held a series of meetings with the local project team to make final arrangements for community participation.

I hadn't heard from Raylene whether she had performed her private blessing, but the Christian ceremony was scheduled for the day before our work began. It happened that the Hawaiian Civic Club was in deep debate over a troubling issue inside the courthouse when the Bible reading began. Surprised by the presence of a minister and the small gathering with a film crew in front of the sculpture, the Native Hawaiian group abruptly terminated their meeting and about twenty people came out to join us. When Kahu Samuel Makaneole Saffery, Jr., finished, he looked around at the expanded group. Recognizing that an important *kupuna* was present, he gave his offering to her rather than to the sculpture. Surprised, she quickly turned

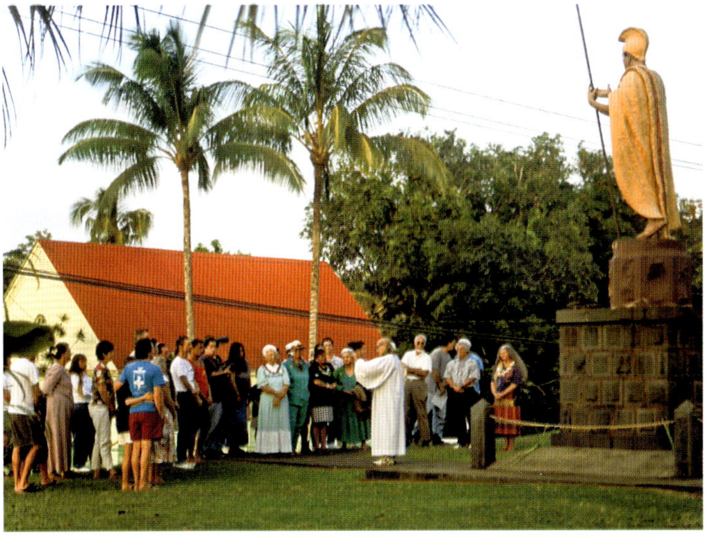

Christian blessing for the project by Kahu Samuel Makaneole Saffery, Jr. Participants include the conservation work crew, Bowden family members, Kohala Hawaiian Civic Club members, and Ki'i Productions video team.

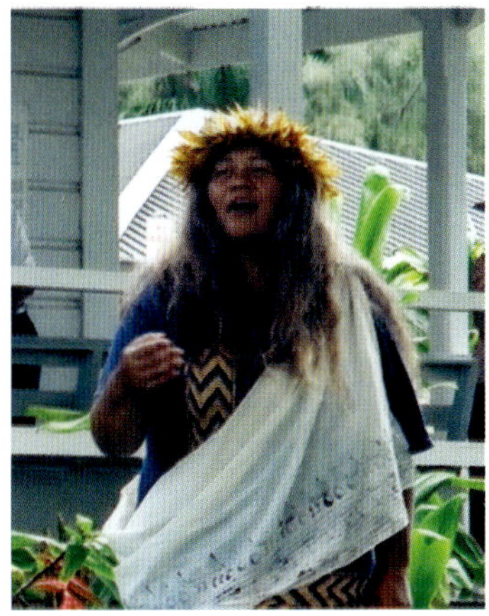

Raylene Ha'alelea Lancaster offers a Hawaiian chant as an offering to the Kamehameha sculpture.

around and placed it on the sculpture's pedestal and an awkward moment of silence followed. *Kupuna* Solomon then turned to Raylene and requested an impromptu offering in chant, to add a Hawaiian blessing to the Christian ceremony. Raylene closed her eyes, opened her arms, and began chanting in a low voice that became increasingly powerful in its cadence. For me, this transformed the moment into something beyond any prior experience. She later told me that the chant came to her slowly, as if in a dream. It filled the air, as the two religious blessings fused into one. This spontaneous blending of cultures provided an auspicious start. It was captured by Tuti's crew and later became part of her film.

The next day Michael, Nalani, and I wrapped the scaffolding with large blue tarps to protect the area from the mess of chemicals and paint residue we would produce. We tied off a large area around the sculpture with caution tape and posted signs created by local artist/teacher Margaret Hoy, asking people to stay back during the conservation treatment. We anticipated frequent visitors with lots of questions, so we posted a sign for talk story sessions about our work progress on Friday afternoons.

I documented the sculpture's condition with archival black-and-white photographs and color high-resolution digital images. We annotated drawings with condition problems such as the crack through the sculpture's base and the isolated patches of bronze disease visible in areas of exposed metal. I took more paint samples, this time cutting off half-inch sections with a scalpel rather than the tiny, unobtrusive specimens of my prior visits. I wanted to perform further paint analysis to better map the history of colors as they changed over the years. I also wanted to provide future researchers with plenty of samples in an archive. After peeling away areas where the paint was lifting, I took further samples of corrosion and placed them in small glass vials. I hadn't been able to access much of the corrosion on prior visits, since it had been hidden under the paint. We looked forward to seeing the entire metal surface after paint removal and discovering any hidden evidence of damage and repair from the 1880 shipwreck.

Our first intervention was to remove the brass spheres that Joe Chang epoxied into the eye sockets in 1978. Our high-pressure water blasting would pop them off, possibly losing them, and I wanted to retain them and let the local team decide whether to replace them or not. I decided to give Nalani the honor. He looked at me, looked at Kamehameha's face, thought for a moment, and said, "Okay, show me what to do." We sat down on the top plank of the scaffolding and I demonstrated the technique of dripping solvent gel behind the eyeballs, waiting for several minutes, adding a bit more, then leveraging them out of the sockets with long wooden skewers from the Asian food section of the nearby Takata Market. Nalani carefully pried the eyes out while I continued taking paint samples and putting them in plastic containers, along with sketches and measurements to note where they came from. Meanwhile Michael tested various techniques to remove the thick crust of paint: methylene chloride gel paint stripper, pressure washing, and steam cleaning. Nalani handed me the brass spheres and I placed them in a film canister in my pocket for safekeeping. The work had begun.

In cultural terms, the most revealing aspect of the conservation treatment came from my decision to temporarily remove the eyeballs. During the prior eighteen months of public and private discussion about the sculpture, no one had mentioned the significance of the eyes. At the end of our first day of work, I met with the team of local decision makers to provide a project update. Exhausted and unprepared for new revelations, I explained that our first step after documentation and sampling was removing the eyeballs. *Kupuna* Marie Solomon looked at me and said:

**OPPOSITE PAGE:** Hilton Nalani Cabrera removes the brass eyeballs added by Joe Chang in 1978, originally check valves from cans of poison purchased in a hardware store.

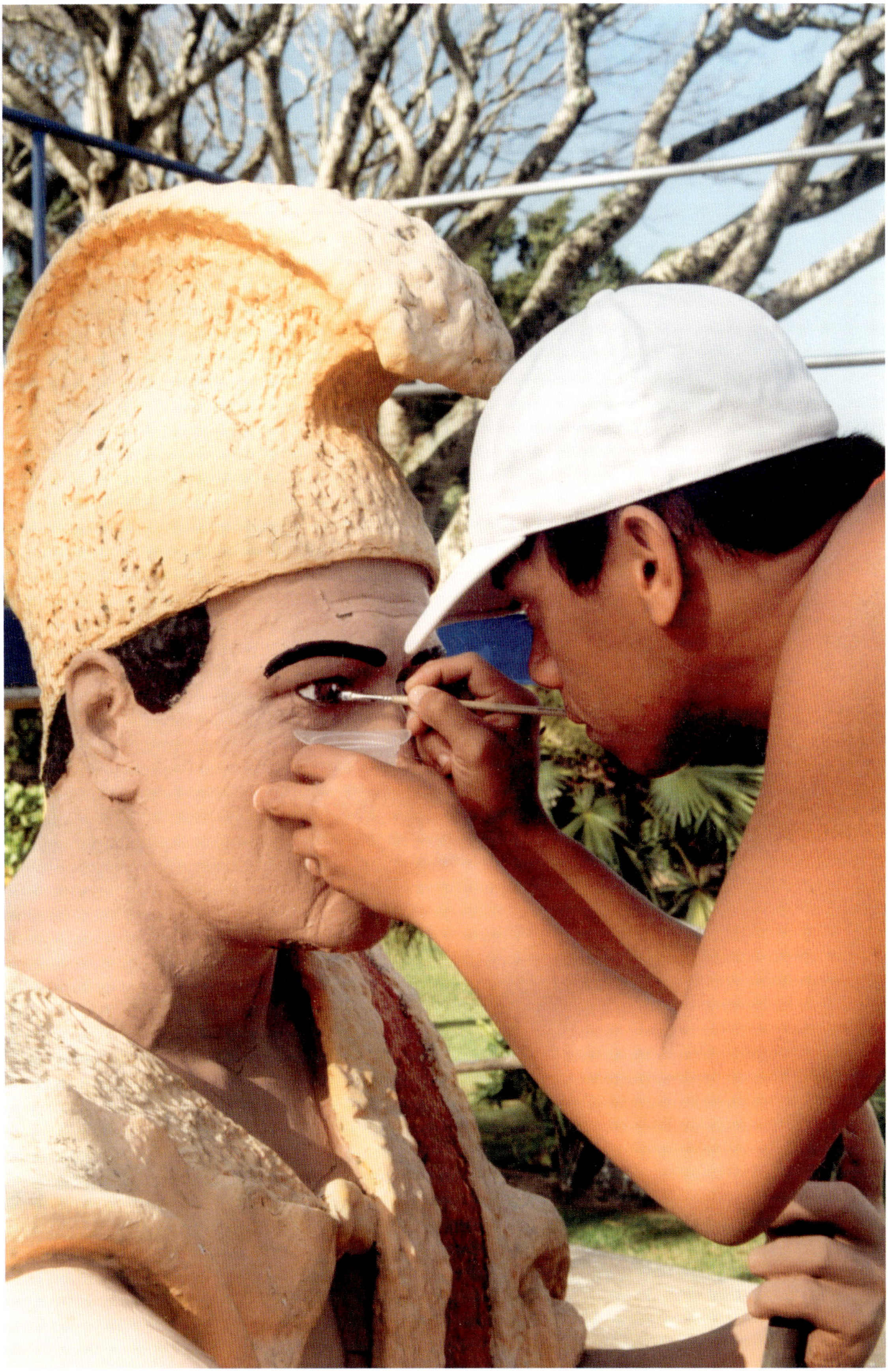

"You took his eyes out?"

"Yes. We took them out to save them, because otherwise they would fall out during the paint stripping."

"Where are they now?"

"They're in my pocket."

"Can I see them?"

She cupped her hands as I rolled the painted spheres out of the film canister. Eyes in hand, she launched into a considered response:

> There's always someone in the background who knows the *kapus* and the forbidden things . . . you folks were going to undress Kamehameha; you were going to strip him of his garments. In our culture, no one touches the *ali'i*'s things, his clothes, or whatever. There is only one person. The one who takes care of his wardrobe, and no *maka'āinana* (commoner) can touch anything. So the blessing that they had was to cut off whatever

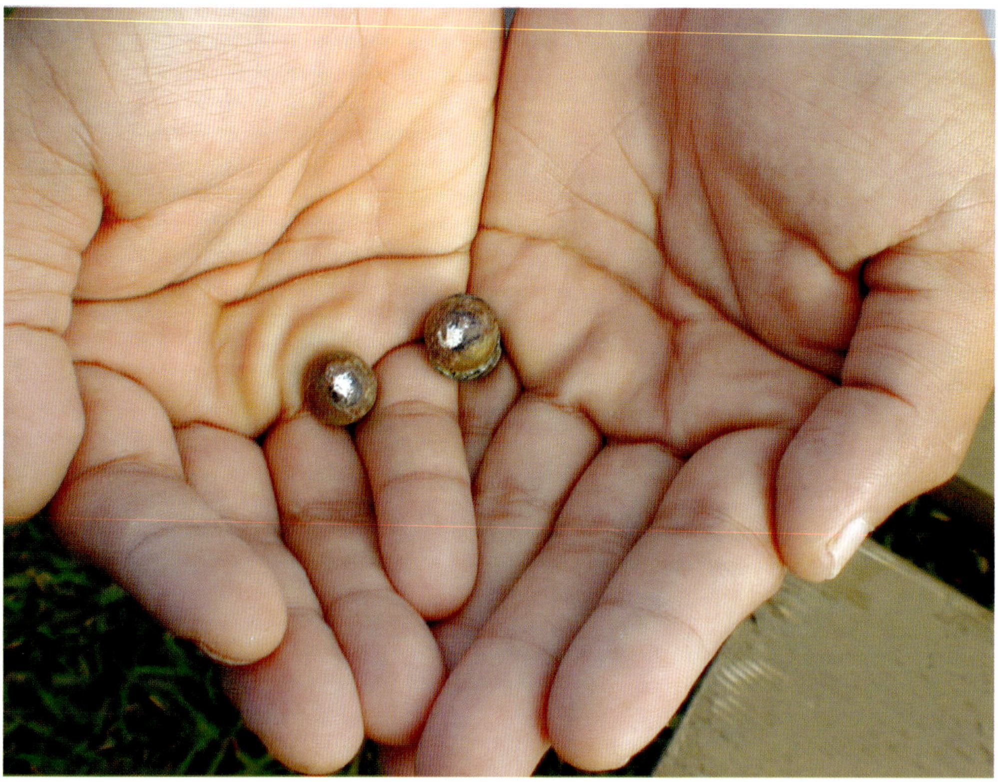

Painted eyeballs from the sculpture held in Hilton Nalani Cabrera's hands.

> *kapus* come from behind. You folks are bringing things out of the grave. We believe in God, that's why the priest came. Now you give me the eyes! You took the eyes out. That means he cannot see. What does that mean, for Kohala, you know, you've got to be careful. I kind of don't want to take part in this thing.

The situation was surreal. We were aware of the video camera and microphone documenting every word of our meeting. Here I was, a haole from the mainland, blundering by asking a Kamehameha descendant to remove the king's eyes as our first step in the conservation treatment. Despite my attempts to tread lightly and be sensitive to cultural concerns, had I transgressed in a way that could not be forgiven? Fortunately, others on the committee agreed with the eye removal. Stephanie Cabinis broke the silence. "Don't worry, Auntie, Glenn had to take them out. Besides, they were put in by Joe Chang, not the artist. They are Joe Chang's eyeballs." Finally, Marie Solomon started to laugh. She, too, realized that we were in new territory without a clear road map, and she agreed to be part of the group that would decide on the future of the eyeballs.

Nalani later described his experience on that first day. "We bow to him and acknowledge him. That is what the Hawaiians do. And then you told me to take his eyes out! I didn't say nothing. But you asked me to take his eyes out. I said 'I'm taking out your eyes for a reason. I *kūlou*ed [bowed the head] and then I took out his eyes. He said 'okay.' And I took out his eyes."

The next day the three of us devoted all our time to paint stripping. First came the surface layers of bird guano, gecko poop, spider nests, embedded soil, and flaking paint. All this came off with a light pressure washing at 3,200 pounds per square inch. The well-attached paint was much more tenacious. We adjusted our techniques for each stubborn area, using repeated cycles of swelling with methylene chloride gel, and blasting alternately with pressurized steam and cold water. Alternating hot and cold treatments caused the metal and paint to expand and contract at different rates, loosening the bond between them. We even used a propane torch to burn off stubborn areas of paint. It was a hot, messy operation that took us seven long days under the blue tarps. During most of the operations we wore full-body Tyvec suits, gloves, toxic vapor masks, and goggles. We kept the tarps closed during these operations to protect the onlookers who were standing and sitting around the site. Despite our attempts to clean up our mess at the end of each day and put all the waste in plastic bags for proper disposal, residents gathered small, scattered paint chips as souvenirs, some with bright patches of gold on the underside.

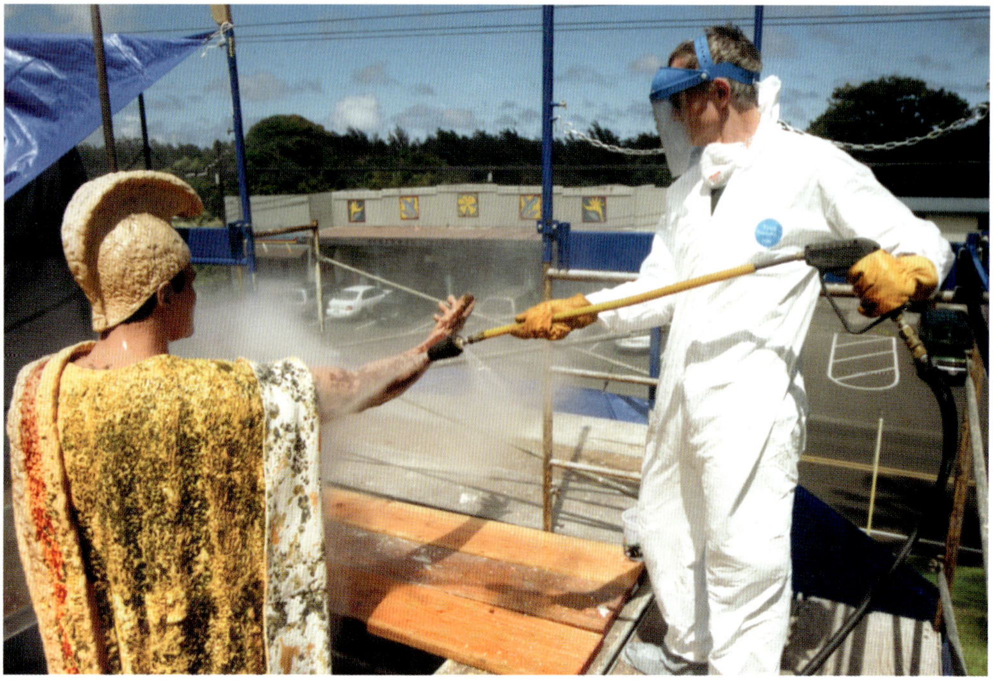

Author removes paint with pressurized steam blasting, one of several methods used in the process.

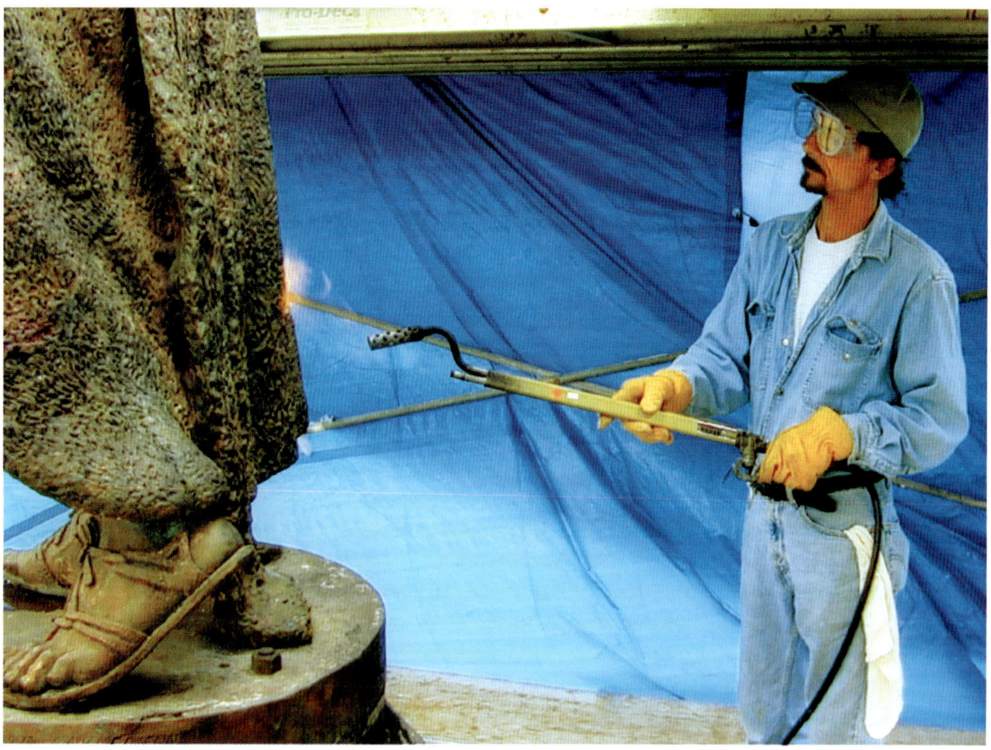

Michael Jones heats stubborn areas of paint with a propane torch.

The paint came off in a series of historic stages. First to go were the faded colors applied by Kealoha Sugiyama in 1996, then the thick crust of paint applied by county and state workers in preparation for bygone Kamehameha Day celebrations. It was difficult to determine when the plantation days took over, then the prior years in which Hawai'i was a U.S. territory, and finally the royal kingdom. We removed approximately 90 percent of the paint during the process. Some residue of lead-white paint in deep crevices proved too tenacious to remove without more toxic solvents. We decided to leave them, along with traces of well-adhered gold adjacent to the letters that spelled "KAMEHAMEHA I" on the circular base. This was information for future researchers to discover. I saved hundreds of paint chips for analysis and archival storage.

We removed the blue tarps whenever possible so onlookers could observe the progress. Tourists would alternately ask us to stand aside or to pose for photographs. After we washed the freshly cleaned metal surface with a pH-neutral non-ionic detergent, many visitors commented on the strong features and deep engraved lines in the cast that gave more character to the face. Previously obscured by the thick crust of paint, deep crevices articulated the feathered garments as well.

As the bare metal appeared, those of us on the scaffolding, the local project team, and casual visitors all shared the excitement. We pored over the surface, taking photographs and making more drawings of corrosion, cracks, and holes. Details became visible that had been covered since the first coat of paint was applied during the 1883 restoration. We traced weld lines telling us that the sculpture was cast in nine separate pieces and joined over an interior iron armature. We saw scores of round plugs in the cast that the Barbedienne foundry inserted to cover casting flaws, such as voids from air bubbles created as the molten brass solidified. They "chased" some of these plugs by hand-engraving to match details of drapery folds. They left others unadorned, a mark of poor craftsmanship. This surprised us, since the Barbedienne foundry was renowned in the late nineteenth century for its craftsmanship. We noted approximately twenty-five small casting holes through the metal that they had not filled in with plugs. These small holes would have allowed water to seep into the interior had they not been filled with paint—an example of how the paint tradition helped preserve the sculpture over the past century. It was a good, solid cast, but not the quality of finish we expected from the foundry used by Rodin and Barye.

We also found the repairs from the shipwreck, executed between

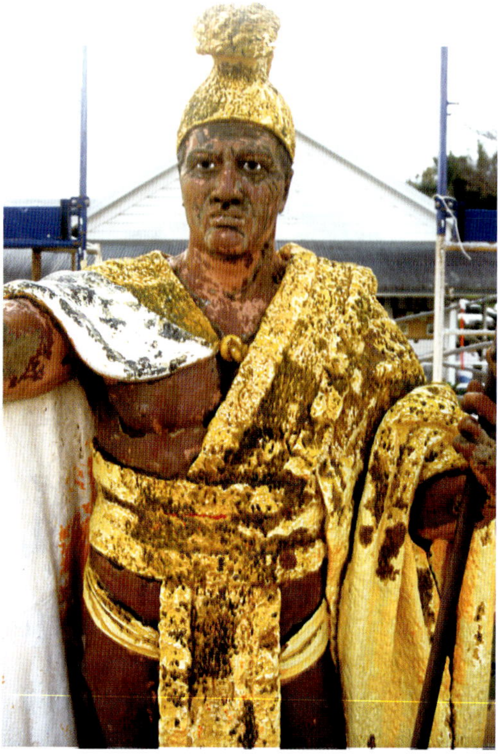

Kamehameha sculpture after partial stripping, revealing color variation in paint layers.

February and April 1883. The primary repair was the new right forearm that replaced the one broken off when fishermen pulled the statue from the sea. The pinned and welded seam was stable, although it was tilted off at an angle by a few degrees. Two gouged areas on the back of the *ʻahu ʻula* were evidence of the damage described in early newspaper articles. According to different reporters, the *ʻahu ʻula* was knocked around during the shipwreck or during recovery. Perhaps both. David Scott at the Getty Conservation Institute analyzed samples of lead-tin solder we found in one of the damaged areas. The alloy, with traces of copper and antimony, was commonly used at the time of the restoration.

We scoured the surface looking for defects in the brass and located a number of "stress cracks" running horizontally through the cloak on Kamehameha's left side. The well-developed corrosion in the cracks convinced me that they were not new and didn't immediately threaten the sculpture's

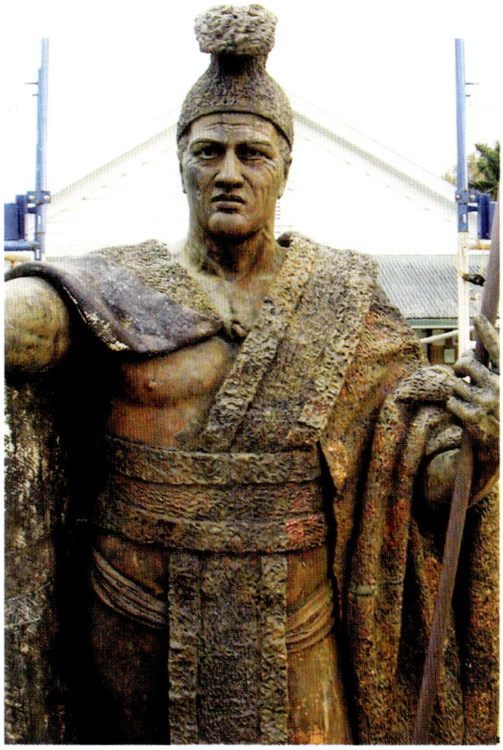

Further details revealed on the brass surface after paint removal.

structure. They most likely developed from the violent descent to the bottom of the sea or from banging against the ship as the fishermen lifted it back out. I was more concerned about a deep dent and complex fracture in the metal base behind his left foot. Iron corrosion stains under this fracture revealed interior corrosion from the iron armature. I could tell that this corrosion was not fresh, since there was no corrosion staining on the surface paint before we stripped it, and because dense copper corrosion covered the edges of the fracture. Assessing all this evidence, I decided that none of the damage was recent. The sculpture would need to be monitored, but it was not in immediate jeopardy. We photographed and measured the cracks, repairs, and other surface features, noting them on sketches in the project notebook for future condition assessment.

I was also concerned about the small spots of bronze disease we noted before cleaning. They were gone after the paint-stripping operation. All that remained was a beautiful layer of black and red oxides, with a few patches of dark emerald green that only a corrosion scientist could love. David Scott at the Getty was surprised that his environmental scanning electron microscope identified complex clinoatacamite and atacamite but no nantokite minerals in the samples of green powdery corrosion I sent him. Backup analysis with x-ray powder diffraction told us that aside from minor chlorides, the rest of this corrosion consisted of straightforward combinations of copper and oxygen. This was good news. We had bronze disease, but very little of it, and very little chloride in the corrosion mix. Once again, the paint seemed to have protected the sculpture over the years.

Since the sculpture needed no major repairs, our next step was to fill all the holes, cracks, and small gaps with pH-neutral epoxy putty. We removed loose grout from the stone base and repointed the gaps with a low-alkali cement mortar. We cleaned the metal components of the sculpture with acetone and misted it with a warm benzotriazole solution. Benzotriazole develops a chemi-absorbed film that helps prevent future corrosion. Since it is a possible carcinogen, we worked with protective gloves and toxic-vapor masks, then properly disposed of all debris. After removing excess benzotriazole crystals the following day with alcohol-soaked rags, we were ready to paint.

We had plenty of time for reflection during this sequence of steps, marveling at the sculpture's dramatic transformation after we had removed up to twenty-five layers of paint. When not wearing our toxic-vapor masks, we talked about our experience on the scaffolding. Nalani spoke about his feelings as the paint gradually came off to reveal Kamehameha's dramatic facial features:

> There is no word that can describe the work. All this stripper and pressure washer. If you look at it now it looks like a warrior. Before he looked calm and mellow, now he looks like a warrior, mean, strong. Like one guy you wouldn't mess with. I have a hard time looking him in the face.

Nalani also revealed his troubled thoughts about working above Kamehameha's head:

> Being above the chief, the *ali'i,* it's kind of interesting. . . . "I'm looking at your face and I am above you, but I am sorry." I just *kūlou* and acknowledge him. Each morning I *kūlou* for all of us, not just for myself.

We attracted a constant ring of onlookers. The film crew's presence, with their video camera, tripods, and boom microphones, may have helped generate some of the attention. Some shouted up questions and made comments; others watched for hours from the picnic tables on the surrounding lawn and benches positioned on the courthouse *lānai*. Tourists complained about the distance they traveled to visit the sculpture only to see a giant box covered with blue tarps. During our breaks, we tied corners of the tarps back with bungee cords for public viewing and engaged people in conversation. We moved aside for photographs when we could and answered questions shouted up to us from the ground: "Is it true they pulled that rascal out of the ocean?" "Is this the real one?" "Are you taking him away?"

Some visitors were part of organized groups, including the high school Hawaiian Studies class, the Girl Scouts, and a local Hawaiian-language immersion preschool class. Sometimes I climbed down from the scaffolding to talk about the technical aspects of the project. Other times Michael or Nalani took over. Once I looked down to see Nalani with his shirt off and a lei around his neck, acting out the story of the shipwreck in an impromptu hula to a group of wide-eyed school children.

Many who watched us knew Nalani and asked questions in pidgin that I could barely understand. Nalani spoke about all this community interaction. "The community is talking. They see the scaffold and the work. Cars drive by. Kids yell, 'You'd better not make a mistake!' or 'You'd better paint him good!'" He also reported back from his experiences away from the site: "people talking and talking. The gossip, they are talking about Kamehameha. By doing this, it's keeping him happy. It's not you who decided you were going to do the statue. You were called by him to do it. It was him. He would have let us know if he didn't want us to do it. He is allowing us to do this."

By the time we began the work, I already knew what paint system I wanted to use. After months of research to select a tenacious industrial coating that could withstand the harsh subtropical sun and constant rain, I chose an automotive epoxy primer, a polyurethane paint, and a polyurethane clear top coat made by DuPont. I selected the specific set of coatings in part because they were locally available, knowing that future touch-ups would be in the hands of volunteers with no funding from the state. I found John Gruell (Big John) at Big Island Marine in Kona, who not only supplied the paint but was willing to engage in long conversations about getting the colors right and getting it shipped on time from the mainland. He loaned me color wheels and provided samples as the local committee deliberated on color choice.

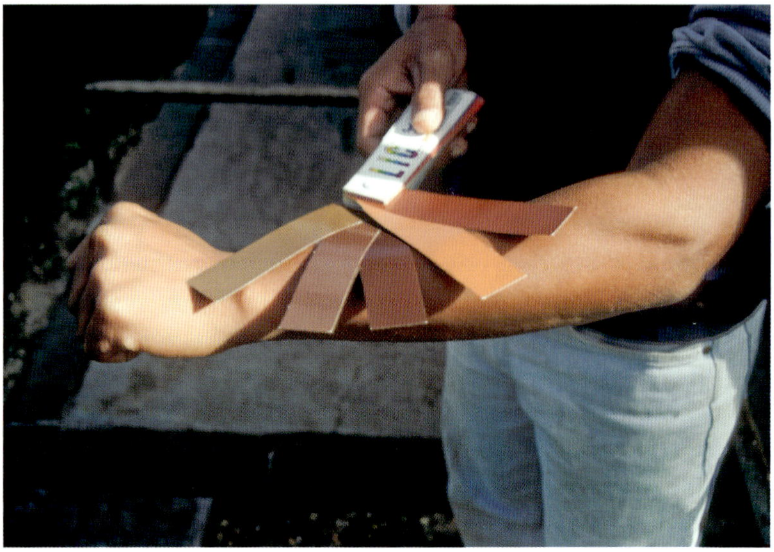

Brown color sample wheel against Hilton Nalani Cabrera's arm, in an attempt to get the skin color "right."

I provided the committee with the DuPont color sample wheels, but they were not satisfied with the options for the brown skin colors. The paint itself became political through their process as we discussed appropriate brown tones and cultural values associated with them. Since the palette of DuPont browns did not represent "Hawaiian" skin tones, Big John loaned me a color wheel from the Valspar brand with a greater range of options. Several committee members suggested using Nalani's suntanned, medium brown skin tone as a basis for deciding. Although he is a descendant of Kamehameha, Nalani is also a descendant of Filipino, Japanese, Portuguese, and British immigrants. *Kupuna* Solomon pointed out that Kamehameha's mother was *keakea* Hawaiian (light-skinned) and his father (either of two possible fathers) had darker skin. In the end, the committee selected a medium-dark brown color based on her recommendations, slightly darker than Nalani's skin tone.

For the feathered garments, the committee decided to match paint samples to actual feathers from the *'i'iwi* and the *mamo* birds. Laddy Shim, a local member of the Royal Order of Kamehameha, located a source for these rare feathers and brought them to the site for matching with paint chips. The committee's discussions reminded me of debates I have had with museum curators and public art administrators over how people perceive colors from a distance and the visual effects of bright versus muted tones. Aside from one member's preference for less bright tones, the decision was unanimous to match closely the vibrant red and yellow feathers and to maintain Kealoha's decision to paint the interior band of the *kā'ei* red. They selected a tan color for the interior of the cloak, representing the woven cordage that supports the feathers on the original garment at the Bishop Museum.

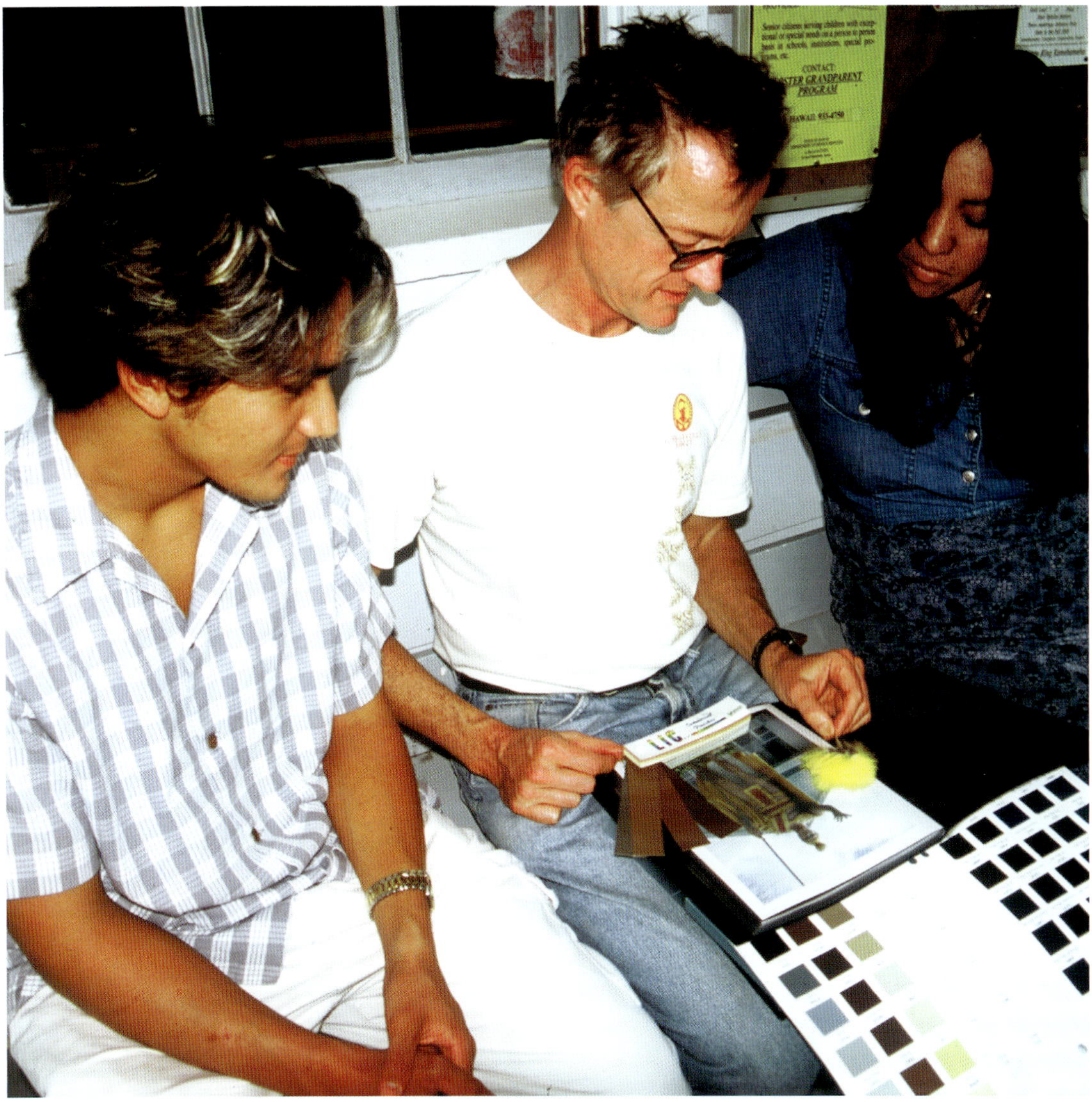

Author meets with Stephanie Cabinis and Daniel Otake with feathers from the *'i'iwi* and the *mamo* birds and brown color samples to discuss color choices for the paint.

The committee also discussed the colors of the stone base under the figure. One option was to paint it black, representing lava and the goddess Pele, who some believe still resides in the nearby Kīlauea volcano. Others suggested gray to evoke the ever-present bluestone in the region, while still others preferred brown for the rich soil of North Kohala. As Stephanie Cabinis recalls the selection of brown for the stone:

> *Kupuna* Solomon reminded us about the legend of goddess Pele and her brother; there is no lava in Kohala, only blue-rock. Every old-timer would agree. For during the years of making home here and digging up of a cesspool, one would always find blue-rock—for this is North Kohala, not South Point which is home to goddess Pele—lava; and as *kupuna* Solomon has stated on tape, blue-rock is blue-rock. She notes there is no brown in blue-rock. However, because Kealoha Sugiyama had his own interpretation, not seeing the "natural" order of blue-rock without brown, she went along with Kealoha.

Before painting the surface, I conducted ASTM standard adhesion tests between the primer and metal by painting on paint samples, letting them set, and attempting to peel them off with adhesive tape. After I was satisfied with the performance of the primer and paint on location, Mark Bowden's team applied the white primer with a high-volume, low-pressure airless spray unit, covering the entire sculpture. The following day began our seventy-two-hour window to hand paint the colors before applying the protective clear coat. Given the significance of this step, I asked Daniel Otake, who led the high school dialogue on gold versus paint, Sharon Hayden, and Kealoha Sugiyama to help the rest of us on the scaffolding. The toxic-vapor masks limited our conversation during this process, providing time for internal reflection as we focused on our task. We finished hand painting the colors just in time before the paint could fully polymerize. Mark Bowden's crew then applied the clear coat with his airless spray unit.

We held the final eyeball meeting during the intense hours of hand painting. I stood on the scaffolding with Joe Chang's brass spheres attached to the ends of two wood skewers. Committee members stood below to judge whether they preferred the figure with or without the eyes. I repeatedly

**OPPOSITE PAGE:** North Kohala High School student Daniel Otake paints a section of the *kā'ei*.

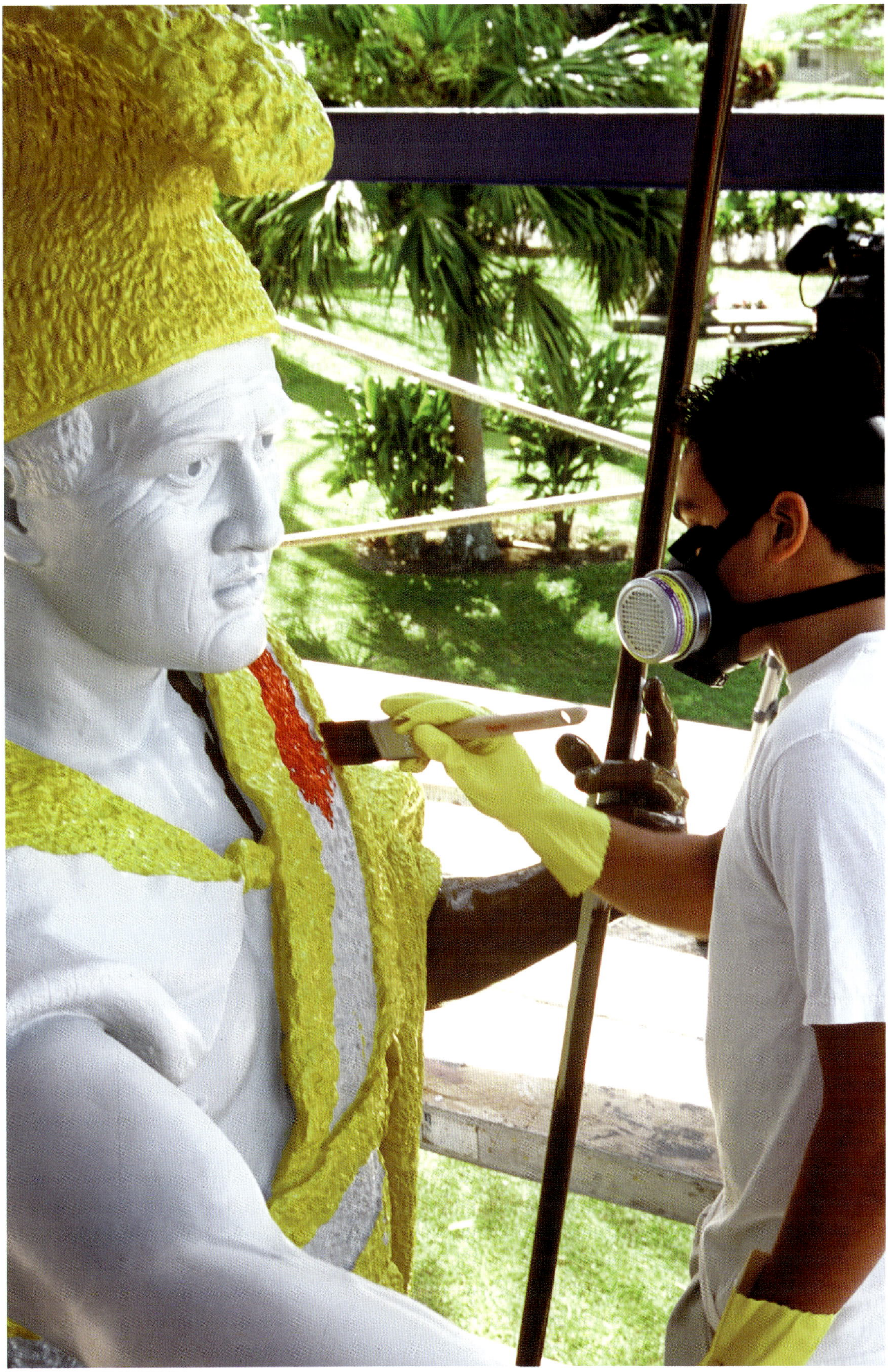

moved the eyes in and out of the sockets, just as an optometrist tests lenses, while the committee discussed whether it looked better with eyes in or eyes out. In the end, the committee decided to replace the spheres. *Kupuna* Solomon turned to me and said, "We have to stop calling them Joe Chang's eyes. They are now Kamehameha's eyes." I reattached the eyeballs with epoxy. Lying upside down on the top rung of the scaffolding, I painted the pupils, irises, and highlights to make sure they gazed out but looked appropriate from below.

The conservation treatment was complete. After another round of documentation photography, we took the scaffolding down and returned all our rented equipment to local vendors. The project team held a celebratory dinner and started planning the rededication and community celebrations for the June Kamehameha Day holiday.

I returned to North Kohala in early June to conduct a maintenance-training session for local volunteers and to participate in the rededication festivities. I trained a team to carefully observe the surface for condition changes each year and document these changes with photographs and drawings. We set up a tool kit and practiced techniques for the annual cleaning. Tuti's film crew taped the training session and created a special "maintenance" video for volunteers to watch.

The local team decided to rededicate the sculpture the day before Kamehameha Day in 2001. Ceremonies began with sunrise prayers and offerings led by the *kahuna nui* of the Puʻukoholā Heiau, the Royal Order of Kamehameha, and the Kaʻahumanu Society. After opening chants and prayers, a long morning of talking story unfolded. Speakers told of Kamehameha's significance, the sculpture's dramatic history, and its conservation. Much was said about the sculpture as a window into the Hawaiian past and how people in North Kohala participated in conservation decision making and intervention. As Raylene put it, "the project is now part of local history."

Pam Korza from Animating Democracy and Susan Nichols from the Save Outdoor Sculpture! funding programs attended the rededication on June 10,

**OPPOSITE PAGE:** Author holds the eyeballs added by Joe Chang during the "eyeball" meeting.

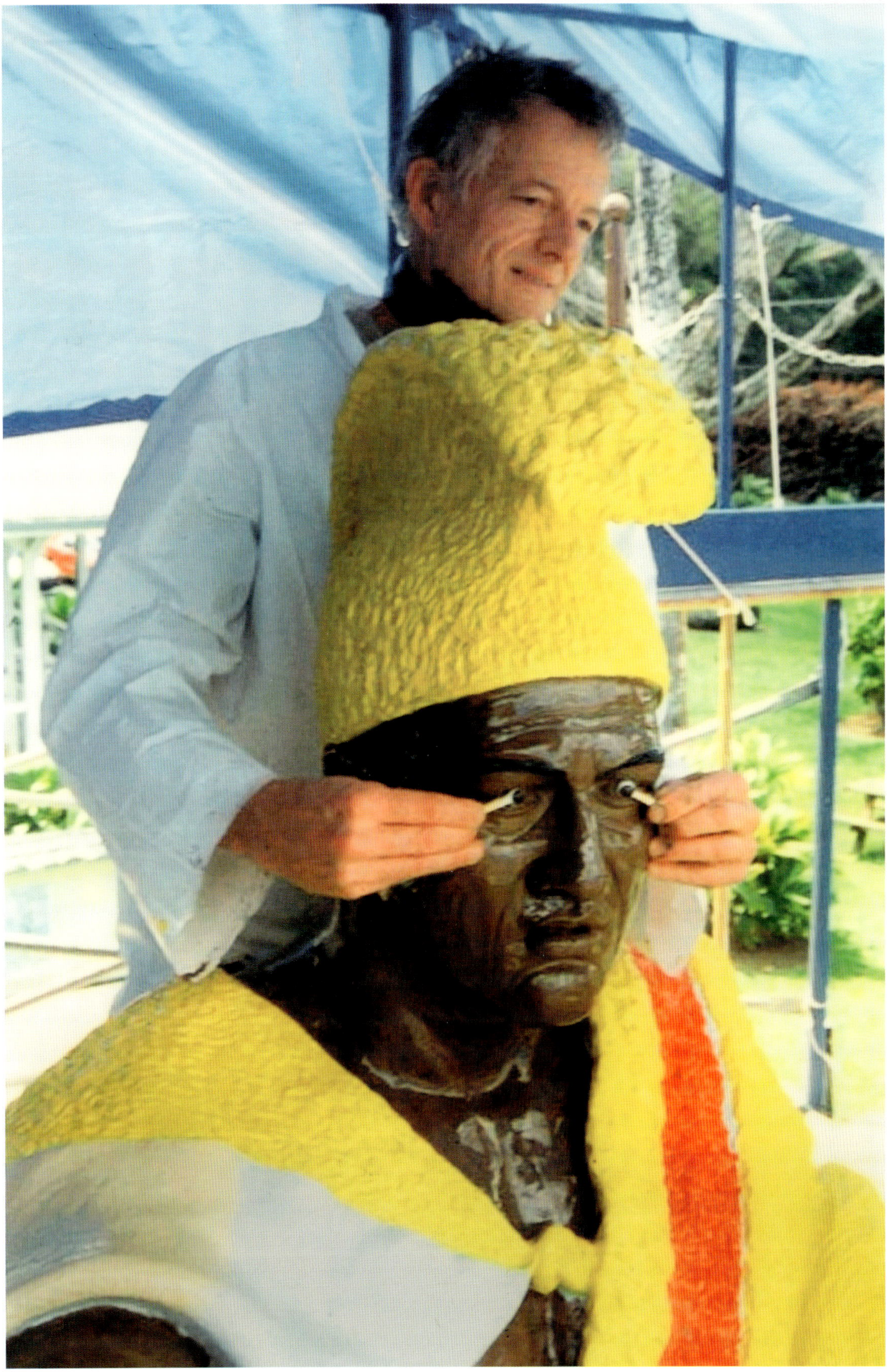

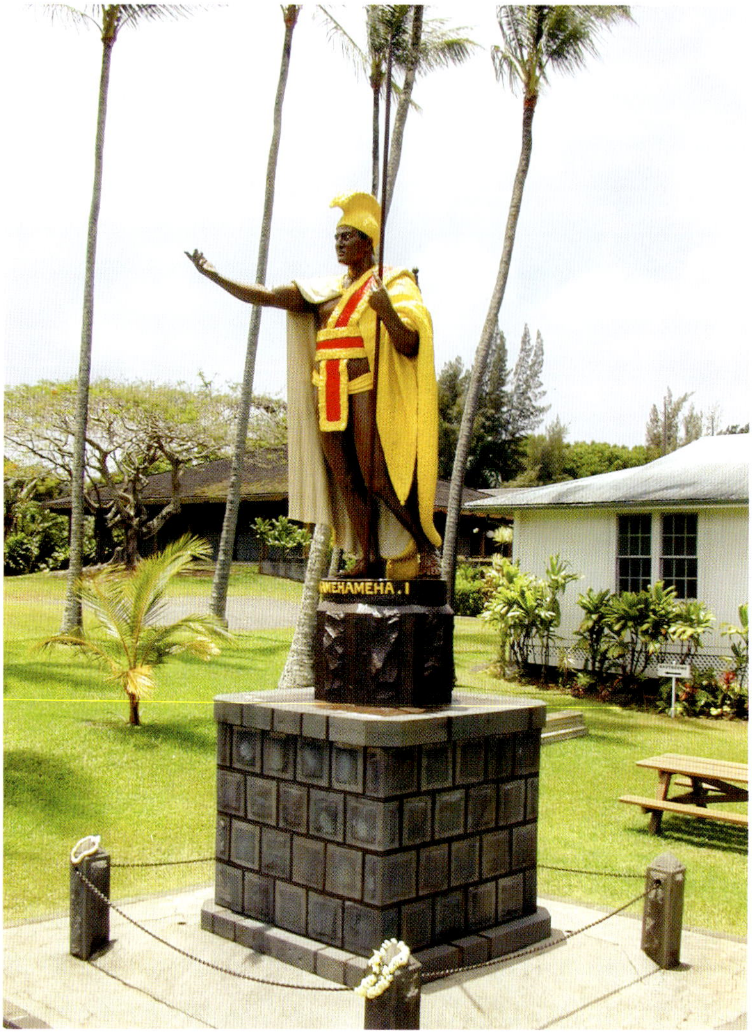

The sculpture after conservation intervention.

along with representatives from the Hawai'i Alliance for Arts Education and approximately 250 locals and visitors.

At the end of the ceremony, Raylene's *hula hālau* performed a new *hula ki'i* that she wrote for the occasion. The new puppet hula was a surprise to me. Participants included preschoolers, the hula group, and a *kupuna* who spoke, sang, and chanted their way through the script. Children voiced questions about technical conservation issues to a *kupuna* and a conservator. A coconut puppet named Mr. Wharton, outfitted with eyeglasses, responded to a series of questions about the conservation project.

"Ke Ki'i Nui 'O Kohala" (The Great Statue of Kohala)

**KUPUNA:** Now let me tell you the story of the king's new clothes.

**KEIKI:** Ka mea lole hou no ka mo'i Kamehameha? (New clothes for King Kamehameha?)

**KUPUNA:** Yes! . . . I know you learned many things about our statue from last year's presentation when Kumu Hula Keola Lake came and taught the hula ki'i and Mr. Glenn Wharton came and shared his research and work about the statue. Who remembers how many statues of King Kamehameha there are, and where they are?

**KUPUNA:** The colors that you see now were chosen by a committee from the community who got together and decided to pick the colors that closely resembled the feathers and clothing that King Kamehameha would have worn in his time. Uncle Laddy Shim had feathers from his kupuna of the 'i'iwi bird and the mamo that were used to help decide the colors.

**KAMA:** Kupuna, we voted in school to see if we wanted the statue painted or to be gold like it was when it was first made.

**KEIKI:** Yes Kupuna, some of us wanted it gold and some of us wanted it painted . . .

**KAMA:** Kupuna, there is Mr. Wharton now, will you ask him what the statue of King Kamehameha was like when he took all of the paint off of it?

**KUPUNA:** Hui! Aloha Mr. Wharton, my two mo'opuna wanted to know what the statue of our King Kamehameha was like without any paint on it. Would you share with them?

**MR. WHARTON:** I would be happy to. The statue without any paint was quite interesting. There were twenty-five or so layers of paint that needed to be removed and underneath all of that paint, gold was found to be present. I had paint chip samples sent for analysis and it confirmed that the sculpture was indeed gilt originally.

**KUPUNA:** You know Mr. Wharton, I came one day when all of the paint was removed. I looked and looked at the statue. I was so impressed with the artist's detail and workmanship. I had not noticed it before, it was quite beautiful even without the paint. Do you feel any different about our statue from when you began your work last year to now?

**MR. WHARTON:** I originally thought I would come and work on the statue as I do on many statuary all over this world. But I soon learned that this small community of Kohala has a very different relationship to its statue than almost any other place that I have ever been to. That is so interesting to me, you all really care about what happens to this statue. I have learned so many things while being here in Kohala, thank you.

**KAMA:** We learned from you, too, Mr. Wharton.

**KUPUNA:** Mr. Wharton, we would like to honor you for your good work and manner that you have presented yourself here to us. It is our small way to say mahalo a nui loa, thank you.

Followed by a Hawaiian chant written and performed by Lancaster, "Eia I Kapa'au Kou Lei Nani" (Here Is Your Beautiful Lei)

Excerpts from the script of *Ke Ki'i Nui 'O Kohala* (The Great Statue of Kohala), written by Raylene Ha'alelea Lancaster and performed by local preschool students, *Kupuna* Audrey Veloria, and the 'O Ha'alelea *hula hālau* during the sculpture's rededication ceremonies.

The *hula ki'i* ended with a Hawaiian chant dedicated to Kamehameha and the project, which brought tears to many in the audience, including project organizers, participants, and myself. I looked over and our two funders had tears in their eyes—this I had never seen before. In a way, the *hula ki'i* marked the significance of the project and how the sculpture was now a conservation object that inspired new forms of thinking about the past. The final events of the day included songs evoking Hawaiian history and culture. Many in the audience joined to sing the familiar lyrics. The rededication ended in a large circle of people holding hands around the sculpture, offering prayers, and singing *Hawai'i Aloha*.

A much larger number of people participated in festivities the following day, the Kamehameha Day state holiday. At sunrise, Hawaiian Studies students draped scores of floral lei over the neck and arms of the sculpture.

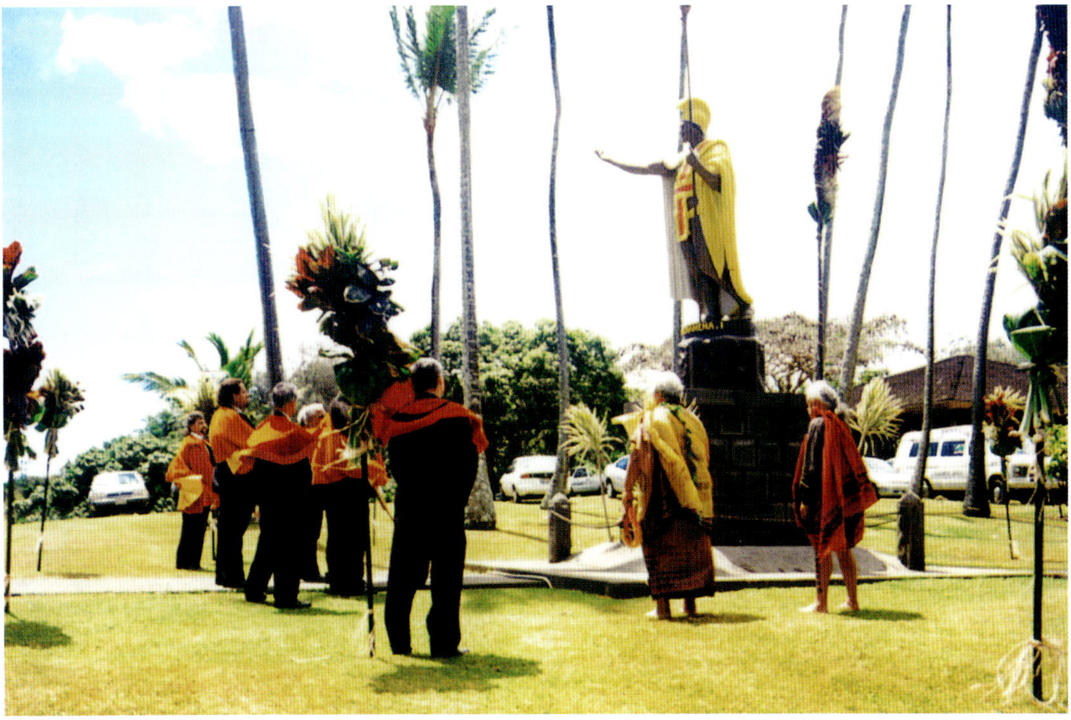

Sunrise offerings by the Royal Order of Kamehameha before rededication of the sculpture.

Soon after the lei draping, *pāʻū* riders and floats arrived at the sculpture to complete the parade from Hāwī. Many brought *hoʻokupu*. Girl Scouts received the *hoʻokupu* and in turn handed them to officials for placement on the sculpture's pedestal. Susan Nichols from Save Outdoor Sculpture! awarded the Girl Scouts with achievement patches for their research and art projects involving bronze technology and the sculpture's conservation.

Following the parade, hundreds of people strolled down the road to Kamehameha Park for an entire afternoon of hula performance and singing. Booths sold food, Kamehameha T-shirts, and other items to raise money for local campaigns. Once again, project members staffed a booth in the high school gymnasium and talked story about the project. This time, our booth included storyboards of photographs, newspaper articles, and samples of layered chips of paint, some with gold on their underside. The booth extended into adjacent exhibits that included art, photographs, and Kamehameha timelines produced by students and community groups during the project. People gathered around our booth and lingered, recounting their own stories about Kamehameha and the sculpture's conservation.

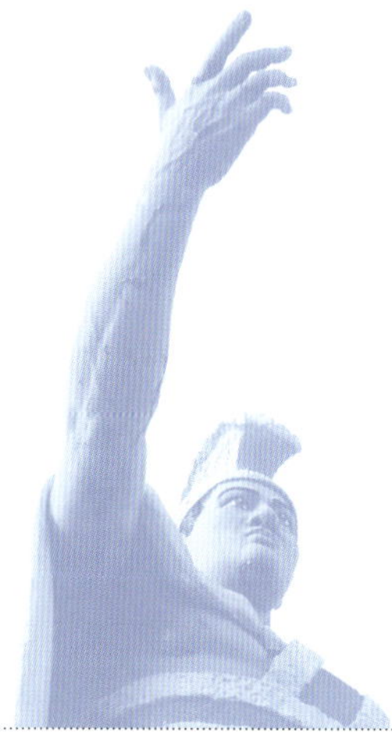

# 10 *Looking to the Future*

AFTER CELEBRATIONS ON KAMEHAMEHA DAY 2001, I returned to my life as an art conservator on the mainland. Yet much had changed for me. I had a new sense of how community participation could influence my practice, but I wondered what effect the project had on the community itself. I also wanted to place what we did in the larger context of heritage preservation. Fortunately I had the opportunity to return to North Kohala one year later on remaining funds from our grants. I was to provide additional training and oversee the first annual maintenance of the sculpture in preparation for Kamehameha Day 2002. I also planned follow-up interviews to assess the impact of the project.

This time returning to Kapaʻau was like coming home. The once-strange plantation architecture, windblown palms, and rural Hawaiian atmosphere now relaxed me. I associated memories with practically every building as I drove along the highway through Hāwī and into Kapaʻau. I now had a long list of friends to visit and plenty of places to stay to keep the project costs down.

With a group of volunteers, I erected a scaffolding tower provided by Ali Fujii of the state maintenance division. After assembling the tower and hefting up the planks to stand on, we climbed up and had a close look. To my relief, the paint remained well adhered. Aside from a few spider nests in the crevices and black spots from gecko poop, the sculpture was in good shape. We took photographs to document the condition and filled out our annual assessment form. We then hosed the figure down and set to work with wash buckets, soft scrub brushes, water, and non-ionic pH-neutral detergent. This time, cleaning took a matter of hours.

Being face to face again with Kamehameha and working with friends on the scaffolding provided a good setting for reflection. As we sudsed the sculpture and worked our brushes into the deep folds of red- and yellow-painted feathers, we spoke about the strained relations with administrators in Honolulu. Although some supported our efforts, especially after seeing Tuti's documentary "King Kamehameha: A Legacy Renewed" on public television, others remained staunchly against our participatory approach. The state continued to provide funds for maintaining the gold-leafed second cast in Honolulu, but refused local requests to help maintain the original cast. This irony was not lost on people in North Kohala, and the subject stirred a fierce local pride.

We noted with additional irony that because the project had been funded from out-of-state sources such as the Getty Trust, the Smithsonian Institution, the Ford Foundation, the National Park Service, Heritage Preservation, and the National Endowment for the Arts, the project had a stamp of authority that was beyond the state government's opposition. The local tradition of painting and the participatory mode of research had, in some ways, been legitimated at a national level.

During our project, we made some changes to prior procedures. Instead of house paint, the sculpture now has an industrial coating that will resist ultraviolet radiation, airborne chlorides, and high humidity levels. We retained other practices, but now an outside conservator, rather than a local maintenance worker, attached the brass spheres from poison can check valves. The tradition of painting pupils with white highlights was further legitimated through a community process of decision making. All of this moved the project beyond state opposition: if they saw painting as an act of vandalism, it is a nationally sanctioned vandalism backed by local support.

In further interviews with people touched by our work, I found that project details were no longer on the minds of many. Yet I learned of lingering effects. Sharon set a baseline for this by exclaiming, "You can bet that no one in our community is unaware of this statue now!"

During this trip, I learned of a heightened sense of impending change in the local landscape. Real estate prices continued to rise as speculators purchased, subdivided, and resold land parcels from the Japanese development corporation that had purchased the Kohala Sugar Company's vast holdings. There was much talk about how the project offered an opportunity for people who had never participated in public dialogue to express their opinions. Some suggested that this gave them experience and confidence to take civic action on issues such as unplanned development. Sharon further commented:

> This project was a high-profile allegory for saving tradition and inclusion in the process of making decisions in a collective manner. [It] empowers people to have the confidence to express themselves in other arenas such as the new general plan for our county and the many development issues we are now facing.

In the words of Boyd Bond, "the process, the balloting, and the discussion were a great model for us as a community. I hope we can continue what we learned here." In the same conversation, he referred to the project as a relatively safe space to learn tools of public expression. "The question was relatively benign when compared to some of the more contentious problems we face like rampant development, water issues, and the continuing drug problem. It gave us a chance to practice community discussion without getting at each others' throats."

People spoke of an increased sense of public ownership of the sculpture and local recognition that North Kohala's traditions are unique and respected outside the community. This was shown by spin-off programming such as a new classroom curriculum that incorporates the sculpture and Kamehameha himself. Such programs potentially lead to a new sense of local identity among students who, whether they leave the region or remain in place, gain a different sense of their background.

Another project spin-off was the *hula ki'i* workshops and performances. Raylene's *hula halau* had plans for a coloring book and accompanying CD of a performance about the sculpture. They also spoke of extending the "new" *hula ki'i* tradition brought by our project to the community with a new script about the life of Queen Lili'uokalani, Hawai'i's last monarch.

The social inclusion in the project not only led to additional public programming and community activism, but it also provided an opportunity to explore public and private memory about the sculpture and Kamehameha. It helped enrich readings of the collective past, not just by getting the past "right" for aesthetic purposes, but also by revealing opposing versions of the past and deciding what to communicate to future generations.

In addition to personal and collective considerations of the Native Hawaiian past, people became aware of the sculpture's existence in material terms. It became a conservation object. The very idea of conserving the sculpture became part of community awareness in ways it hadn't been before. Among all its other meanings, it was now understood as a cast brass object that was originally gold-leafed and chemically patinated, suffering from structural damage and chloride-induced corrosion. Just as I learned about its cultural associations, local residents came to know the results of scientific analysis and ways the incoming data might influence its physical longevity. Dilemmas I face daily came to people's attention.

One of the most interesting occurrences was how participants, including myself, absorbed new knowledge as it came to our attention. As research results came in, my investigations and the understandings of participants interacted with one another and continually shaped our decision making. For instance, knowledge that a state maintenance worker had attached the figure's eyeballs created a new path of research and a new decision to make: whether to replace them. This led to new considerations about material authenticity and symbolic meaning. Similarly, confirming that the sculpture had bronze disease justified removing the paint layer, at least to treat the surface with corrosion inhibitors before recoating it. Discovering gold beneath the twenty-five-plus layers of house paint strengthened arguments for gilding rather than painting.

In our search to get the conservation right, in one form or another, we were presented with new pieces of information that altered our prior thinking. Driven by the need to conserve an object, I learned how it was made and how it physically altered over time. I shared this technical knowledge with community members, who produced their own knowledge of its social, economic, spiritual, and political function in North Kohala. As various forms of knowledge came to the table, they served to reinforce, complement, and question each other. The result was a dynamic process of investigation and intervention, with each modality looping back upon the other. Both cultural and material knowledge affected the direction of the research and the material outcome of how the sculpture ended up being treated.

In community discussions about conservation, many people voiced opinions based on some version of "authenticity." In fact the very notion of authenticity, a canon of conservation, became a topic of public debate as residents discussed honoring artist intentions, honoring cultural tradition, and getting the skin tones and feather colors "right." Some voiced preference for maintaining a painted surface, suggesting that it made him more lifelike. Some pointed to the veracity of the yellow and red colors of the original bird feathers in the garments. On the other hand, the general theme in the pro-gold camp was the greater art historical propriety in honoring the nineteenth-century artist's original intent. Authenticity could swing both ways.

As awareness of diverse interpretations increased, another process that took hold was the adoption of more complex views of what the sculpture should be. In the beginning, some residents latched on to one simple framing or another: follow the artist's intention and gold-leaf the garments, or follow the local "tradition" and continue painting the figure. But over time, as the public forum developed and people learned about contrasting opinions, absolutism tended to erode. Some attained a deepened awareness of their own constructions of the past, as well as other, multiple ways of knowing. For those who came to understand the object in its cultural hybridity, initial formulations of it representing one primary value or another broke down. Some adopted positions that promoted multiple understandings, perhaps recognizing that their own views were constructed from their own social circumstances.

Of course, not all residents got to this level of awareness. Inevitably, people I spoke with experienced the project in different ways, some as thoughtful participants, some as casual observers, and some with a complete lack of interest. And for some, the process only served to ratify their initial position, which may have come to at least be a more thoughtful stance than it otherwise would have been.

Contrary to my prior assumptions about what I would find in North Kohala, no clear patterns emerged between treatment preferences and people's ethnicity, age, religion, or length of time in the community. Within a heterogeneous demographic setting, people struggled to come to terms with a culturally hybrid sculpture in ways their own backgrounds did not predict. Cultural strands of the Hawaiian past blend within individuals who are ambivalent about how to honor elements of their identity through this representation of a Native chief.

Agendas from inside and outside the community combined with other spiritual, economic, political, and social forces. There isn't just one way to know or use the sculpture, there are many, and they change over time. One scholar suggests that a way to think about expanding and shifting meaning in cultural objects is to view them as “slow events” rather than static manifestations.[1] As sociologist Howard Becker argues, works of art are never “finished”; they are constructed and continually modified amidst the needs and constrictions of overlapping worlds.[2] Some scholars advancing these views about objects find authenticity in every stage of an object’s life, not just in its original appearance. It follows, as we learned from this project, that objects with multiple constituencies do not have primary values that are easily designated for conservation purposes.

If this continuously changing complication of meanings and use is characteristic of the conservation object, then how does a conservator decide what it should look like? Our traditional theory and professional guidelines are not very helpful, since they presuppose a primary value that can be defined for conservation purposes. The conservation field is underpinned by a belief stemming from European philosophy that cultural objects have an *essential nature* and that the task of conservators is to render an appearance that represents that nature. Conservation literature encourages conservators to recognize the “intrinsic nature,” or “essence” of the object.[3] Suzanne Keene points out, “At the foundation of the conservation ethic lies the precept ‘thou shalt not change the nature of the object.’ ”[4] Codes of ethics developed by professional organizations advocate a respect for the “integrity” of the object.[5] Until it was recently expanded, the United Kingdom Institute for Conservation’s code read, “Conservation is the means by which the true nature of an object is preserved. The true nature of an object includes evidence of its origins, its original construction, the materials of which it is composed, and information as to the technology used in its manufacture.”[6]

Conservators specialize in built structures, cultural sites, archaeological and ethnographic materials, archival materials, or fine arts. For those of us who work with fine arts, essential nature is linked to both the “artist’s intent” and the original appearance of the work. Throughout the twentieth century, conservation theorists considered the essential characteristics of art objects and approaches to conserving these characteristics. For instance, the influential Italian philosopher and art historian Cesare Brandi described a principle of restoration as “re-establishing the potential unity of the work of art.”[7] He emphasized the uniqueness of artworks and argued that the material form and its image can only be restored through an aesthetic approach.

This focus on the essential nature of artworks and the aesthetic vision of the artist does not easily accommodate changes the artworks experience over time. Their appearance shifts through exposure to the environment, as lacquers yellow, dyes fade, and metals corrode. The "true nature" approach also conflicts with communities that actively use objects from the past and invent new traditions for their care. Our project went against this single-nature conservation approach and opened the door to multiple meanings in order to negotiate a public decision. The concrete need to decide "one way or the other" led participants to engage in larger determinations and inscription of cultural meaning. This meant engaging in issues of local identity and historic forces.

Alois Riegl, an Austrian philosopher and conservation theorist, articulated an early relativism in conservation research one hundred years before our project. He categorized monuments according to social values invested in them, such as *art value, historical value, age value,* and *use value.*[8] He argued that we must understand these values in order to make conservation decisions. He was a product of his time, however, and did not take on the potential for public negotiation and the empowering effect it could have on communities. Nor did he anticipate the fractious identity politics of today's multicultural present laid over traditional pasts.

My own attempts to assign one social value over another in order to understand relationships with the sculpture gave way to accepting more and more complex interpretations. I witnessed a similar process among other project participants. As we were exposed to different attitudes, remembrances, and expertise, many of us took on a more complex vision of what the sculpture embodied.

The problem of deciding who gets to decide brought up an additional set of issues for an object with a hybrid nature. It neither clearly represented Native Hawaiians nor those who have joined them in today's multicultural landscape. Almost all those who identify as Native Hawaiian in the community at least partially derive from other ancestry. To further complicate matters, many of the strongest advocates for preserving Hawaiian culture are Caucasian malihini. Many Native Hawaiian elders are practicing Christians, and strongly express allegiance to U.S. patriotic values. Others participate in the renaissance of Native Hawaiian culture and the sovereignty movement.

Sorting out complexities of such a mixed population led to multiple options for structuring conservation decision making. The mechanism of decision making evolved with the changing dynamics of community events, including a certain degree of slippage and misunderstanding that occurred along the way. The outcome was contingent on many factors, including the sculpture's physical condition as revealed during analysis and treatment, budgetary constraints, and interests of participating groups. The decision making, like everything else, was hybrid. We made choices in almost continuous interaction with findings from analysis, local preferences, and cultural practices.

In devising a method of decision making, local residents had to negotiate "who counts" in the postplantation landscape of North Kohala. This led to expressions of who is and who is not Native Hawaiian, or Hawaiian of any sort. Notions of who "belongs" also affected protocol for project blessing—producing dialogue over Christian prayer versus Hawaiian chanting. The possibility of *kapu* placed on the sculpture became part of the research, negotiation, and hands-on work of conservation. Comments on access to decision making led to opinions about local organizations and their roles in the project and in the community. Talk also involved issues seemingly unrelated to the sculpture, such as the "fairness" of local media, the need for land-use zoning to protect the surrounding landscape and its spiritual and historical significance, and problems like drug abuse that reportedly increased with the erosion of Hawaiian values. The hybrid decision-making process that evolved and the substantive expressions to which it led conformed to the hybridity of past migrations and current cultural makeup of the region.

One clear benefit of the project was the cultural knowledge produced at all stages of research, discussion, and hands-on work. Removing the sculpture's eyeballs as a first step would be a routine procedure in conventional conservation, since they would otherwise fall out as solvents and heat dissolved their epoxy adhesive. In addition, since they were added in the late 1970s and are not in keeping with the artist's intent, the eyeballs are "inauthentic." During eighteen months of community involvement and discussions, no one mentioned any significance of the eyes to me. The knowledge that for some people in the community the spheres allowed the *ali'i* to watch over his community would not have come to me had I not removed them. Similarly, the reluctance to physically work above Kamehameha's head came as a revelation, informing me of a depth of concern about which I would have otherwise been ignorant.

This knowledge benefited the conservation process as it fed into our discussions, but it also has potential to inform a larger public. Conventional conservation research can produce cultural information, but this occurs as a by-product of analysis rather than as a goal in itself. Unlike other investigations that start with objects, such as material culture studies in social anthropology,[9] conservation research typically arises from concrete concern about the care and disposition of tangible things and does not investigate larger questions about the human condition. Cultural knowledge does play a role in traditional conservation research, but in very applied ways.

Through participant observation and deeper ethnographic investigation, material culture researchers learn about relationships between people and things. In addition to my participatory research, I conducted forty semistructured interviews with strategic informants (Native Hawaiian, Asian, and Caucasian) that represented important groups in the community: elders, activists, teachers, students, local businesspeople, and *keiki o ka ʻāina* (young people born in the region).[10]

I selected these groups as I learned that people in North Kohala categorize one another by ethnicity, birth location, and length of residency, along with more standard categories of age, occupation, and income. I repeated some of these interviews during the course of the project and selected ten of these people to re-interview in June 2001. In most cases, I taped the interviews in order to select quotes and abstract thoughts. Using what sociologist Mitchell Duneier calls an "extended place method" of ethnography, I interviewed thirty-eight people elsewhere in Hawaiʻi with specialized knowledge, including conservators, archaeologists, cultural administrators, anthropologists, and Hawaiian activists.[11] The purpose of these interviews was to gather a range of attitudes, rather than to obtain "statistically representative" or "random" samples. In this sense, the research was more characteristic of qualitative ethnography than quantitative sociology.

Compared with that of standard ethnographic research, the position of a conservator offers a few special advantages. First of all, I gained access to people who don't ordinarily share their concerns with outside researchers. I had a job to do that everyone agreed needed to be done, and I asked for advice. Of course, access was gained slowly, and acceptance was not always immediate or universal. Some people expressed initial distrust of an outsider haole "expert." As recalled by Emma Glory, president of the Senior Citizens Group:

> Initially, especially the Hawaiians here in Kohala got very suspicious. Everyone said "don't tell him any stories." But at the gathering at the

> gym, you did so well because you were right in there with the flowers trying to string the leis. We have had people just show up and stand there and that didn't go over very well, but you were right in there. I think that you related so well in Kohala that's why we say "hey Glenn"—it feels like you have been here with us forever.

Over time, people heard about the project and wanted to share their concerns with me about how the sculpture should look. Once we were in conversation, it wasn't a great leap to discuss spiritual and other values they associate with the sculpture, nor their thoughts about relationships between the multicultural present and the Native Hawaiian past. We naturally moved on to other topics of concern, including land use, development, and the influx of recent immigrants from the mainland.

Over the course of my work in North Kohala and reporting back to colleagues on the mainland, I received criticism about the design of the project. One conservator argued that enhancing community consciousness is not an appropriate mission for the profession, especially given the scarcity of resources for conservation. I heard arguments that opening the door to nonprofessional participants erodes professional authority and leads to decisions that contradict conservation principles such as honoring artists' intent and other versions of a settled "historic" value. Another colleague warned me about the risks of "going native," stressing that I could be influenced by a clamor of voices that did not take on the careful application of scientific methods in conservation analysis.

Challenges to conservation come from outside the field as well as inside. One example is scholarly criticism about the heritage industry. Some people complain about hegemonic practices of governments and organizations that package the past for tourism and invent traditions about the past to support those in power.[12] By implication, conservation exists to serve this selective preservation and exhibition of objects from the past. Our field is sometimes charged with disempowering the lay public through the smoke of science and professionalism.[13] The participatory practice as it evolved in the Kamehameha project responds to these challenges by opening up the process to voices otherwise muted in conventional expert discourse. It provides a vehicle for wider communities to debate the social implications of material analysis and technical interventions—an answer to Lowenthal's claim that heritage run by a small elite is "socially barren."[14]

A more profound challenge comes from scholars who question the core assumptions of conserving any version of reality. Lowenthal also charges that conservation is a method of segregating the present from the past, of freezing or reifying periods of history and their associated artifacts.[15] Taking the postmodern argument to its extreme, any attempt at establishing authenticity is a relative construct, implying that the meaning of any object is completely open. It follows that there is not much to lose if the object disappears in the sands of time. Some say there is little value in any enterprise that strives to represent objects as they "might, could, or should have been."[16] If the past is constantly reconstructed in the present anyway, we might as well construct something morally and politically appropriate to the current moment rather than try to conserve some version of "irreplaceable" remains.[17] Simulacra[18] can be built to represent the past instead of using resources to keep old stuff around.

The participatory conservation model we developed in North Kohala offers a response to these extremes of postmodernism as well. There are clear reasons to conserve objects from the past, but they are not necessarily those typically provided by conservators and other professionals within the heritage industry. The justification for conservation is found within its process as much as its product. It gives purpose to conservation as a method for continually reconstructing public memory and questioning authority in heritage management. It offers a tool for memory work and activism within a public forum. It is not so much about getting the past "right"; it is about finding value in an active process of exploring versions of the past and analyzing the power dynamics in deciding what the past should look like. Right down to patination of skin color and fix of the gaze.

# *Appendix 1* HAWAIIAN GLOSSARY

The following definitions are primarily drawn from Mary Kawena Pukui and Samuel H. Elbert's *Hawaiian Dictionary* (Pukui and Elbert 1986).

| | |
|---|---|
| *'ahu 'ula* | cloak (the feathered cloak on the sculpture) |
| *'āina* | land, earth |
| *akua* | god, spirit, divinity |
| *ali'i* | chief, chiefs, officer, ruler, monarch, noble, aristocrat |
| *aloha* | love, affection, compassion, mercy, sympathy, pity, kindness, sentiment, grace, charity; greeting, salutation to show kindness; to venerate |
| *aloha 'āina* | love of the land |
| *'aumakua* | family or personal gods, deified ancestors |
| *haole* | Caucasian (in contemporary parlance); formerly haole referred to any foreigner or foreign object introduced to Hawai'i |
| *hapa Hawaiian* | part Hawaiian |
| *heiau* | place of worship, shrine; some *heiau* were elaborately constructed stone platforms, others simple earth terraces |
| *ho'okupu* | offering, gift |
| *hula* | traditional Hawaiian dance |
| *hula ki'i* | image dance; a combination of art forms used together to tell stories through song and dance; often the storyteller uses puppets, or dancing images to assist them in recounting a legend or tale |

| | |
|---|---|
| *iwi* | bone |
| *kaʻao* | tale, legend |
| *kāʻei* | sash (tied around the sculpture's waist and draped over the left shoulder) |
| *kāhili* | feathered standards |
| *kahuna* | priest, sorcerer, magician, minister; expert in any profession |
| *kapa* | barkcloth; also called *tapa* |
| *kapu* | taboo, special privilege, sacredness, consecrated |
| *keiki* | child |
| *keiki o ka ʻāina* | child of the land (a young person born in the area) |
| *kiʻi* | image, statue, picture, photograph, drawing, diagram, illustration, likeness, idol, doll, petroglyph |
| *kūʻauhau* | genealogy, lineage |
| *kuleana* | responsibility, right, privilege |
| *kūlōa* | prayers associated with hula |
| *kumu* | teacher, tutor |
| *kupuna* | grandparent, ancestor |
| *kūpuna* | grandparents, ancestors |
| *lāhui* | nation, race |
| *lei* | garland or wreath with flowers, leaves, or feathers, generally worn around either the head or the neck |
| *loʻi* | irrigated terrace, especially for taro |
| *mahalo nui loa* | thank you very much |
| *mahiole* | helmet (the feathered helmet depicted on the sculpture) |
| *makaʻāinana* | commoner |
| *mālama ʻāina* | caring for the land |
| *malihini* | newcomer, stranger, foreigner |
| *malo* | loincloth |
| *mana* | supernatural or divine power |
| *mele* | song, anthem, or chant of any kind |
| *mōʻī* | king, sovereign, monarch |
| *moʻolelo* | myth, tale, story |
| *ʻohana* | family |
| *ʻokina* (ʻ) | Hawaiian diacritical mark, or glottal stop, produced by a momentary complete closure of the glottis |
| *pololū* | long spear (referring to the spear in Kamehameha's left hand, as depicted on the sculpture) |
| *pono* | goodness, uprightness, morality, moral qualities, correct or proper procedure |
| *puka* | hole |
| *tapa* | barkcloth, also called *kapa* |

# *Appendix 2*

Significant Dates in the Early History of the Kamehameha Sculpture

| | |
|---|---|
| Sept. 1878 | The Hawaiian legislature contracted with Thomas Ridgeway Gould to create the sculpture |
| 1880 | The Barbedienne foundry in Paris cast the sculpture |
| Aug. 21, 1880 | The ship *Geo. F. Haendel,* carrying the sculpture, left Bremen for Honolulu |
| Nov. 15, 1880 | The *Geo. F. Haendel* sunk off the coast of the Falkland Islands, near Argentina |
| Feb. 22, 1881 | Honolulu residents learned of the shipwreck |
| July 23, 1881 | The Hawaiian legislature commissioned the second sculpture |
| Nov. 1881 | The Barbedienne foundry cast the second sculpture |
| Nov. 26, 1881 | Thomas Ridgeway Gould died |
| Dec. 1881 | The artist's son, Marshall S. Gould, completed four reliefs depicting the life of Kamehameha |
| March 27, 1882 | The first sculpture (found in the Falkland islands) arrived in Honolulu on the ship *Earl of Dalhousie* |
| April 1, 1882 | A fence was built around the first sculpture in Honolulu for future repairs |
| Jan. 31, 1883 | The second sculpture arrived in Honolulu, along with a new |

| | |
|---|---|
| | forearm for the damaged first sculpture, on the ship *Aberman* |
| Feb. 14, 1883 | The second sculpture was unveiled in Honolulu during the coronation of King Kalākaua |
| May 1, 1883 | After restoration, the first sculpture was sent to Māhukona (Kohala's port on the island of Hawai'i) on the ship *Likelike* |
| May 6, 1883 | King Kalākaua arrived in Kohala on the Russian ship *Nayezdnik* |
| May 8, 1883 | The first sculpture was unveiled in Āinakea, Kohala |

# *Notes*

## **CHAPTER 1:** *A Painted King*

1. Kamehameha I was followed by Kamehameha II, III, IV, and V. I drop the ordinal (I) and refer to him simply as Kamehameha.
2. The modern districts of North and South Kohala were established in 1859. Prior to this division, the region was referred to as Kohala. Local residents today use the terms "North Kohala" and "Kohala" interchangeably, as I do in this book.
3. The Honolulu Mayor's Office of Culture and the Arts obtained the grant from the Save Outdoor Sculpture! project of the National Heritage Foundation and Smithsonian American Art Museum.
4. Kamehameha's date of birth, recorded through oral Hawaiian tradition, is contested. For the purpose of this writing, I accept Kuykendall's calculation as reported in Kamakau 1992: 66.
5. Relational aesthetics refers to contemporary art that engages social context in its production and often invites interaction from the public. Nicolas Bourriaud coined the term. Bourriaud 2002.
6. Muñoz Viñas 2005.
7. Obeyesekere 1997; Sahlins 1995.

**CHAPTER 2:** *Creating a "Pacific Hero"*

1. The original correspondence and contract documents are now located in the Hawai'i State Archives. Adler (1969) wrote an excellent secondary source.
2. The Hawaiian population at the date of Cook's arrival is a matter of heated debate. Lieutenant King, of Cook's expedition, estimated the population at 400,000. Stannard (1989) revised the estimate to 800,000 based on archaeological evidence. Venereal diseases, tuberculosis, and influenza killed four out of every five Hawaiians within the first half-century after contact. Mid-nineteenth-century epidemics of measles and smallpox further decimated the population (Kuykendall and Day 1961: 127). The 1878 Hawaiian (and part Hawaiian) population figure of 47,508 is from Kuykendall and Day 1961: 306.
3. Kame'eleihiwa 1992.
4. Gibson's life is critically appraised in Adler and Kamins 1984.
5. Thrum 1879.
6. The other members were Archibald S. Cleghorn, John M. Kapena, Simon K. Kaai, and Joseph Nawahī (Thrum 1880; McConnel 1898: 137).
7. Edward M. Brewer, Esq., and former Honolulu resident James W. Austin, Esq.
8. Charlot 1979.
9. Other Western visitors in the late eighteenth century and early nineteenth century provided similar descriptions of Kamehameha. Captain George Vancouver described him "in form and stature of a herculean savage" (Jarves 1843: 159). Archibald Campbell provided a more detailed description: "In 1809 the King seemed to be about fifty years of age, he is a stout, well-made man, rather darker in the complexion than the natives usually are, and wants two of his front teeth" (Campbell 1816: 211).
10. King Kalākaua later published his own description of Kamehameha as "a man of tremendous physical and intellectual strength. . . . He was so strong of limb that ordinary men were but children in his grasp. . . . He had a harsh and rugged face, less given to smiles than frowns, but strongly marked with lines indicative of self-reliance and changeless purpose" (Kalākaua 1888: 384–385).
11. Walton 1969.
12. Rose 1978.
13. Kaumuali'i was the chief of Kaua'i that Kamehameha had twice attempted to conquer and finally brought under peaceful submission in 1810 (Kuykendall 1967: 48–51). During their historic meeting in Honolulu, it is believed that Kamehameha gave Kaumuali'i the *mahiole* and two feathered *'ahu 'ula* (Brigham 1899; 1918: 31).
14. Brigham 1918; Charlot 1979; Rose 1978.
15. Kū is the Hawaiian god of war, fishing, and all related activities (Valeri 1985: 11). Representations of Kū, at least at the time when Europeans first appeared,

also referenced sovereignty. Kū was the source of a ruling chief's political power (Cox and Davenport 1988: xv).

16. Kamakau 1992; Malo 1898: 83.
17. X-Ray fluorescence analysis was performed on a sample I removed from the interior of a crack in the sculpture. The alloy is 93.9 percent copper, 4.5 percent zinc, and less than 1 percent each of tin, lead, and iron. The analysis was conducted by David Scott, J. Paul Getty Museum.
18. *Kūʻokoʻa* (Hawaiian newspaper), December 18, 1880.

## CHAPTER 3: *Shipwreck*

1. Jarves 1843.
2. Queen Liliʻuokalani provides another favorable description of the coronation in Liliʻuokalani 1898.
3. Thrum 1880: 65.
4. George Kaiwiea Koalii published the original collection. See Charlot 1979.
5. The *Honolulu Advertiser* reports that King Kalākaua asked Princess Kekaulike to pull the cord to unveil the sculpture, rather than Kalākaua himself.
6. Daws 1968.
7. Newman 1970.
8. Father Elias Bond established the Āinakea missionary school in 1860. In 1878 it merged with the boys' boarding school (opened in 1842) and was called the Government English School. It taught missionary students. One of its teachers in 1902 commented that it also served the affluent and the teachers' children in the community (Stephenson 1977: 52).
9. I found no reference describing the details of moving the sculpture. The connection between the school closing and relocating the sculpture is based on interviews with old-timers (a local term) Sadie Rodenhurst, Navas Santiago, Albert Solomon, and Kindy Sproat.
10. Damon 1927; Tomonari-Tuggle 1988.
11. Early population counts of North Kohala vary widely. The 1832 figure is in a letter from a missionary at Waimea to the Board of Commissions for Foreign Missions. A missionary census in 1834 estimated the population of North Kohala at 6,175 (Schmitt 1977; Tomonari-Tuggle 1988).
12. Chang 1977.
13. Tomonari-Tuggle 1988.
14. The population of North Kohala was 6,275 in 1920 and 3,386 in 1960 (*Data Book* 2000; Schmitt 1977).

### CHAPTER 4: *Return to Kohala*

1. Barrère, Pukui, and Kelly 1980: 55, 62–63; Luomala 1984.
2. Many historical references refer to Hale o Kāʻili Heiau as the personal *heiau* of Kamehameha and his family (Stokes 1991: 181).
3. Oral and written accounts of the circumstances of Kamehameha's birth vary. Leading sources include Fornander 1969: 136; and Kamakau 1992: 66–68.
4. *Data Book* 2000: Table 1.29.
5. Kehau Cachola-Abad, of the Kamehameha schools, and Ross Cordy, state archaeologist of the State Historic Preservation Office.
6. Kaeppler 2008: 185; Kaeppler 2010.
7. Kameʻeleihiwa 1992.
8. Wharton 2004.
9. Kanahele 1986: 3–5.
10. Trask 1999: 2.
11. Jolly 1992; Keesing 1991; Linnekin 1990, 1991; Ross 1994; Trask 1991; Thomas 1991.
12. Kameʻeleihiwa 1992: 22–23.
13. Trask 1999: 164.
14. *Data Book* 2000: Census of Population, 1960 and 1970.
15. Ariyoshi 1991.
16. Ibid.
17. *New York Times,* October 8, 2000.

### CHAPTER 5: *Local Style*

1. For additional reading on Hawaiian values, see Kanahele 1986.
2. Hall 1996: 4.
3. Williams 1973.
4. Takaki 1994: 86–89.
5. Osorio 1994: 236.

### CHAPTER 6: *How People Think about Their Sculpture*

1. Pukui and Elbert 1986.
2. Cox and Davenport 1988: xx, 14.
3. Valeri 1985.
4. For a better understanding of these protocols and traditions relating to *kiʻi,* see commentaries on earlier texts from Īʻī, Kamakau, Malo, and Wilkes in Valeri 1985: 264–279.
5. Donat 1996.

6. In legislation passed in 1864 (Sec. 187 of title 40 of the United States Code, 1864), the old hall of the House of Representatives became an exhibition space for sculptures donated by each state. Title 40 of USC 187 states that "the President is authorized to invite all the States to provide and furnish statues, in marble or bronze, not exceeding two in number for each State, of deceased persons who have been citizens thereof, and illustrious for their historic renown or for distinguished civic or military services, such as each State may deem to be worthy of this national commemoration" (*King Kamehameha I and Father Damien* 1969: 6). Cast in bronze with gilt feather garments, the figure was unveiled in 1969 at a dedication ceremony presided over by Senator Daniel K. Inouye of Hawai'i (*King Kamehameha I and Father Damien* 1969; Mitchell 1969).
7. Adler 1969.
8. The 1791 killing of Keoua, Kamehameha's cousin, and the subsequent sacrifice of his body at the Pu'ukoholā Heiau is described in Kamakau 1992: 156–158.
9. My thoughts on how communities perform their culture through material objects are shaped by Kirshenblatt-Gimblett 1998 and Shanks 2001: 299, among others.

### CHAPTER 7: *The Community Takes Sides*

1. Articles about the conservation project in Hawaiian media include *Honolulu Advertiser* (September 24, 1999; October 9, 2000; December 12, 2000; May 30, 2001); *Honolulu Star Bulletin* (September 21, 1999; September 22, 1999); *Hawai'i Island Journal* (July 1–15, 2000; December 12, 2000; June 10, 2001); *Hilo Tribune-Herald* (June 10, 2001); *Hawai'i Westways Magazine* (June/July 2001); *Kohala Mountain News* (March 1, 2000; June 12, 2000; August 16, 2000; September 20, 2000; October 4, 2000; November 1, 2000; December 6, 2000); and *North Hawaii News* (July 12, 2000; June 7, 2001; June 14, 2001).
2. Kamehameha '*E Kahi* (The Lonely One) is a nickname given to Kamehameha (McKinzie 1982; Mellen 1949).
3. Brinkman and Wünsche 2007.
4. Dening 1980; Gosden and Marshall 1999; Thomas 1991.

### CHAPTER 8: *Decision*

1. Also see Ayau 2004; Young 1998: xi.
2. Cachola-Abad and Ayau 1999; Cordy 1999; Kirch 1999.
3. U.S. Supreme Court Case Number 15373.
4. Shook 1985.
5. Samuel Manaiakalani Kamakau's *Ruling Chiefs of Hawai'i,* written during the late 1860s to 1871 by a Native Hawaiian historian, is widely read as a resource

on chiefs and royal leaders from 'Umi-a-Liloa in the sixteenth-century through the reign of Kamehameha III (Kamakau 1992).

6. The number of residents eighteen years old and older in North Kohala in 2000 was 4,564 (*Data Book* 2000; Pdf file 1.13 Residential Populations of County Divisions and Census Designated Places (CDPs), Hawai'i County by Age: 2000). The number of registered voters in North Kohala in 2000 was 2,810 (*Data Book* 2000; Pdf file 8.1 Registered Voters, Hawaii County, by Districts: General Elections, 1992 to 2002). The number of votes cast in the general election in November 2000 was 1,273 (*Data Book 2000*; Pdf file 8.3: Votes Cast, Hawaii County, by Districts: General Elections, 1992 to 2002).

**CHAPTER 10:** *Looking to the Future*

1. The description of an object as a "slow event" was described to me in communication with Katharine Young (November 5, 2001), who reports that it was formulated but never published by Stanley Eveling (now deceased).
2. Becker 1982.
3. Clavir 2002.
4. Keene 1994: 19.
5. Sease 1998: 102.
6. United Kingdom Institute of Conservation 1983: 2.
7. Brandi 1963: 231.
8. Riegl 1903: 70.
9. Kingery 1996; Miller 1998.
10. Wharton 2004.
11. Duneier 1999: 344.
12. Holtorf 2001; Layton and Thomas 2001; Treanor 1997; Walsh 1992.
13. Lowenthal 2000.
14. Ibid.: 23.
15. Lowenthal 1995: 404, 410.
16. Tunbridge and Ashworth 1996: 8.
17. Holtorf 2001: 294.
18. Baudrillard 1983.

# Bibliography

Adler, Jacob. 1969. "The Kamehameha Statue." *The Hawaiian Journal of History* 3: 87–100.

———. 1986. *The Fantastic Life of Walter Murray Gibson, Hawaii's Minister of Everything.* Honolulu: University of Hawai'i Press.

Adler, Jacob, and Robert M. Kamins. 1984. "The Political Debut of Walter Murray Gibson." *Hawaiian Journal of History* 18: 96–115.

Ariyoshi, Rita. 1991. *Spirit of Aloha.* January 1991, 16–19.

Ayau, Edward Halealoha. 2004. "Rooted in Native Soil." Hui Malama I Na Kupuna O Hawai'i Nei (Group Caring For the Ancestors of Hawai'i). http://huimalama.tripod.com/. Accessed September 19, 2010.

Barrère, Dorothy B., Mary Kawena Pukui, and Marion Kelly. 1980. *Hula: Historical Perspectives.* Honolulu: Bishop Museum.

Baudrillard, Jean. 1983. "The Procession of Simulacra." *Art & Text,* September 11, 3–47.

Becker, Howard. 1982. *Art Worlds.* Berkeley: University of California Press.

Boggs, Stephen T., Georgia McMillen, and Karen A. Watson-Gegeo. 1985. *Speaking, Relating and Learning: A Study of Hawaiian Children at Home and at School.* Norwood, N.J.: Ablex Publishing Company.

Bourdieu, Pierre. 1993. *The Field of Cultural Production.* Translated by R. Johnson. New York: Columbia University Press.

Bourriaud, Nicolas. 2002. *Relational Aesthetics.* Dijon: Les Presses du réel.

Brandi, Cesare. 1963 (1996). "Theory of Restoration, I, II, & III." In *Readings in Conservation: Historical and Philosophical Issues in the Conservation of Cultural Heritage,* edited by N. Stanley-Price, M. K. Talley, and A. M. Vaccaro. Los Angeles: The Getty Conservation Institute.

Brigham, W. T. 1899. "Hawaiian Featherwork." *Bishop Museum Memoirs* 1: 1.

———. 1918. *Additional Notes on Hawaiian Feather Work, Second Supplement, (Memoirs of the Bernice Pauahi Bishop Museum),* vol. 7, no. 1. Honolulu: Bishop Museum.

Brinkman, Vincenz, and Raimund Wünsche. 2007. *Gods in Color: Painted Sculpture of Classical Antiquity.* Munich: Stiftung Archäologie Glyptothek.

Buck, Elizabeth. 1993. *Paradise Remade: The Politics of Culture and History in Hawai'i.* Philadelphia: Temple University Press.

Burman, P. A. T. I. 1997. "Hallowed Antiquity: Ethical Considerations in the Selection of Conservation Treatments." In *Saving Our Architectural Heritage: The Conservation of Historic Stone Structures,* edited by N. S. B. R. Snethlage. Chichester: John Wiley & Sons.

Cachola-Abad, C. Kehaunani, and Edward Halealoha Ayau. 1999. "He Pane Ho'omālamalama: Setting the Record Straight and a Second Call for Partnership." *Hawaiian Archaeology* 7: 73–82.

Campbell, Archibald. 1816 (1969). *A Voyage Round the World from 1806 to 1812.* Amsterdam and New York: N. Israel and Da Capo Press.

Caple, Chris. 2000. *Conservation Skills: Judgement, Method and Decision Making.* London: Routledge.

Chang, Betty. 1977. "Churches of Kohala." In *Kohala Keia (This is Kohala): Collected Expressions of a Community,* edited by L. K. Stephenson. Kohala: Reprinted by the Kohala Library Fund.

Charlot, Jean. 1967. "Letter to Jacob Adler on the Statue of Kamehameha by Thomas R. Gould." *Honolulu Star-Bulletin,* May 10, 1967, C1–1.

Charlot, John. 1979. "That Statue of Kamehameha." *Honolulu* 13 (9): 35–40.

Clark, John R. K. 2002. *Hawai'i Place Names: Shores, Beaches, and Surf Sites.* Honolulu: University of Hawai'i Press.

Clavir, Miriam. 2002. *Preserving What Is Valued: Museums, Conservation, and First Nations.* Vancouver: University of British Columbia Press.

Clifford, James. 1988. *The Predicament of Culture.* Cambridge Mass.: Harvard University Press.

Cordy, Ross. 1999. "Hawaiian Archaeology: A Post-Colonial History." *Hawaiian Archaeology* 7: 83–89.

Cox, J. Halley, and William H. Davenport. 1988. *Hawaiian Sculpture.* Honolulu: University of Hawai'i Press.

Damon, Ethel M. 1927. *Father Bond of Kohala: A Chronicle of Pioneer Life in Hawaii.* Honolulu: The Friend.

*Data Book.* 2000. Hilo: County of Hawaii Department of Research and Development. <http://www.hawaii-county.com/databook_current/section01.htm>. Accessed September 19, 2010.

Daws, Gavan. 1968. *Shoal of Time.* Honolulu: University of Hawai'i Press.

Dening, Greg. 1980. *Islands and Beaches: Discourses on a Silent Land: Marquesas, 1774–1880.* Honolulu: University of Hawai'i Press.

Donat, Charlotte H. 1996. "Kokoiki to Awini: A Walk in Ancestral Footprints." *Waimea Gazette,* July 1996, 12–15.

Duneier, Mitchell. 1999. *Sidewalk.* New York: Farrar, Straus and Giroux.

Forbes, David W. 1992. *Encounters with Paradise: Views of Hawaii and its People, 1778–1941.* Honolulu: Honolulu Academy of Arts.

Fornander, Abraham. 1969 (1878–1885). *An Account of the Polynesian Race: Its Origin and Migrations (three volumes in one).* Tokyo: Charles E. Tuttle Company.

Freire, Paolo. 1996 (1970). *Pedagogy of the Oppressed.* Translated by M. B. Ramos. New York: Continuum.

Gosden, Chris, and Yvonne Marshall. 1999. "The Cultural Biography of Objects." *World Archaeology* 31 (2): 169–178.

Graham, Brian, Gregory J. Ashworth, and John E. Tunbridge. 2000. *A Geography of Heritage.* London and New York: Arnold and Oxford University Press.

Halbwachs, Maurice. 1992 (1941). *On Collective Memory.* Translated by L. A. Coser. Chicago and London: The University of Chicago Press.

Hall, Martin. 2001. "The Archaeology of Memory: Cape Town's District 6." In *Destruction and Conservation of Cultural Property,* edited by R. Layton, P. Stone, and J. Thomas. London and New York: Routledge.

Hall, Stuart. 1996. "Introduction." In *Questions of Cultural Identity,* edited by S. Hall and P. D. Gay. London: Sage.

Handler, Richard, and Jocelyn Linnekin. 1984. "Tradition, Genuine or Spurious." *Journal of American Folklore* 97 (385): 273–290.

Hayden, Dolores. 1995. *The Power of Place: Urban Landscapes as Public History.* Cambridge, Mass., and London: MIT Press.

Hobsbawm, Eric, and Terence Ranger, eds. 1985. *The Invention of Tradition.* Cambridge: Cambridge University Press.

Holt, John Dominis. 1997. *The Art of Featherwork in Old Hawai'i.* Honolulu: Ku Pa'a Publishing Incorporated.

Holtorf, Cornelius J. 2001. "Is the Past a Non-Renewable Resource?" In *The Destruction and Conservation of Cultural Property,* edited by R. Layton, P. L. Stone, and J. Thomas. London and New York: Routledge.

Jarves, James Jackson. 1843. *History of the Hawaiian or Sandwich Islands.* Boston: Tappan and Dennet.

Johnson, Jessica S., Susan Heald, Kelly McHugh, Elizabeth Brown, and Marian Kaminitz. 2005. "Practical Aspects of Consultation with Communities." *Journal of the American Institute for Conservation* 44: 203–215.

Jolly, Margaret. 1992. "Specters of Inauthenticity." *The Contemporary Pacific* 4 (1) (Spring): 49–72.

Kaeppler, Adrienne. 2008. *The Pacific Arts of Polynesia and Micronesia.* Oxford; New York: Oxford University Press.

———. 2010. *Polynesia, the Mark and Carolyn Blackburn Collection of Polynesian Art.* Privately printed. Distributed by University of Hawai'i Press.

Kalākaua, David. 1888 (1972). *The Myths and Legends of Hawaii.* Rutland, Vt.: Charles E. Tuttle Company.

Kamakau, Samuel M. 1992. *Ruling Chiefs of Hawaii (Revised Edition).* Honolulu: The Kamehameha Schools Press.

Kame'eleihiwa, Lilikalā. 1992. *Native Land and Foreign Desires: Shall We Live in Harmony? Ko Hawaii Aina A Me Na Koi Puumake A Ka Poe Haole: Pahea Lā E Pono Ai?* Honolulu: Bishop Museum.

Kanahele, George. 1986. *Kū Kanaka Stand Tall: A Search for Hawaiian Values.* Honolulu: University of Hawai'i Press and Waiaha Foundation.

Karp, Ivan, Christine Mullen Kreamer, and Steven D. Lavine, eds. 1992. *Museums and Communities: The Politics of Public Culture.* Washington D.C.: Smithsonian Institution Press.

Keene, Suzanne. 1994. "Objects as Systems: A New Challenge for Conservation." In *Restoration: Is It Acceptable? Occasional Paper No. 99,* edited by A. Oddy. London: The British Museum.

Keesing, Roger M. 1989. "Creating the Past: Custom and Identity in the Contemporary Pacific." *The Contemporary Pacific* 1: 19–42.

———. 1991. "Reply to Trask." *The Contemporary Pacific* 3 (1) (Spring): 168–171.

*King Kamehameha I and Father Damien: Hawaii's Presentation to the National Statuary Collection Proceedings in the Rotunda United States Capitol April 15, 1969. Washington D.C.* 1969. Flyer for the event.

Kingery, David W., ed. 1996. *Learning From Things: Method and Theory of Material Culture Studies.* Washington D.C.: Smithsonian Institution Press.

Kirch, Patrick Vinton. 1985. *Feathered Gods and Fishhooks.* Honolulu: University of Hawai'i Press.

Kirshenblatt-Gimblett, Barbara. 1998. *Destination Culture: Tourism, Museums, and Heritage.* Berkeley and Los Angeles: University of California Press.

Kopytoff, Igor. 1986. "The Cultural Biography of Things: Commoditization as Process." In *The Social Life of Things: Commodities in Cultural Perspective,* edited by A. Appadurai. Cambridge, UK: Cambridge University Press.

*Kū'oko'a* (Hawaiian newspaper), December 18, 1880.

Kuykendall, Ralph S. 1967. *The Hawaiian Kingdom, Vol. III, 1874–1893: The Kalakaua Dynasty.* Honolulu: University of Hawai'i Press.

Kuykendall, Ralph S., and A. Grove Day. 1961. *Hawaii: A History From Polynesian Kingdom to American State.* Englewood Cliffs, N.J.: Prentice-Hall, Inc.

Latour, Bruno. 1987. *Science in Action: How to Follow Scientists and Engineers Through Society.* Cambridge, Mass.: Harvard University Press.

Layton, Robert, and Julian Thomas. 2001. "Introduction." In *The Destruction and Conservation of Cultural Property,* edited by R. Layton, P. G. Stone, and J. Thomas. London and New York: Routledge.

Lili'uokalani. 1999 (1898). *Hawaii's Story.* Honolulu: Mutual Publishing.

Linnekin, Jocelyn. 1990. "The Politics of Culture in the Pacific." In *Cultural Identity and Ethnicity in the Pacific,* edited by J. Linnekin and L. Poyer. Honolulu: University of Hawai'i Press.

———. 1991. "Text Bites and the R-Word: The Politics of Representing Scholarship." *The Contemporary Pacific* 3 (1) (Spring): 172–177.

Lowenthal, David. 1995 (1985). *The Past Is a Foreign Country.* 2nd ed. Cambridge: Cambridge University Press.

———. 2000. "Stewarding the Past in a Perplexing Present." In *Values and Heritage Conservation,* edited by E. Avrami, R. Mason, and M. d. l. Torre. Los Angeles: The Getty Conservation Institute.

Luomala, Katharine. 1984. *Hula Ki'i Hawaiian Puppetry.* Honolulu: Brigham Young University–Hawaii Campus. Distributed by the University of Hawai'i.

Malo, David. 1951 (1898). *Hawaiian Antiquities.* 2nd ed. Translated by Nathaniel B. Emerson. Honolulu: Bishop Museum Press.

McConnel. 1898. "The Great Kamehameha." *The Paradise of the Pacific* 9 (9): 131–132, 137.

McKinzie, Edith Kawelohea. 1982. *An Original Narrative of Kamehameha the Great Written in Ka Na'i Aupuni (19–5-1906) by Joseph M. Poepoe: Hawaiian Text with English Translation and Brief Comparative Reviews of Earlier Historical Biographers of Kamehameha I.* MA thesis, University of Hawai'i.

Mellen, Kathleen Dickenson. 1949. *The Lonely Warrior: The Life and Times of Kamehameha the Great of Hawaii.* New York: Hastings House.

Miller, Daniel, ed. 1998. *Material Cultures: Why Some Things Matter.* Chicago: University of Chicago Press.

Mitchell, David D. 1969. *The King Kamehameha Memorial Statue.* Honolulu: The Statuary Hall Commission.

Molotch, Harvey. 2003. *Where Stuff Comes From: How Toasters, Toilets, Cars, Computers, and Many Other Things Come to Be as They Are.* London and New York: Routledge.

Muñoz Viñas, Salvador. 2005. *Contemporary Theory of Conservation.* London: Elsevier Butterworth Heinemann.

Newman, Thomas Stell. 1970. *Fishing and Farming on the Island of Hawaii in AD 1778*. Honolulu: Department of Land and Natural Resources, Division of State Parks.

Nordyke, Eleanor. 1989. *The Peopling of Hawai'i*. Honolulu: University of Hawai'i Press.

Obeyesekere, Gananath. 1997 (1992). *The Apotheosis of James Cook: European Mythmaking in the Pacific*. Princeton, N.J.: Princeton University Press.

Osorio, Jonathan Kamakawiwo'ole. 1994. Review of "Native Land and Foreign Desires: Pahea Lā E Pono Ai" by Lilikalā Kame'eleihiwa. *The Contemporary Pacific* (Spring): 233–236.

Park, Peter, Mary Brydon-Miller, Budd Hall, and Ted Jackson, eds. 1993. *Voices of Change: Participatory Research in the US and Canada*. Westport, Conn.: Bergin & Garvey.

Pearce, Susan. ed. 1994. *Interpreting Objects and Collections*. London and New York: Routledge.

Philippot, Paul. 1986 (1996). "Restoration from the Perspective of the Humanities." In *Historical and Philosophical Issues in the Conservation of Cultural Heritage*, edited by N. Stanley-Price, M. K. Talley, and A. M. Vaccaro, 216–229. Los Angeles: The Getty Conservation Institute.

Pukui, Mary Kawena, and Samuel H. Elbert. 1986. *Hawaiian Dictionary*. Honolulu: University of Hawai'i Press.

Pye, Elizabeth. 2001. *Caring for the Past: Issues in Conservation for Archaeology and Museums*. London: James and James.

Riegl, Alois. 1903 (1966). "The Modern Cult of Monuments: Its Essence and Its Development." In *Historical and Philosophical Issues in the Conservation of Cultural Heritage*, edited by N. Stanley-Price, M. K. Talley, and A. M. Vaccaro. Los Angeles: The Getty Conservation Institute.

Rose, Roger G. 1978. *Symbols of Sovereignty: Feather Girdles of Tahiti and Hawai'i*. Honolulu: Bernice P. Bishop Museum.

Ross, Andrew. 1994. "Cultural Preservation in the Polynesia of the Latter-Day Saints." In *The Chicago Gangster Theory of Life: Nature's Debt to Society*. London: Verso.

Sahlins, Marshall. 1995. *How "Natives" Think About Captain Cook, For Example*. Chicago & London: University of Chicago Press.

Said, Edward W. 1978. *Orientalism*. New York: Pantheon Books.

Schmitt, Robert. 1977. *Historical Statistics of Hawaii*. Honolulu: University of Hawai'i Press.

Scott, David A. 2002. *Copper and Bronze in Art: Corrosion, Colorants, Conservation*. Los Angeles: The Getty Conservation Institute.

Sease, Catherine. 1998. "Codes of Ethics for Conservation." *International Journal of Cultural Property* 7 (1): 98–114.

Senie, Harriet F., and Sally Webster, eds. 1992. *Critical Issues in Public Art.* New York: Harper Collins Publishers.

Shanks, Michael. 2001. "Culture/Archaeology: The Dispersion of a Discipline and its Objects." In *Archaeology Theory Today,* edited by I. Hodder. Cambridge, UK: Polity Press.

Shanks, Michael, and Ian Hodder. 1995. "Processual, Postprocessual and Interpretive Archaeologies." In *Interpreting Archaeology: Finding Meaning in the Past,* edited by I. Hodder, M. Shanks, A. Alexandri, V. Buchli, J. Carman, J. Last, and G. Lucas. London and New York: Routledge.

Shook, E. Victoria. 1985. *Ho'oponopono.* Honolulu: University of Hawai'i East-West Center Press.

Staniforth, Sarah. 2000. "Conservation: Significance, Relevance and Sustainability." *The International Institute for Conservation of Historic and Artistic Works Bulletin* 6 (December): 3–8.

Stannard, David E. 1989. *Before the Horror: The Population of Hawai'i on the Eve of Western Contact.* Honolulu: Social Science Research Institute, University of Hawai'i.

Stephenson, Larry K., ed. 1977. *Kohala Keia (This Is Kohala): Collected Expressions of a Community.* Kohala: Reprinted by the Kohala Library Fund.

Stokes, John F. G. 1991 (1919). *Heiau of the Island of Hawai'i: A Historic Survey of Native Hawaiian Temple Sites.* Honolulu: Bishop Museum Press.

Sully, Dean. ed. 2007. *Decolonising Conservation: Caring for Maori Meeting Houses Outside New Zealand.* Walnut Creek, Calif.: Left Coast Press.

Takaki, Ronald. 1994. *Raising Cane: The World of Plantation Hawaii.* New York & Philadelphia: Chelsea House Publishers.

Thomas, Nicholas. 1991. "Alejandro Mayta in Fiji: Narratives about Millenarianism, Colonialism and Post-colonial Politics." In *Clio in Oceania: Toward an Historical Anthropology,* edited by A. Biersack. Washington D.C.: Smithsonian Institution Press.

Thrum, Thomas G. 1879. *Thrum's Annual (All About Hawaii) Hawaiian Annual and Almanac.* Honolulu: Thomas Thrum.

———. 1880. *Thrum's Annual (All About Hawaii) Hawaiian Annual and Almanac.* Honolulu: Thomas Thrum.

Tilley, Christopher. 1989. "Interpreting Material Culture." In *The Meaning of Things: Material Culture and Symbolic Expression,* edited by I. Hodder. London and New York: Harper Collins Academic.

Tomonari-Tuggle, M. J. 1988. *North Kohala Perception of a Changing Community: A Cultural Resources Study.* Honolulu: Division of State Parks, Outdoor Recreation and Historic Sites Department of Land and Natural Resources, State of Hawai'i.

Trask, Haunani-Kay. 1991. "Natives and Anthropologists: The Colonial Struggle." *The Contemporary Pacific* 3 (1) (Spring): 159–167.

———. 1999. *From a Native Daughter: Colonialism and Sovereignty in Hawaii.* Honolulu: University of Hawai'i Press.

Treanor, Paul. 1997. *Archaeo-spatial Europe.* http://web.inter.nl.net/users/Paul.Treanor/archaeo-spatial.europe.html. Accessed September 25, 2010.

Tregaskis, Richard. 1973. *The Warrior King: Hawaii's Kamehameha the Great.* New York: The Macmillan Publishing Co.

Tuan, Yi-Fu. 1977. *Space and Place: The Perspective of Experience.* Minneapolis: University of Minnesota Press.

Tunbridge, John E., and Gregory J. Ashworth. 1996. *Dissonant Heritage: The Management of the Past as a Resource in Conflict.* Chichester, N.Y., Brisbane, Toronto, and Singapore: John Wiley & Sons.

United Kingdom Institute of Conservation. 1983. *Guidance for Conservation Practice.*

Valeri, Valerio. 1985. *Kingship and Sacrifice: Ritual and Society in Ancient Hawaii.* Chicago and London: University of Chicago Press.

Walsh, Kevin. 1992. *The Representation of the Past.* London and New York: Routledge.

Walton, Maryann Baker. 1969. "Who Was the Model?" *Honolulu* 4 (1): 26–27.

Wharton, Glenn. 2004. *Heritage Conservation as Cultural Work: Public Negotiation of a Pacific Hero.* PhD diss., University College London.

———. 2005. "Indigenous Claims and Heritage Conservation: An Opportunity for Critical Dialog." *Journal of Public Archaeology* 4: 199–204.

Whyte, William Foote, ed. 1991. *Participatory Action Research.* Newbury Park, London, and New Delhi: Sage Publications.

Williams, Raymond. 1973. *The Country and the City.* New York: Oxford University Press.

Young, Kanalu G. Terry. 1998. *Rethinking the Native Hawaiian Past.* New York & London: Garland Publishing, Inc.

## NEWS MEDIA REFERRED TO IN THE TEXT

*Boston Evening Transcript*
*Daily Bulletin* (Honolulu)
*Hawai'i Island Journal*
*Hawai'i Westways Magazine*
*Hawaiian Gazette* (Honolulu)
*Honolulu Advertiser*
*Honolulu Star-Bulletin*
*Honolulu Tribune Herald*
*Hilo Tribune-Herald*
*Ka 'Elele Pō'akolu* (Honolulu)
*Kohala Mountain News*
*Kū'oko'a* (Honolulu)
*North Hawaii News*
*New York Times*
*Pacific Commercial Advertiser* (Honolulu)
*Paradise of the Pacific* (Honolulu)
*Spirit of Aloha*
*Saturday Press* (Honolulu)

# *Index*

*Page numbers in italics refer to figures.*

## *About the Author*

After performing the work described in this book, Glenn Wharton moved to New York, where he holds dual positions at the Museum of Modern Art (MoMA) and New York University (NYU). At MoMA he serves as time-based media conservator, where he cares for video, performance, and electronic collections. At NYU he is a research scholar in the Museum Studies program, teaching graduate courses on the conservation of cultural heritage. Dr. Wharton received his MA in Conservation from the Cooperstown Graduate Programs and his PhD in Conservation from the Institute of Archaeology, University College London. He is a Fellow of the International Institute for Conservation and the American Institute for Conservation, and was the founding executive director of the International Network for the Conservation of Contemporary Art—North America.

*Production Notes*

Wharton / **THE PAINTED KING**
Cover/Jacket design by Julie Matsuo-Chun
Interior design and composition by Julie Matsuo-Chun
in Arno Pro with display type in Corbel
Printing and binding by Everbest Printing Co., Ltd.